Women Police: Portraits of Success

Women Police: Portraits of Success

Patricia Lunneborg

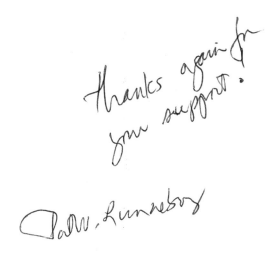

iUniverse, Inc.

New York Lincoln Shanghai

Women Police: Portraits of Success

iUniverse, Inc.

For information address:
iUniverse, Inc.
2021 Pine Lake Road, Suite 100
Lincoln, NE 68512
www.iuniverse.com

ISBN: 0-595-32075-9 (pbk)
ISBN: 0-595-66474-1 (cloth)

Printed in the United States of America

Contents

Foreword

Patricia Lunneborg has added another important work to the understanding of the integration of women as full partners in policing. At the time this book is published, women only comprise 13% of the work force in city and county agencies and only about 5% in state police organizations. They also hold only about 13% of the federal law enforcement positions. The first few women entered policing in the early 1900s. They were not considered "real" police officers by their male coworkers. They were usually in plainclothes and worked mostly with women and children. The second large wave of women entered policing in the 1970s and 1980s. Their entry into the uniformed ranks sent shock waves through those paramilitary organizations. They faced blatant discrimination and most paid a high price for their insistence on being treated as equals. Today's women in law enforcement are part of the third large wave of women in policing. They expect to be treated as equals.

At the beginning of 2004, we have five women who are chiefs of major city police departments and two who are heading state law enforcement agencies. We estimate that there are about 100 more who are chiefs of small departments and campus law enforcement agencies. This sounds impressive until we realize that there are 18,000 police chiefs in the U.S. We have made some changes, but we have a long way to go.

Because of the low numbers of women in law enforcement, the women who are there now still face daily challenges to be recognized for their excellent work and to be considered equal to their male partners. Although a lot of the discrimination is subtler, it still exists and in some places is still blatant.

The women in this book step boldly out of these pages as multidimensional people who are changing the definition of police work. They are mothers, daughters, sisters, wives and partners, lesbian and straight, representing all racial categories and all belief systems. Their hopes and fears, triumphs and tragedies help us understand the challenges they face. We gain an appreciation for their bravery on the streets of our communities and in the police stations. They are kicking down the last doors that bar women from full integration. They are joining SWAT teams, motorcycle squads and anti-terrorism units. And, as they open these final frontiers, they are showing that women indeed can perform any role in policing and do it well. And, as we have seen since the first women entered policing, they are bringing their feminine values and styles to these jobs. They use excessive force much less often than their male counterparts, receive fewer citizen complaints and epitomize a style of policing that is more community oriented.

We owe these women a debt of gratitude for sharing their stories with us. An added bonus is the helpful advice they share for recruiting and retaining women. Chiefs and sheriffs would be smart to read this book and learn about the challenges these women face and their innovative ideas for improving policing.

It is rewarding to know that, as I and other women of my generation retire from the world of law enforcement, there are thousands of bright, eager, and brave young women stepping in to replace us and build upon what we started. We salute our sisters in law and wish them well.

Chief Penny Harrington

Penny Harrington is the former chief of police of Portland, Oregon and the first woman in the nation to head a major city police department. She is also the Founding Director of the National Center for Women & Policing.

Preface

"What attracted me was the adventure, the courage, the sheer guts of it."

"You're very independent. It was my patrol car, my district, my responsibility and I had to think on my feet."

"I learned integrity from her. I learned about tact and how to be assertive and not be considered a bitch."

"I'd rather investigate a case and put the bad guy in jail than supervise whiny babies telling on each other."

"I was never afraid to say, I'm a little confused here. Can you help me out?"

"You win more fights with your mouth than with your hands, is what I tell all new people."

"She has these little come-to-Jesus meetings in the parking lot when she has an issue with one of her officers. What a great way of doing management."

"If it were possible to be a part-time officer, I'd be there in a heartbeat."

Motives—adventure and independence. Mentors, essential. A downside to promotion. Handling things a woman's way. Why women leave—children. These are just a few of the expected and unexpected themes my interviews with women police revealed.

Here are a few facts behind why I put this book together. In 1999, women made up 14.3% of officers in police agencies with 100 or more sworn personnel, but in 2001 their percentage had declined to 12.7%. If we combine small and large agencies, women only represent 11.2% of all sworn law enforcement personnel in the U.S., which is dramatically less than the 46.5% of women in the labor force (*Equality Denied*, National Center for Women & Policing, 2002). This report also says that more than half (56%) of large agencies have no women in top command positions, while 97% of small agencies have no women in top command positions. The report concludes that given the difficult challenges facing modern police agencies (such as excessive use of force), the imperative to hire more women has never been more urgent. There are increasing fears among police administrators that the number of female chiefs has peaked (Leinwand, 2004).

Two of my earlier books, *Women Changing Work* (Greenwood Press) and *Women Police Officers: Current Career Profile* (Charles C Thomas), found that women were changing the way male-dominated work was done in three ways. They had a strong service orientation to the public, a caring, nurturing attitude toward coworkers, and a steady need to balance work and family. But if the workplace ignores the necessity for childcare, flexible work schedules, job sharing, and job-protected family time off, women will leave the job. Ironically, men police benefit even more than women from family-friendly policies because of their sheer numbers.

To attract more women to the police service, I had several goals in mind for this book. For young women contemplating career choices and older women contemplating career change, here is what they need to know about women in law enforcement. For women officers, the book would share ideas about how to improve recruitment, training, retention, and promotion of women. These ideas are also intended for police administrators concerned about the declining percentages. And lastly, I wanted the general public to learn what women police are really like and how they succeed in this nontraditional occupation.

So I put out the call, starting in, of all places, the little towns on Washington's Olympic Peninsula. My sister is a senior volunteer officer in Sequim. She regularly mails me local newspaper articles that feature women officers. Why not pilot-test my interview schedule where I felt comfortable? When I was satisfied with my questions, I asked the International Association of Women Police, to which I now belong, to email my pitch to the membership and in October 2001 my husband and I started a trek across the country. I solicited interviews with the following email:

I am a retired professor of psychology and women's studies at the University of Washington. Two of my books concerned women police: *Women Police Officers: Current Career Profile* and *Women Changing Work*. I am now putting together a book based on interviews with women police—*Women Police: Portraits of Success*. I have a three-fold audience in mind—women considering a career in law enforcement, police officers who could use an aid in recruiting, and police executives who make policies that affect women police. My questions cover the decision to join, recruitment strategies, how to prepare for training, ideas about retaining officers, and promotion. As I did in my previous books, I also want to document the unique qualities women bring to law enforcement and how they balance home life and work life. I am happy to listen to war stories but that's not what the book is about. My goal is to attract more women to law enforcement by clarifying what the job is really all about.

Between September 2001 and May 2003, I taped interviews with over 50 women all told, 38 in Washington State, 15 in Oregon, Arkansas, Oklahoma, New York, Texas, and Alaska. Six of the Washingtonians had worked in other states—Illinois, New Mexico, Florida, Nevada, Hawaii, Oregon. Six were African American, Hispanic, or Asian. Other demographics about the group are sprinkled throughout the book: Types of agencies employed by, Chapter 4; ranks, marital status, and number of children, Chapter 5; college majors and years education, Chapter 6; age at joining and years in the police, Chapter 9.

Retired Kent, WA, Officer Trisha King-Stargel felt, "Everybody's going to get the nudge from a different place. I remember lying in bed reading this true story about a woman officer for the NYPD transit authority. After that book, I was positive I wanted to be a police officer." If this book succeeds, more and more women will be positive.

My apologies to this group of wonderful women and readers for any errors that may have crept in. They are totally mine.

1

Introduction

To attract more women to law enforcement, I have taken an in-depth look at the lives of women officers from tiny rural Western towns to Brooklyn South, NYC. Here readers into career decision-making or craving career change can learn what draws women to the job and what keeps them on the job. What daily challenges and satisfactions can you expect? How can you balance police work and family responsibilities? *Portraits* also deals with recruitment, training, retention, and promotion issues through firsthand accounts of how these women successfully dealt with each in turn.

This is the place where a woman can learn if the police service is for her. It also serves other audiences as well—the general public seeking answers about what the job is really like, career counselors, police recruiters, and law enforcement agencies at the city, state, and federal levels trying to attract more women to protect and serve.

Here is a run-down on the book's organization and a glimpse of what lies ahead. The chapter, "The Housewife, the Dancer, and the Pilot," is about changing careers and illustrates the wide variety of jobs women leave. Other women had worked as a travel agent, school bus driver, newspaper editor, phlebotomist, flight attendant. If they could make the switch, you could too.

"Patrol and Family Life" testifies to how very difficult it is to balance family and job. Here, officers who love police work explain how sometimes the children have to come first, and later the job can come first. If balance is important to you, you can do it.

Three detectives who work in radically different departments talk about their lives in "Life as a Detective." One detective had a trying time at the academy, while another had a field training officer who had serious "issues" with women. The third is the de facto chief in her little town as she is its only cop. With whom do you most identify?

The idea of sitting behind a desk for some sergeants remains anathema to the freedom and independence of riding in a patrol car. In "Sergeants in the Field," three women out in the field supervising teams of officers describe their satisfactions. Demographics for the whole group including marital status, physique, and number of children are also here. Is out in the field where you'd like to work?

One way sergeants end up as "Sergeants in the Office" is to recover from injuries. Others create a new position, a perfect fit for their talents, interests and values. A third motive is the recognition that the higher they go, the more they can shape department policy. So, which is it for you, the field or the office? The women's educational background is also presented.

Three sergeants who solved the problem of balancing childrearing and policing detail how they do it. Highlighted in "Sergeants and Family Life" is the importance of a woman researching different agencies to find which one has the most family-friendly attitudes. But if you're looking for something else in an agency, this research is still vital.

Sometimes women's fascination began watching TV cop shows. "Starting Early" can also result from a criminal justice course or a friend's badgering, "Come on, take the test with me." Then there are those parents who say, "You need to get a job." So at 21, these women became cops. How like these early starters are you?

In "Starting Late" you'll meet a county deputy who joined at 43, a sergeant who began at age 37, an officer who left dental assisting at age 41, and a sergeant who was in marketing for 14 years until she got sick of being behind a desk and joined at 36. Here is inspiration for women who think, Oh, it's a young person's job.

"You know what you have to do and you do it. I like the freedom to do my job." "I wanted to be on my own, making my own decisions." "I miss being out and about and involved finding out what's going on." Women police have downright "Independent Personalities." How important to you are independence and making your own decisions?

Two chiefs in "Command Thoughts about Recruitment" describe the intern programs they use in recruiting. All of my interviewees said that word of mouth—everybody playing the role—was the number one way recruitment could be expanded. But you don't have to wait for them to come to you. What do they think? Is policing a good fit for you?

"A Suburban Commander and a Small Town Chief" see their role as being there for different groups in their communities, out and about where they can be seen and talked to. They have been able to implement more social programs than they could have working as state social workers. Do you share their passion for the community?

"Command Thoughts about Family Life" tackles the crucial issue of childcare. Women cops use parents, grandparents, sisters and brothers, neighbors and friends when duty calls. It also helps to have an understanding, flexible boss, and, for some, a stay-at-home husband. Are children in your life plans? How are you going to care for them?

"What ended up working in recruitment was the department's reputation for being family-friendly. I always told my staff that you can't do this job and survive psychologically unless you have support," so said a retired chief in "The Importance of Family Support." What's your family situation? Where will you get your support?

The president of Oklahoma Women in Law Enforcement and the president of the International Association of Women Police speak out in "Support from Women's Organizations." Their organizations' conferences offer all kinds of training, but what the women get most from these gatherings is camaraderie. Does membership in women's organizations appeal to you?

"Where Are They Now" is a great illustration of the flux in women officers' lives, while "Summary: Expected and Unexpected Themes" is just that.

After all this, readers will be in a position to ask themselves, "With which women do I most connect? Whose life most inspires me? Whose personality is closest to my own? Whose interests mirror mine? How high would I like to go? Do I have what it takes to succeed in today's male-dominated police service?"

2

The Housewife, the Dancer, and the Pilot

Many women sergeants and above wistfully recall their early days as patrol officers. They allow as how, under pressure from above, they finally tested and were promoted, but what they most enjoyed was cruising around in that car and taking calls. So patrol is missed by lots of people. Patrol means you are very independent. It's your car, your district, your responsibility, and you have to think on your feet. You have to size up situations on your own and decide what action to take and whether to involve other officers. You like being out in the field and you don't like sitting behind a desk. When women in their thirties join up, it is often because they can't stand being stay-at-home moms any longer or are sick of corporate management. They don't join the police to rise in the ranks. They join to escape the tedium of their present careers.

Not surprisingly, I found a significant relationship between age at entry to law enforcement and whether or not this was a career change. Of the 16 women who had not made a career change, fifteen had entered at age 26 or less. And of the 37 women who had made a career change, twenty joined after age 26. Because these officers came from such a wide range of occupations, readers need to get a flavor of that variety so they, too, can say, "If she could make the change, I could, too." What follows are three portraits of women who left widely diverse occupations to become police officers.

The Housewife

Master Patrol Officer L. Jean VanLandingham was born in 1944 in Ft. Smith, Arkansas, and is one-sixteenth Choctaw. She and her husband had been next-door neighbors all their life. When he graduated from college, she married him as a junior in high school and finished her diploma by correspondence. Her husband is an assistant mayor. Their daughter is now 39, their son 34. Jean has 122 credit hours in police science, the equivalent of a bachelor's degree from Oklahoma State University. She joined the Tulsa, OK, PD in 1978, the ninth female hired by the city to work the street in uniform. The squad she currently oversees has 12 members (three women) who police one-twelfth of the city. This is what Jean had to say.

Nobody Took Me Seriously

When my daughter was a senior in high school and my son an eighth-grader, I told my family I was enrolling in college and that I wanted to be a police officer. Nobody took me seriously. Their attitude was, If you get through school, we'll see. It wasn't a discouraging attitude, it was just, Well, you've never had a career and that's what you're talking about. You're not talking about working until you get Christmas money and then quitting.

If my mother could have had an abortion 35 years after the fact, she would have. She was always asking afterward, When are you going to get a desk job? Mother, I'm not. My father used to say, I guess I did something right. They could either be cops or criminals, because my brother was a state trooper. He was very proud of both of us. It was my mother, who was an office manager and worked until she died, who taught us strength—you can do it if you say you can do it.

I was a housewife and a mother before I joined the police department. The day I got my badge and my husband pinned it on me was my proudest moment. It meant I had to go to college and I'd never been in a college atmosphere. I had an age restriction. I had to get on before I turned 35. I had to compete with men who were closer to my children's age than mine. This was a goal that I wanted, a career, not a part-time job.

Officer Mom at the Academy

The academy class graduated on February 28, 1978. I turned 35 on February the 10th. I had to be sworn in before my thirty-fifth birthday. The captain at the academy, a sergeant, and the deputy chief called me in on the tenth of February and the deputy chief swore me in as a police officer and told me never to tell a soul. He gave me his badge. I have his badge to this day. When he was killed in a car wreck after his retirement, I tried to give it back to his wife but she wouldn't take it. My husband knew it and I knew it and those guys knew it and the paperwork knew it. But for years I didn't tell a soul.

Most of the 16 weeks of training I went through was scholastic. I was proud that I was number two in my class, the only female of the 12 in the class. I was Officer Mom, ten years older than the next person in my class. But the men weren't going to defeat me, they weren't going to beat me down. You've got to conduct yourself with the attitude that you're the boss. The public or whoever I'm dealing with is not going to intimidate me. I've got the gun, I've got the badge, and by George, you're going to do what I say.

I'd Rather Work the Field

Seniority-wise when I came on, graveyard was the only thing I could get. It was the best thing that could happen to me because I was home in the morning to get my children ready for school. I'd sleep from eight in the morning until two in the afternoon. I had time for their after-school activities and evening programs—my son was a swimmer, my daughter was in Job's Daughters. We had dinner as a family. We watched a little TV. I slept through it but they watched it. They did their homework, they bathed and went to bed. I bathed and went to work. The only person it really affected was my husband and he learned to sleep by himself for five nights a week. Then on my days off, I would stay up all day and just be dead.

What I put up with at first was we'd be at a call and it's my call, my decision. And the guy walks in front of me and starts taking over. When I arrived first, people would talk to me. But the minute my male backup got there, they ignored me. The guy I work with now tells them, This is her call. It's her decision. I'm listening, but you talk to her.

I got hurt last April and I couldn't count how many guys said, Just wait till he gets out of jail. It was a drunk huffing carburetor cleaner. He threw the carburetor cleaner on me and tried to set me on fire with a lighter. Then he jumped on me and grabbed my ears, tore my earrings off, ripped my earlobes out. I finally broke his hold and he fell down and the only thing I could think of was, He's not getting away. I rode him like a dog. I jumped on his back and locked my feet around him. I got a handcuff on one arm and thought, If nothing else, I'm going to handcuff him to me. About that time civilians came running and pushed him down so I could handcuff him. We have an emergency button and the first guy to get there was a cycle officer and he was really ticked off. Why did you handcuff him? Because he wanted to beat the pulp out of the guy and couldn't if he was handcuffed. My uniform was ripped off and there was blood everywhere. As long as anyone could remember, nobody got that much jail time for an assault on a police officer, but the guy got five years. The judge asked me, Can you settle for that? I said, Yes, I can. I'll be gone by then.

I've had two plastic surgeries. I also broke my thumb which could be a career-ending injury. I'm going to have surgery on it but when I do, my career will be over. They'll take out a bone that means I will have no grip. I probably won't be able to shoot left-handed and can't qualify at the range. I'm playing it by ear.

Our department has an incentive for acquiring higher education, money, so those 122 college credit hours I earned meant I earned more. I chose not to be a supervisor. I stay working in the field as an officer, a "slick sleeve," meaning no rank. That's another incentive the department offers. We get a little bit more pay. We lose maturity and experience in the field through promotion. When you get to be a supervisor, you don't work with the people. I'd rather work the field than do paperwork.

Equality with the Men

The number one reason why a female should consider the police is that it is about the only occupation, from my experience in the Bible Belt of America, where we get equal pay for equal service. The radio that assigns us a call doesn't know our gender. It doesn't care whether you're male or female, or whether you're nearly 60 or 21. You've got a number and that number is associated with an area in town and if there's a call from that area, you're going to get that call.

I feel a lot of satisfaction knowing that I can shoot as well as a man, and I used to fight as well as a man. I'm very strong-willed and I won't be discriminated against. I'd speak up before it happened. It's very important to women that we have equal opportunity to promote, to advance as high as we want to, or stay where we are and do the work we want to do. Women don't have to act like men but you've got to be able to conduct yourself with the attitude that you're the boss.

Several years back, I was working at the police booth at the state fair and met a very nice Black female who worked for the city already. She was a chemist with a master's degree, she tested the water we drink. She was from New York, and her father was a retired police officer. She talked to me about the job and said, Oh, it looks like a lot of fun. I said, You ought to put your application in. She did and she's been in the department five years in the detective division. It works, just meeting people who ask, Why did you pick this job? What do you do? A lot of women today don't want to be desk jockeys. When they find out I drive a police car by myself and answer calls by myself, as women, they're interested. When I compare my early volunteer work at a hospital with police work, the hospital's got boundaries, but out here, there are no boundaries. It says City of Tulsa on my sleeve and I can go anywhere I want.

My New Job

I became editor of *Women Police* because I wanted something that would challenge me both mentally and physically and be fun, too. The magazine has always interested me, it has always been very professional. I also like the recognition. I enjoy the IAWP conferences. I'm getting close to retirement so if younger women coming into the department asked to go to a conference, the department would send them before they'd send me. The magazine was a way to guarantee that I could go without paying for it myself, or the department sending me. Our chief likes for his officers to be recognized nationally and internationally. Our department is well-educated, professional, and all-round.

What I enjoy most about the meetings are the close friendships. I also like getting to know women from other countries, and having experiences like going to China in 1988. We were the first group of women police officers in China. I get a lot of gratification from the fact that Tulsa PD doesn't have the problems other departments do. When I come back, I say, Thank you, Lord, for letting me choose this department. One group of women from Texas all worked desk. They were officers, but they never got field assignments. Why would you want to qualify yourself every year at the range to sit behind a desk?

Family Issues

A fourth of the women who join the department leave. Baby-sitting is a terrible burden. We work 24 hours, seven days a week, we work holidays, we don't know what a holiday is. My weekend is Sunday, Monday. For years my weekend was Tuesday, Wednesday. When I began, my shift was graveyard, eleven until seven, so my days were nights, and my nights were days. It can be very confusing for family life. Women's husbands encourage them to quit and stay home and raise their families. Some, as soon as they have put in twenty years, leave to stay home. A friend who quit when she got her twenty in, commented, My girls are in high school. I have missed the last ten years of their lives and I want to be part of the last two years, the proms, graduation, everything.

We need to get childcare for the men's sake too. There are several single dads here. I have a friend who has been a single dad for twenty-odd years who has raised two boys on his own. I was talking with a woman in her forties with a 14-year-old and a 10-year-old who said how lucky she was to draw dayshift because there's no daycare on graveyard. The weighing of family life is so important and that's what takes women before it takes men, that guilt, that motherly instinct.

Paulette's Legacy

My favorite mentor died last October. We remained very close friends even after she retired from the police department. She joined four years before I did. I rode with her as a volunteer in the traffic division every Tuesday night. That began in 1972 in the auxiliary police, which is the reserves today. I had to qualify at the range every year just like everybody else. Paulette's shift was from 3:30 in the afternoon until 11:30. That was my night out, mother's day off. I'd put on my police uniform and go ride with her. One day she said, Why are you doing this for free? Why don't you get paid for it? You like it. You're good at it. I said, But I'd have to go to college. She said, Big deal. Go to college. Paulette was very professional and very much a lady. She was my role model. I wasn't the only person she mentored. She had a real good life. She meant a lot to a lot of people.

The first woman I mentored was a young college woman who was a ride-along with me and said, I want to be a police officer. I'm going to join the auxiliary. I told her what Paulette told me, Hey, do it for money. If this is what you want to do, don't wait until you're 35. Do it now. She put in her application and flunked the physical. They decided she had curvature of the spine even though she'd never been diagnosed. She called me and I told her, Fight it. Don't take no for an answer. To be a good cop, you can't take no for an answer. It had never affected any part of her life and then a city physician who practices in the basement of a police department and sees nothing but bruises, says, You've got curvature of the spine. She fought it and she's in the department, married to an officer.

The Right Mindset for Promotion

A woman needs to adopt an I-can-do-it attitude. She's got to be able to be the boss. Because when she's promoted, 90% of the people in the area she works will be men. And while women are known to be better test-takers than men, our oral interviews aren't graded as highly as the men's. The reason is that lots of men have had military training and experience with taking orders and, if they've been supervisors, giving orders. Women don't have that experience. Women need verbal command training. But the only way to go through the assessment process is to take the test. A lot of male officers will take the test without studying because everybody who takes the test goes through the assessment center and they want to get a feel for the oral interviews. We have in-service training on taking the stand as a witness and on report writing. We should have in-service training strictly on promotions—the skills you need to work on so you aren't blind-sided or terrified about what's going to happen.

Women who really want to be promoted don't have to study for it. They think they do, but they make those decisions every day in the field. You don't have an hour to sit down and figure a situation out. You have to make decisions in an instant. And it has to be the right decision, not only for your protection and the other person's protection, but for the police department's protection, too, from civil liability. You make them for yourself, but when you become a supervisor, you're making decisions for everybody in your squad. Women can do it, they just have to have the right mindset.

The Dancer

Retired Auxiliary Sergeant Judith Rock, born in 1946 and married to the Director of Interfaith Relations for the National Council of Churches, has a BA from Duke University in religion, an MA in divinity from San Francisco Theological Seminary, an MA in dance from Mills College, and a Ph.D. in Theology and Art from the Graduate Theological Union in Berkeley.

In 1991, after twenty years as a dancer, Judith became a part-time auxiliary officer for the NYPD, for which she worked a total of four years. She also was a part-time officer for Northfield, Minnesota PD for three years and is a graduate of the Florida State Academy. She is now an artist and continues to use her police experience through performing in her one-woman show called *Response Time* and through writing a novel with a female cop protagonist. Here is what Judith had to say.

The Sheer Guts of It

I began my working life as an ordained clergywoman in the Presbyterian Church. I was the only woman who graduated in my seminary class. This was early '70s in Berkeley and I was dealing with a lot of feminist issues and coping as a woman in what was still an almost entirely male world. This is one of the reasons I became fascinated later on with women police.

It was when I had a dance company in the Bay Area, mid-70s, that I began to notice female police officers on patrol in San Francisco. Often small, Hispanic women wearing two tons of equipment and I thought, What on earth can it be like as a woman? I wanted to know more about them, but I was in the middle of my career in dance and it never occurred to me that I could enter that other world. What attracted me was the adventure, the courage, the sheer guts of it. And there were times when I wished I had a weapon on my belt in dealing with some guys.

I tried to join the NYPD, but I was too old. Their age limit was 35. But I found out there was an auxiliary unit that didn't have an age limit so I began auxiliary training in January 1991. Got my shield in May and had a few months with them before moving to Northfield, MN. Because my dance career was coming to an end because of a knee injury, I took on a four-year teaching stint at St. Olaf College in the dance department. I questioned whether it was what I wanted to do for the rest of my life, but it was tenure track, it was money, it was my field.

So now I was an assistant professor, but very early on I was trying to persuade myself I could do this job. I had had that taste of police work in New York and I absolutely loved it down to the ground. When I got to Northfield, I lost something and had to go to the police department to report it and I met their only woman officer and we really hit it off. I found out there was a reserve unit, so I joined it. About a year later a part-time slot came up and I bothered the chief until he hired me. My field training officer was the female officer who was the only woman full-time at that point.

Troubles with Training

I was part-time for three years. Then I decided to try for a full-time slot. The college was having financial difficulties, my job was taken off the tenure track, and when I got that news my immediate response was not, Oh, dear, how terrible. It was, Oooh, I get to leave. In 1994 I tested for LAPD and got a provisional offer. They'd done a gender equity report with the Center for Policing and were recruiting women. I went out to their academy and watched and I knew this wasn't going to work, watching them run straight up the side of a canyon. I also tested for Berkeley but I couldn't make it over the bloody wall.

I grew up in Florida, which doesn't have an age limit so I went through the full-time academy in Florida in the fall of 1995. I did as much running as I could.

I went to a stadium and ran up and down the bleachers. You had to be able to drag a 200 pound weight, so my husband let me drag him around the gym floor by his T-shirt. I was really good at weight-dragging. I practiced beforehand as much as I could but it was still pretty hard. I was way the oldest, 49, most of them were in their twenties. But I did the whole nine yards and graduated and I was proud of myself for having the guts to see it through.

Partly because I had realized this was probably not going to work out, and I didn't have much to lose, I started being aggressive about confronting men. Two young men from a SWAT team were teaching officer survival. One of them prefaced his lesson by saying, Being a cop, you don't have a lot of free time. There you are at home and you gotta cut the grass, feed the dog, beat the wife. I looked around at these people in their twenties and I thought, I am as old as this guy's mother and this is going no farther. I pulled age rank on him, went up afterward and repeated back what he said. He was astounded. It was new information to him that anybody minded. I said, You're teaching, these are young people, feel free to report me if you want to, but you cannot do this.

My Ultimate Decision

As I said, in the course of the academy I realized that my chances of actually landing a job were very small. My knee was telling me that I was getting closer and closer to the edge. Although I never had trouble on the job when I was working, I became concerned that I was not going to catch the 17-year-old kid if it was up to me to chase him. Or if my partner was in trouble and I had to run to help him, I might not make it. It wasn't going to be safe for me or my partner. And as a woman sergeant said to me in Berkeley, Do you really want to have a 30-year-old training officer pounding on the desk and screaming at you? It was going to be psychologically harder to start fully in the system than I had realized. Part-time is one thing, reserve is another, but being completely inside the system at age 50 and starting at the bottom? It was very hard to say, Okay, I'm not going to take this farther, but it was the right decision. I returned to New York in December 1995, rejoined the auxiliary unit, was made a sergeant and worked until 1998.

I Am Exactly in the Right Place

NYPD auxiliaries don't have firearms. You look the same, you wear the same uniform, unless you get up close and read the patch and the brass. We used to joke about being decoys, equal opportunity targets. Every precinct has an auxiliary unit. You do foot patrol in pairs at night and you're assigned to a post with a sergeant as supervisor. You're out there as a deterrent, you do a lot of question-answering, what anybody does on patrol. When something happens, it's your job to contain the situation, call it in, and hold the fort until the regulars get there. But if people are shooting at each other, you get out of there because you don't have the ability to deal with that.

Being a sergeant is not as much fun as patrol because you're involved more in supervising than handling situations and I'd rather handle situations. But I liked being a supervisor partly because I had some say in the direction of the auxiliary program. I liked being able to step in with a female voice and say, Let's look at this alternative. A lot of the young guys had never had a female supervisor so they were always testing.

When I was at Northfield, we got a call that someone was sitting in a kitchen, threatening to commit suicide with a shotgun. Some officers hated dealing with potential suicides. They weren't patient, rather they got angry. So I was the person who ended up doing all the talking. This night I managed to talk this young retarded man into putting down the gun. Then I took him to the emergency room and I stayed in the examining room with him while the doctor was out looking for a placement. The guy started talking about how ever since he was a little boy he'd wanted to be a police officer because he wanted to help other people and make them safe. But he knew that he wasn't bright enough to do that. That's what had gotten to him that night—he thought he wasn't good for anything. I had a lot of struggles in Northfield as someone who was fairly different. It wasn't easy to fit in as a cop there, and sometimes I felt sorry for myself. I stood there listening to him and I thought, I am so lucky that I get to do this. The kid really gave me a gift. The doctor came back and I went out in the hall and standing there, in the middle of the night, in this deserted hospital corridor, I was flooded with the feeling of, I am as happy as a human being gets to be. I am exactly in the right place.

Women in the Male Police Culture

I learned from my FTO at Northfield that one way women are changing the police culture has to do with the importance of talking to deal with situations. She could get as hardnosed as the next cop when she had to, but most of the job is about talking. She was really good at that and she taught me to be good. She was one of those patient, unemphatic Midwestern people, she didn't get ruffled. We had different major skills. It was a good combination.

She also had a good sense of humor, like one night we were called to a domestic. A Hispanic guy was very drunk, angry about some perceived insult to his family and on his way to avenge the insult. We arrested him. I speak some Spanish and she was learning Spanish so we would speak Spanish together. A lot of Hispanics were coming there to work in the vegetable and chicken packing houses, so their presence was creating some new situations for the PD. I tried to calm this guy down in Spanish, explaining why he was being arrested, and he had these big thick glasses and he started yelling at me that I was just a Tejana from South Texas and I couldn't talk to him like that. I said, Sir, in addition to your other problems, you need to get your glasses changed. We put him in the car and started to take him back to the station for processing, when a bunch of kids got into a fight at the Taco Bell. So we had to go to the Taco Bell with the guy in the back seat. I was told to stay in the car with him and he thinks we've stopped there to get him something to eat so he's yelling out what he wants. Policing is mostly about people and a lot of it goes from heartbreaking to hilarious.

When I would walk into a situation, I tended to hang back a little and watch, if the world wasn't coming to an end, which it usually wasn't, to get a sense of what is going on. Who are the players? How serious is this? Probably the most mortified I ever was publicly was at a disturbance in a bar. There was a crowd and I was taking a minute to size up the situation. All of a sudden I felt hands on my arms. My sergeant was behind me and he just set me aside and waded into the situation. I was so embarrassed I wanted to die, and angry too because it wasn't like I wasn't going to do anything. He interpreted my taking a minute to look as incompetence, not knowing what to do. I remember how much that hurt and there was no way I could say, Hey, wait a minute. I was too new and too low on the totem pole.

It's not easy to cross the huge wall between NYPD auxiliaries and regulars, which makes my perspective that of an outsider. Some people are really friendly and open, other people feel auxiliaries threaten their turf. Chatting with the women regulars I sensed that many of them were stuck "trying to be one of the guys." They seemed to be under a lot of pressure. I asked them from time to time if they were part of the IAWP or the New York Region and mostly the answer was no. I came to feel that the gender situation in the NYPD, in terms of progress and changing, is running behind some other departments, certainly behind Berkeley, Madison, and Portland. What is 110% true is that if a department wants to recruit women, the more women it has, the more women it will recruit.

Sometimes cultural differences were harder to deal with than gender challenges. I come from a working class family but because of my educational background and what I've done professionally, people made assumptions that weren't true. It was like making my way through a jungle to communicate sometimes. They were doing a background check in Florida before the academy and I was interviewed by a retired Long Island cop. I had even considered not giving all my educational history because I sensed that this was not going to be cool. But he was going to find out anyway so I thought, I'd better not give him a reason for me to have a problem. I told him the whole story, and he listened, and before I was done talking, he threw his pencil down and looked me right in the eye and said, Well, there went your chances for a job. When I told him I had a doctorate, instead of saying, That's interesting, and thinking, Maybe this person has some skills that we could put to use, you could see the disgust on his face. He was saying, Nobody's going to hire you. You have too much education. You're too different. If I had said, I have high school and two years of military service, that would have been great.

Women's Organizations, A Godsend

When I was in Northfield, the other thing that was important to me besides my training officer, this woman who became a good friend, was the Minnesota Association of Women Police. It was a godsend. I went to meetings held various places around the state and the big annual meeting usually around the Twin Cities. There would be trainings and I felt so welcomed, accepted, and supported. These women were less startled and put off by my different educational and professional background than men were. The women were simply interested, if it came up at all, whereas men were often threatened. I heard other women's stories, mostly full-time women, about their moments of being pushed out of the way or being misinterpreted. I learned how awful field training can be for new women officers. These women were so committed, both to policing and to transforming policing in ways that they thought were right.

I've stayed connected with them and help support them. The state groups and the regional groups within the IAWP perform a fundamental service for women police officers, particularly for young women coming in. It used to be that if you joined and there were only two or three women in the department with the men not so sure about this, you got your consciousness raised quickly. Now if you join and there are 14% women in your department, it is less obvious to somebody who is 21 that there is a problem. So it's essential that these local groups recruit young women.

An enticement is scholarships. To get training, either you have to have enough seniority for the department to pay for it, or you have to be able to afford it yourself. Most people starting out in law enforcement can't afford it. I was in a position to give the MAWP money to start a scholarship fund. So they're able to give some people a little bit of help. My intention is to contribute more to that. If you say, Here's a scholarship, take your days off, come stay in a hotel, have fun, someone's more likely to do that. And a scholarship also feels like, Oh, I'm special.

You also have to have women who are part of these organizations talk about it. I did that when I was in the auxiliary because there were women who wanted to go through the academy and I gave them copies of the IAWP magazine. We could give a free subscription to *Women Police* to every academy graduate.

I went back and performed *Response Time* for the MAWP, which was so scary to do for a room full of women cops. But women are more open about their inner lives as police officers. After I did the show I had a talk-back time. This one deputy from some rural county in northern Minnesota just blew me away. There's a point where I talk about how I roll up on something, get out of the car, and pieces of life script are blowing around my feet, as if some library had collapsed and a forgotten language was flying about in the street. Because one of my experiences was, I'd get to a situation and have no idea what people were talking about, and what they were talking about was passionately important to them. Even if it was a felony. This rural deputy was the last person I would have expected to understand, but she raised her hand and said, When you said that about the pieces of life script blowing around your feet, I feel like that every time I roll up on something.

Response Time is connecting with what this job means to people because it means an enormous amount to most cops and there are very few venues in which they can talk about it. When I went back to do the show they also had a poetry session where everybody sat on the floor with wine and cheese. St. Paul's police chief's wife was there, reading. I couldn't believe it. Women had brought their poetry, most of it about being cops and we were crying and laughing. I thought, Do men do this when they go to meetings? Most departments would be happier places if they did.

Coming to police work from a background in dance, choreography, and theology, I always wanted to know what things meant. My Northfield partner would tease me about it. She came to see the show, and I knew she was coming to that performance so I dedicated it to her. I heard her talking to someone afterward who said, You two worked together, didn't you? She laughed and said, Yeah, we'd be driving along and I'd be watching the traffic and Judith would be watching how the light falls on the trees.

The Pilot

Julia Grimes was appointed head of Alaska State Troopers on May 29, 2003, four days after our interview. She forwarded to me a newspaper editorial headlined "A good choice for the top." It went on to say that Governor Frank Murkowski had done his bit to rectify the poor record of law agencies in having women in command positions. Now a Colonel/Director, Julia Grimes was born in 1957, has an AA degree in aviation flight technology and is married to a retired state trooper. When we met she had just graduated from the FBI National Academy. Because 17 of Julia's 20 years with the State Patrol were spent as a trooper, I'm putting her here with Jean and Judith.

We Need Women. You Should Apply.

I give my Dad complete credit for bringing me up with the attitude that I could do anything I wanted to do. I was always impatient. I started flying when I was 14 because my older sister Debbie had gotten her license. I was in that I-gotta-do-whatever-Debbie-does stage. He thought it would be a quick flight, I'd get sick, I wouldn't like it. But he was always supportive of my flying and my career as a pilot. However, he was not happy when I took the job of trooper.

I got my AA degree in 1976; it took me only a year. Then I went into flight instructing, because to become a commercial pilot you need to build time. I did that for two years and when I was 21 I got hired by United Airlines as a flight engineer/pilot. I worked for them for three years. Then the controllers went on strike and there was an oil embargo, which hit the airlines very hard and United started furloughing pilots and flight attendants. It took a year to get to me in my seniority number. I was based in New York, living on Long Island, so I found a float plane base and got my float plane rating. It was something I had always wanted to do.

I ended up working for this little air taxi company on the north shore of Long Island, float-instructed for them for a short time and then flew air taxi and charter in and out of Manhattan and the East River and all around the East Coast. In the winter they laid me off so I went to work for the FAA at the air traffic control center. I met a person who knew somebody in Fairbanks who had an air taxi company. Over the phone I got hired as a flight instructor with the expectation that come summer I'd get back into float operation. In January 1982 I packed everything I owned into the back of my Subaru and moved to Fairbanks and worked for this flying service until May. The float plane job didn't materialize. He gave the job to his brother.

So my girlfriend and I drove down to southeast Alaska, got on the ferry, and went to Ketchikan. Along the waterfront there were six air taxi companies. I went from one to the other, looking for a job and got hired by Tyee Airlines and flew de Havilland Beavers and 185s for them for the remainder of that year. On my passenger manifest were a lot of Alaska state troopers. I took them from Ketchikan over to all of the different villages. That's how I got recruited. We need women. We need pilots. You really should apply.

My Career in Law Enforcement

I took the job never having thought for a second of being a cop but I was drawn by the promise of flying, the benefits, the adventure. I went to the academy in January 1983. I spent a year in a very deep, undercover role in Juneau. I stayed in drugs for ten years. I did everything that we do in Alaska in drug enforcement, canine handler, more undercover, airport interdiction. In 1993 I was recruited by the current captain of C detachment, which is the west coast, the bush areas, the Aleutian chain, because they needed a trooper pilot in King Salmon.

With a lot of anxiety I bid the position and moved out to the bush. I was nervous because I had worked patrol only eleven months. Am I going to remember how to do misdemeanor law enforcement? In drugs it was all huge, major felony cases. My first bush post was King Salmon. I was there with one other trooper. He took all the villages south to Chignik Bay and I took the villages north along the Kvichak River and up into Iliamna. We shared the airplane. Although we had a marked patrol unit, all we did with it was drive from our house to our office and to the airport. The airplane is our patrol car from our post out to the villages where we did every type of law enforcement there is. We could write a traffic ticket if there was a state road out there to a homicide. It was full service law enforcement. That assignment was very, very exciting and I stayed in King Salmon for a year and moved in 1994 to Dillingham where I stayed five years. As a trooper pilot, the airplane went with me, same job, just different villages. Lots of dead bodies, airplane crashes, drownings.

Have you heard the term, VPSO? Part of the job out there was oversight for our Village Public Safety Officers, a program started 25 years ago. We have for-profit native corporations and non-profit native associations. The non-profits are responsible for all the social programs administered to the villages with federal money. The troopers and the non-profits came up with a plan to take state money and fund it through the Department of Public Safety to these non-profits which would then hire and employ local people, usually Alaskan natives from the village or surrounding villages and occasionally plain old white guys. They were our first responders in the villages doing misdemeanor law enforcement, fire protection, search and rescue, EMT. There are not now, nor will there ever be, enough troopers to put in every village. And because we fly to our villages, there could be a homicide late one night in the wintertime and it could be days before we get there. These VPSOs investigate misdemeanor crime and can make arrests and are first responders for the felony stuff that happens. They secure the scene and do the initial steps until we can get there. So they are very valuable employees.

I also taught DARE in two schools. One school I had to fly into to give the classes and at the other I would drive to the end of the road where there was a lake and the village of Aleknagik, which had a south shore community and a north shore community with the school on the north shore. In the summer I would take a skiff to the school and in the winter when the lake was frozen I would go across with the kids from the south shore in the dark in a giant version of a wooden dog sled pulled by a snow machine.

In 1999 I was ready to get back to civilization, which I did in an investigator position in our criminal investigation bureau here in Anchorage. I did that for a year, mostly homicides, major sexual assaults, sexual abuse of minors, lots of autopsies. Then in November 1999 I got promoted to sergeant, at which point I had been a trooper for almost 17 years. I then went to our judicial services unit here in town and worked in prisoner transport function, then moved over to the fugitive/extradition side of it for a year. Then I was reassigned from the JS unit back to our statewide drug enforcement unit. I was put in charge of our airport interdiction team in November 2000 and was there for a year as sergeant of that team. Then in November 2001 I competed for lieutenant's promotion and received that. I was now on the Director's staff and was chosen for a position to handle the legislative liaison work. I also administered two large federal grants for traffic enforcement. I went to the FBI National Academy from January to March of this year and in April I competed for the captain's position and was promoted a month ago.

As a captain I supervise six lieutenants in charge of various programs—concealed handgun permits, sex offender registry, security guard licensing, judicial services, equal opportunity commission, recruitment. Plus all the myriad duties that a recently retired major had. The headquarters staff is a field operations support unit so we handle whatever the field needs as far as equipment, writing grants for overtime for special enforcement projects, administering the distribution of the overtime. The Department of Public Safety is made up of five divisions. One is the division of Alaska State Troopers, which is 250 or so commissioned, then the division of Fish and Wildlife Protection, which is 91 commissioned. The missions right now are separated. AST does all of the regular public safety, criminal investigations of people crimes. Fish and Wildlife Protection does resource enforcement. A total of about 350 of which 17 are women.

A State Trooper Marriage

Eighteen years of my husband's career in the state patrol were spent in drug enforcement. He retired in 1994 but the troopers needed an experienced narcotics investigator so he has been doing that for the last one and a half years. I was about ten months on the job as a state trooper when we met. I was asked to participate in a very, very secret undercover drug investigation. They needed a female to be part of the team, someone no one knew, and I was brand new. Throughout our careers and married life, we're used to being apart, used to working on cases in different parts of the world, so for him to come back and do undercover stuff, it's just part of our life.

We got married in 1985. Jim was my sergeant in drugs and he was chosen to run Operation Snow White. We had had a complaint about drugs being used by lobbyists and the possibility that drugs were being used to influence the legislature. It was called Snow White because it had to be, down the line to every single letter, done perfectly. We got in with the people who were selling drugs and eventually we got to the level where cocaine was being distributed a line at a time like you'd buy one another drinks in a bar. We're not talking about street-level dealing or dealing for profit. It was simply use and distribution. Jim and I worked our way undercover into this crowd to where they were comfortable with us and we made several cases.

Major Mentors

For my leadership class at the National Academy I had to write about, How is it that you are who you are today? Who influenced you and how? I identified my Dad and my husband as my major mentors. Young people starting in a career in law enforcement hear the terms courage, integrity, and honor. You know what they mean but you may not necessarily have lived those values, and you're not fully in touch with what it means to live them.

Jim, through his actions and the way he did his work, taught me what it means to always do the right thing, to always take the right path, and be a person of integrity. There's no halfway. This has to be who you are. He is ten years older, he'd been there, and he'd been in the military. Those values are a part of being military, where men, and now women more and more, learn about these values to a greater extent than the average kid who graduates from high school, goes to college, and then goes out and gets a job. I admired him and respected him. We were friends and coworkers for two years before we got married. I developed such great respect for him and he was one of the most popular supervisors the troopers ever had. He was very, very good at what he did.

Family Issues

You will not find any other agency in the country that does police work the way we do. We expect our people to transfer to the bush. That is a huge part of what we do. It is difficult to move a large family out there. The housing is usually not great. Then if your spouse has any kind of a professional job, you're taking them into a tiny community where the opportunity to work is very slim. So the spouse goes and works at something they really don't want to do, or they stay behind, and you now have a trooper working out in the bush by himself or herself with the family elsewhere, which is very stressful. Depending on the ages of the kids, it's almost impossible.

Then there's the issue of female troopers trying to reconcile shift work with being pregnant. It's difficult when you have a two-person post and one of those troopers is out of commission for many, many months. We arrange for light duty if we can. The way the policy is written is that you're not entitled to it, but if there is some light duty somewhere, they'll try to accommodate you. Generally they are not working patrol. There are concerns now about shooting when pregnant.

We don't have a policy that says you get to be on a different shift because you're a parent. Because how many men are parents? If your seniority is such that you can't pull day shift, you're going to have to work swing and work your daycare around it. There are millions of women all over the country who have shift work as a part of their lifestyle and they make it. But a lot of the women we have lost couldn't make it work for whatever reason and felt it was more important to be a mother than a trooper.

There's the point of view that, when you became a trooper, did you have plans to have kids? If you did, you obviously thought you could work it out then. And now after we've invested all this time and money in you, you're quitting. It's hard because we've had very good female troopers leave. You can give guidance to new female police officers to help them make the right decisions, but there's no way to predict what's going to happen in that person's life that would cause them to have children earlier or later or pick certain career paths.

In our agency the women who have been successful in promotion and moving around have been married to troopers and with no children. We have the ability to be flexible. I try to be very frank with young women and say, You have got to understand that shift work is going to be a part of your life until you are senior enough to be out of it.

Why Join Women's Organizations?

I went over with four other women from Alaska to the IAWP conference in Australia. We had two conferences in Anchorage, in 1985 and 1998, and most are training conferences. However, the conference in Australia focused on the status of women in policing, and women police in Third World countries and how difficult their lives have been. A lot of women officers don't want to make an issue of gender. They go out and they do what they do. That is definitely me. I have never wanted anything I didn't earn.

Some women at the conference were a little put off by the emphasis on gender issues. But the speakers were excellent. There were a lot of male speakers talking about women's place in law enforcement and their progress, which added credibility. There wasn't a lot of whiny, we're poor women being put upon by men, because that is old news.

All told it was very good and I enjoyed the camaraderie. This was my fourth conference and you get so stoked meeting the most outstanding women and having lots of common things to talk about. I signed up for the San Francisco conference while I was there and they've already contacted me to be on a panel on promotional issues.

A lot of younger women aren't joiners and it's very difficult to convince them that the camaraderie and mentorship that come from being a part of the organization are worthwhile. We locally have the Women Police of Alaska of which I was the president for two years. We cannot get young women to become part of the organization. They say, Why? When we fight so hard to just be one of the members of the department, doing law enforcement, and don't want to be noticed. We just want to go do the job. I know that feeling. That's why it took me 17 years to promote because I wasn't interested in anything except doing the job. Young women view joining these organizations as women separating themselves out again, and bringing light upon us. But that is not the point of any if these organizations.

The Message

Readers now know that women come from all walks of life to police work. These women had been a karate school manager, accounts payable clerk, school bus driver, PBX operator, newspaper editor, board of trade floor manager, dental assistant, travel agent, phlebotomist, flight attendant, waitress, nurse's aide. Usually they got lured away by friends, colleagues, family members who said, "You really ought to try this."

Readers can ask themselves, "Who do I most identify with—the housewife, the dancer, or the pilot? Who do I most admire? Would I be as enthralled by patrol as they were? Am I as interested in being out of doors and on my own? How would I feel about riding around alone in a patrol car on graveyard shift? Do I have what it takes to make it through a police academy? Do I have what it takes to balance police work and family responsibilities?"

3

Patrol and Family Life

We've seen with Jean VanLandingham how having first the family and second the career plays out. As a mom you don't resent graveyard. You welcome it because then normal daytime family life can go on. Now for two women who tried to do the job and the family at the same time and what happened. This chapter presents readers with both the difficulties of this balancing act and the fact that there are alternative activities out there for keeping a hand in police work.

Dispatcher Mel Larson

Mel was born in 1959 in Butte, Montana. She is married to a firefighter and they have a son, 17, and a daughter, 14. At the age of 19 Mel became a dispatcher and at 20½ she tested and got hired by the Bellevue, WA, PD for which she worked nine years. She gave up being a commissioned officer and became a part-time dispatcher for the city in 1989 when her second child was born. She's been on the radio ever since.

Mel says she could never be a stay-at-home person. She could never have gone from police work to nothing. Patrol is in her blood and she has to keep her fingers in it enough to, as she says, get that little fix. I finally had to ask her to turn off the radio because my tape recorder was picking up music and news as much as Mel. She always has it on, even when she sleeps, a holdover from those days in the patrol car.

From Dispatcher to Patrol Officer

I first thought about law enforcement as a career when I was sixteen. I have an uncle who was a deputy sheriff and state patrolman in Montana. I thought, I like that, I can do that. He's a great guy, a big teddy bear. I also had a very good friend, already working for the Bellevue Police Department, who helped bring me along, because I'd go ride with her and other people and it strengthened my decision. I got my foot in the door as a dispatcher to make it easier for me to hire on as an officer.

Most of what I did to prepare for the academy was physical—running, sit-ups, push-ups, lifting weights. I've been in sports my whole life. My girlfriend and I helped the other women get over the six-foot wall. We'd sit on top of the wall and have them hit the wall and we'd pull them over so they could get a feeling for it, and after that it was all technique. By the time we got out of there, we could get over the wall three different ways. The first time we did it my girlfriend was the only one who made it. She got her chin on top of that wall and pulled herself over with her chin. The only part of the academy that intimidated me was running, not because of lack of endurance but I'm not a speedster. I've been shooting guns since I was four years old, and usually outshoot anybody I'm shooting against.

Nine Years as a Patrol Officer

The job is a good fit for me because I'm happy-go-lucky, easygoing. I've got a pretty long fuse. I can be patient, I have a lot of empathy and a lot of ingenuity that comes in handy, and common sense. I'm fair. I treat people like I want to be treated. Even if they are bad guys, they still need to be treated with respect. And for the most part with the men I worked with, as soon as they knew I could do my job, as soon as I'd proved myself, they were behind me 110%. They knew that if shit hit the fan, I was going to be there right in the middle of it. Those are the same guys asking me to come back to work.

I did routine patrol, whatever came up. I was involved in the evidence technology program we got started and I was also an FTO. We developed evidence training classes for our patrol officers so that when they went to a crime scene they could do a good job. We put together better kits to go in our cars. Our old fingerprint kit was like a community pot, a big hodge-podge. Some people were careful with it, some people weren't. Whoever used the car used this kit, so lots of times there were things missing. Fingerprint powder is very messy so eventually the whole kit would get trashed.

As an FTO, whether the person was a lateral transfer from another department or a newbie right out of the academy, my job was to teach them how to be a cop. You'd have them for two or three weeks and then they'd move on to another person. That way they could glean a little bit from each person and put together their own style. You wanted them to be themselves, picking up a little bit of good from each person they came in contact with. Laterals went through the program quicker because they just needed to know how we did our paperwork and what our protocols were. If you go to this type of call, this is what we expect. We had a lot of laterals from California and there are a lot of differences between California law and Washington law. Yeah, we can do that here. No, we can't do that here.

My goal was to go out there and be the best cop I could be and have acceptance. I don't have the patience for supervision and all the game-playing and baloney that goes with it. When you are a field training officer, you're helping. You're not their superior, you're their peer and you're helping make them succeed. A supervisor is a boss and the officers are subordinates. It's like the mommy-daddy thing. You've got your boss telling you to make your guys do this and you may not agree and you're in the middle. It's too much.

There were certain things I got called in to do just because I was a female, like searching female prisoners. Did I call a male officer to search my male prisoners? No. But if they had a female prisoner, I'd be right in the middle of doing something and they'd call me in. Any kind of sexual assault stuff, they also want women to do. But no one ever gave me the shit detail because I was a woman; they never did that to me.

Women's Changing Priorities

The other night I went to a going-away party for a guy I worked with in patrol. And I worked with his wife in radio. I saw people that I'd worked on the same squad with and people who I had trained. They are lieutenants now, one is a captain. One of my laterals in particular is a very good cop and he's progressed through the ranks and is now a lieutenant in traffic, and every time I see him he says, When are you coming back?

My son graduates this year and my daughter starts high school this fall so I am seriously thinking about it. The only problem is the academy. It's like being pregnant again. You've been there, you've done it, you don't want to do it again. Although from what I've heard, it's like going to college now. It's a much different animal than what I went through when it was like boot camp. My only reservation is the time commitment. Do I really want to go back into that jungle? It's not a jungle as far as the job is concerned. I love doing the job. I like helping people, having that freedom, being out there, always in the know. When I say jungle, I mean administrative things like having to go to court on your day off and the bad guy not showing up. I mean vacations getting messed up and switching shifts every three months.

See, my part-time job allows me to work out and attend my kids' functions. I like being able to coach. I coached basketball, baseball, and softball for both my kids. I coached two all-star teams. I umpired as well. I have been very involved in sports since I was a kid. I was the first athlete in my high school, male or female, to earn nine varsity letters, volleyball, basketball, and softball. The first year of Title IX, I made the boys' varsity baseball team in junior high. Sports are my gig. I also played on the police department's team. They picked me up for tournaments several times. The first couple of times it was all men and me. They'd yell, Bring that guy in, Mel, and I'd crank one over their heads. Every year we have a city tournament, the police department has a team, the fire department has a team, utilities has a team. My main sports now are soccer and golf.

If it were possible to be a part-time officer, I'd be there in a heartbeat. The main reason women leave law enforcement is because you hit that part in your life when you feel, My kids need me. I don't understand why we can't do job shares. A lot of women would stay in law enforcement and be good contributors to their departments if there was some way to work out the kid thing.

On the other hand, this department has always been progressive about recruiting women, minorities, and laterals. When I worked on patrol I went to a couple of IAWP conferences in Denver and in Canada, where we set up a booth and sat there recruiting women to lateral to Bellevue. Another officer and I put together a slide presentation and we had pamphlets to recruit.

What Friends Are For

Each of us wants to be really good at her job and a good wife and a good mom. But it's very hard to balance the three if your job is police work, because it pulls you in so many directions—responsibilities to your squad members, training, going to court. You don't want to end up doing a half-assed job of everything. When you want to be good at everything, there are only so many hours in the day and you only have so much energy. I got to that point where I'd had it.

My best friend is also a police officer and we've been close ever since the academy. We support each other emotionally. We do things as families. She's the godmother of my kids and I'm her son's godmother. We're like sisters. It's not just because we're both police officers, although it helps that we've got that additional bond so that whatever happens in life, we're there for each other.

The most important time she helped me was when I was getting ready to quit, whether I should do it or not. She's still trying to get me to come back. But back then I felt she was behind me whatever way I went. She wanted me to think about everything that went into resigning. Did I really want to give this or that up?

Emotional Involvement

Being a dispatcher is harder nowadays than being a cop. When you're a police officer you get a call and you go handle the call. You've got to have heads up or you could get hurt or get somebody else hurt. But a dispatcher has to multi-task big time. You can be handling three different calls at the same time, police- and fire-related. When I started dispatching, you flew by the seat of your pants. You'd sit with somebody and she would say, This is how you do it.

I have gotten more emotionally involved with victims of crime in dispatch than when out on patrol. You only have verbal contact with people and you don't have control. In patrol you're out there, you can see it, you can touch it, you're a part of it so you can be empathetic yet not sucked in. One time I really got sucked in by my emotions. I was so angry. I'd had a previous contact with this woman at an Al-Anon club the week before. She was drunk and creating a disturbance and they called the police. So I knew this woman. A week later I was working nights and it was pouring cats and dogs and this car just about took me out head-on. I flipped around and got her pulled over. It was the same woman and she was so drunk and she's got her little seven-year-old with her. I wanted to rip her out of that car. I had to step back and say, Okay, before I do something stupid here, or something bad, I need to back off. I called another officer and he took the child so he didn't have to see mom being arrested, and when I calmed down I arrested her.

I also got emotionally involved in dispatch on a SIDS call. I took the call from a daycare facility so it wasn't the woman's child. I walked her through CPR, the whole deal. Afterward, she sent me a card, and right then it began to be personal. Then she called and wanted to talk to me and I talked to her and it became even more personal. Before I really didn't have an emotional bond other than I felt bad because this child died and this woman had had to go through it. Now I'm talking to her and my little shield goes down and it hurts. She continued to call. She needed to talk to me so I did it for her until she had closure.

Then there was this call about a boy who had had an accident with a rope and ended up hanging himself. His dad found him. I didn't know at the time that this was the son of a very good friend. It was a bad call to begin with and you could tell from the voice of one of the guys who was out on it that he wasn't in very good shape. I began to realize that my child probably goes to school with this boy. All this is going through my mind and this guy on the radio didn't sound very good so I had him call in and asked him how he was doing. He told me who it was and I said, Oh, my God. I know this child, I know his mom, and all I could think of was, His mom's coming home to see her kid in a body bag. I've been out on calls like that. They zip the person up in a body bag. I couldn't get past her coming home and seeing this kid. It was the first time in twenty years that I broke down at work and cried. I was a mess.

Reservist Tania Kohlman

Tania was born in 1966 in Akron, Ohio, and has a BA in counseling psychology from Kent State. She is married to a federal agent with the border patrol and they have two daughters, 2 and 4. She is currently finishing a correspondence course in private investigation through the Detective Training Institute in California and will shortly start her own PI business. But she made sure that her business plans would not interfere with continuing to patrol the streets of Sequim, Washington.

My Time in Blaine

I graduated from Kent State in 1990. I worked in mental health until I became a full-time police officer at Blaine, WA, PD in February 1995. I worked there for four years, my last year as a plainclothes detective assigned to the DEA (Drug Enforcement Agency) doing narcotics. During that time I met my husband who was with the border patrol and he transferred to Port Angeles. I was pregnant with my first child so I took some time off. I joined the Sequim reserves in January 2002.

When did I first think about being a police officer? I was working for CPS (Child Protective Services) and they were going through a layoff period. There was less funding and I was looking at being unemployed. I was sitting in a park in Bellingham, looking out at the bay, thinking what do I do now? It literally popped into my head, How about law enforcement? I went to my apartment, looked in the newspaper and the sheriff's department was taking applications and it closed the following day. I put in my application making me eligible to take the written test that would qualify me to be hired by seven different jurisdictions in Whatcom County.

I placed number two on the list. It happened so quickly that I was in the academy before I knew what had happened to me. This reporter came down to talk to me when I was in the academy because I was the first female for Blaine, first ever, which shook the department up. When I talked to men about getting into law enforcement, most of them had spent years in the reserve to get in the door or had taken the written test over and over and never got hired. I kept quiet about how easily it had flowed for me. There was no affirmative action. It was just placing number two. I was the only female in the top twenty.

There is a pretty rigorous physical agility test you have to pass in the hiring process to meet Washington State standards. On the first day of the academy you have to pass this test again. Plus they tested us half the way through, a surprise test. We had been so bogged down with our studies, a lot of us hadn't been training and working out. They said if you don't pass it, you're going back to your department. They really kept the pressure on. You were always on edge. I had spent a month in the department before there was room for me at the academy so I was doing sit-ups and running and I talked to as many police officers as I could about what to expect. I rode with one of the senior officers as a sidekick. Blaine is on the Canadian border. We had two ports of entry, customs, immigration, DEA, border patrol, Secret Service. There are so many agencies in town I spent most of my time meeting people.

My mother asked me why would I do something so dangerous? So I never told her about the dangers I faced or what I saw on the job, suicides, homicides. She was very happy when I became a plainclothes detective because she never realized how much more dangerous it was. My five siblings were also very worried and when they heard I was going back into the reserves they begged me not to do it. Why can't you get a normal job? However, my youngest sister did a stint as an investigator with a public defender's office and loved it and calls me all the time for advice on how to break in.

When I first started out, it was very hard. You go to looking very not feminine in a male uniform and bulletproof vest with your hair starkly pulled back. You can't wear jewelry. When you're out dealing with people, you're always on alert. Any one of those people could potentially hurt you. You're constantly thinking about who is behind your back. When you go out to a restaurant, you don't ever want your back to the door. Once you get comfortable with this change in your physical persona, and it becomes who you are at work, you're able to brush it off when you go home. But until you're done making that transformation at work, it morphs into your personal life.

Dealing with Men

They were very worried about how they might have to change because a female was coming in. Would they be able to talk the same way, tell the same jokes, act the same way? It took a few months for them to realize their worries were needless and for them to say, Oh, she's like one of the guys. I wasn't overly sensitive. I had no desire to shake up how they behaved, although I could look at them and say, That was a stupid joke.

I had to have a talk with the captain because he was the one making it uncomfortable. The guys would be joking, we'd all be having fun, and he would come out and say, Don't talk like that in front of a woman. It was very uncomfortable for me to continually be separated. So when he and I were having a very casual conversation I said, Incidentally, I am completely comfortable with the joking and the way we get along together and you don't need to do that.

There was at least one male officer at Blaine who didn't want me there. He wouldn't speak to me, he wouldn't return a hello. I knew there was no way I was going to convince him verbally that I was a good police officer. I was just going to have to show him. It was like I didn't exist when I was on duty with him, until one night I got him out of trouble. We were struggling with this guy, taking him off a boat, and if this particular officer had had a male officer there, he would have been fine with the other man taking one arm and he taking the other arm, but he made it very clear I was not to get involved. The guy started to fight and spit on him and I jumped right in and threw the guy on the dock and handcuffed him and he screamed and kicked and spit the whole way up. We got him into custody and I thought the officer would be even madder at me because I took away his masculinity or something. Luckily he didn't perceive it that way. He didn't make a complete turnaround after that, but he had trouble with everyone.

Then there was an officer who truly believed that he had to protect me. He was a super nice guy and was doing it out of chivalry. I had to take him on face to face. He said, Are you going to go arrest that guy by yourself? Wait, wait, until someone can go with you. I looked at him and said, Someday you are going to need me to protect you and don't you ever question my ability to go out and arrest somebody. Do not follow me around. I pointed out how ridiculous it was because I had more experience on the road than he did. He was one of those guys who needed to hear that I wasn't weak and that when we put that uniform on, we're all equal. He never did anything like that again.

Things turned around my first year in Blaine when we got a new chief. Our old chief had been there 28 years, had never dealt with a female, felt he was doing something very innovative by hiring me. He told me that when he got hired, there was no academy, no testing. He was asked simply, Can you fight? Yeah. Have you been in any bar fights? No. Okay. Here's your gun. Here are your keys. Go at them. He said, It's no longer about whether you're tough. It's about so many other things. He was talking about what I was bringing to the department, but he still felt females only belonged in areas like DARE. When we got our new chief, he was gave me every opportunity I wanted.

I kept my troubles to myself and developed horrible ulcers. I didn't do anything about them for a long time and one day on duty I was very, very ill and the captain said, I have ulcers from years of doing this and you have ulcers and you need to get on some medication. My husband always encouraged me to do something about these situations. I'd say, No, that would be my career, that would be the end of me. When you get a little bit older, you realize you do have to stand up for yourself and don't care if anybody knows it. We have a fairly young full-time female officer here who is very feisty. I admire her for standing up for herself and not taking anything from people.

The politics of the job still get to me and unfortunately I will never be like her. I beat myself up so much. If I do anything wrong on the job, I go, Oh, you are such an idiot. On the one hand that makes me a better police officer because I won't accept anything less than what I know I can do and I learn from my mistakes. I told this to another officer who you would not think second guesses himself at all and he said, I'm the same way. I beat myself up on everything. I was shocked. I said, No, you don't. He said, No one knows it because I don't let it show. In hindsight, you look back and it is not worth it to let the job eat you up.

Coming to Sequim

Sequim has a reserve program unlike many, which is why I joined them. When civilians join, they go to the reserve academy. I didn't have to because of my commission. You go through three levels. At Level 3 you are with another officer, a field training officer, you're being FTOed. You eventually make it to Level 2 where you are out in your own car patrolling the city but you are a secondary officer, you still are meant to take directions and do backup. When you reach Level 1 you are regarded the same as a fully-commissioned officer and you fill in for officers who are on leave, you work shifts, you go out and handle all the calls. I came in at Level 3 and now I'm at Level 1. My FTO got me acclimated as to how they do things here, geography, paperwork, computer system. They had a wonderful training program for me. I wouldn't have wanted to be thrown directly into Level 1. There is a requirement that you have to put in 16 hours a month. But if you have the time and the means, they would gladly accept you every day, especially when you reach Levels 2 and 1 and can help field calls and are not just a second body in the car.

They had never dealt with an ex-officer coming into the reserves. My training officer said, This is going to be hard. I don't know how to approach this. But he was very perceptive and he wanted me to go at my pace. He never treated me like I didn't know anything or like I knew everything and he didn't need to teach me. I have told him so many times he was the best FTO I have ever had. He's so competent, organized, and he's one of those officers that everybody looks up to. He knew where I was coming from, intuitively, and even though he didn't think he'd be a good training officer, he was phenomenal. I never felt like I couldn't go to him with a question, that he'd look at me disgustedly and say, Typical female officer. She doesn't get it.

On the other hand, one senior reserve officer made very demeaning comments and finally there came a time and a place for us to talk. As a female, you have to carefully gauge when and how you approach a problem like this. You can't do it emotionally. I had to say, Do not ever question my abilities again. I am not a brand new civilian who just walked in off the street. If I were, I'd leave this program right now because of how you talk to me. I don't want there to be a perception that I feel I'm better than other people or that I can't handle supervision, because I can.

Sequim Reserve Duties

Last Friday another officer and I served search warrants. We spent eight hours pounding the pavement looking for stolen property at pawnshops. You need a warrant if you want to search the premises, but many places cooperated with us and didn't want a search warrant. A couple of shops we knew weren't going to be cooperative, so we had search warrants. We recovered a lot of stuff but there is still a lot missing. The owners of the property had a really good memory and gave us good descriptions. Their entire household was taken. We had a notebook full of jewelry, furniture, precious paintings and prints, photo albums, baby pictures, wedding dresses. They took everything that meant anything to this couple. So our hearts were really in it and all during the day we kept saying to each other, What if this were us? Wow.

My favorite thing is to be proactive, doing drug enforcement or serving search warrants. You have a plan, you know what you're doing, you're going in to do this drug arrest or you're going in to do this search. That is an advantage of reserve. You get to come in and do these specific activities. We just hired two new reservists. I was one of the tac officers for the reserve academy and that was great, helping train these new people coming into the world of police work. However, reservists are also expected to cover basketball and football games. After having been a full-time police officer, it's very hard to do detail like that.

My biggest adrenaline kick was the report of a residential burglary. When we got there and were crawling under the windows we heard a man in the house saying, I just broke into the house. He was clearly on the phone. The window was open so we just snuck our guns in through the window and surprised him. It turned out he was talking to his mom and telling her that he had just broken into her house. And mom didn't care.

Private Investigating on the Peninsula

My private investigator business is all going to be about the geographics and demographics of this area and its needs. Right now I'm focusing on security issues because of what's happening in the world. I worked for several years for CPS as a mental health case manager. I did investigations and worked in the schools as a counselor. I'll be putting on a seminar soon on how to help children get through this time of crisis, how to help them deal with the fact that we're going to war, possible terrorist attacks, and their fears. I hope to develop other seminars on helping businesses prepare security-wise and how to respond to any type of attack. I found out that the department is going to change my status to a specially commissioned officer and through that position I'll be putting the seminars on through the police department.

I talked to the sergeant last week, told him everything I'd been thinking, and said I had strengths that I could bring to the department that I didn't feel were being utilized as a reserve. This specially commissioned officer position just started. They created it for ex-police officers who had a specialty and can help the department when their particular expertise was called for. My proposal was very positively received.

I had announced to them six weeks ago that I was planning to go into private investigation, which they were also very supportive of. The chief gave me his blessing. I thought I might have to take a leave of absence because there might be a conflict. But instead they are willing to look at melding those two activities together. I had been somewhat afraid of how the department would receive my private investigation plans because I didn't want to leave the reserves. It meant a lot to me to be back in law enforcement. I missed it terribly for the couple years I was gone from it. It was in my blood and I couldn't let go of it. Before I told them of my plans I really increased my time on the road because I wanted them to get to know me, my skills, how serious I am, how much I love police work, but also how much I wanted to pursue a new direction full-time.

For the children and their coping I've found coloring books and little stories that help parents work with their kids on different issues. I'll talk about how each age level perceives things and how to talk to different age levels. I have a whole power-point presentation ready for community disaster preparedness. The government has said clearly that we need to have the resources for surviving three days on our own without help. I have special segments of what that means to the elderly, people with mobility problems, mothers with infants.

I'd also like to talk to businesses and churches about being prepared and more aware of their security. We feel very isolated over here and very safe compared to Seattle, but really we're not, as we saw with the ferry incident in Port Angeles.

The bulk of my PI work will be insurance fraud investigation and background investigations for employers hiring new people. I'm going to contact all the attorneys over here and give them my business card and flyers about what my specialties are. Attorneys need process servers and it pays well and it's easy work. They also need investigators to do witness interviews before trials. I'll start with what I feel comfortable with. If there were a PI firm in town, I would probably join it, but the private investigators here all work by themselves. One does only government work, another only does criminal defense. I'll be the only woman.

Dealing with Children

If I didn't have children, I would be back in law enforcement full-time. My four-year-old has cried when she saw me in uniform. Mommy, don't go. On the other hand, she has asked, Can I be a police officer? I told her she can be anything she wants. I want her to know that the sky's the limit for her. We've discussed where she got the idea my job was dangerous. It may be from things I said, not realizing how she was going to take them. I have said if somebody is really bad or hurting other people, I have to put them in jail. She could extrapolate from that that if a person is really, really bad and they are going to hurt somebody, they could hurt me. I picked her up the other day from pre-school in uniform and the kids went, Wow, a police woman. And she stomped her foot and said, That is not a police officer. That's my Mommy.

I had a flak jacket on that said Police when we were serving search warrants in pawnshops the other day. I used to work as a counselor in school with a little girl who comes from a very sad family that probably has dealt with the police a lot. She was in the pawn shop with her mother and saw the front of me and ran into my arms. She was so glad to see me. But when I turned around to talk to my partner she saw Police on my back, and the tears started rolling down her cheeks. I said, Yeah, sweetie, I have two lives. I help kids and I also help people as a police officer. Her mother looked over and screamed at her to get away from me. I was a behavior interventionist for the Port Angeles school district and saw that child for home and social problems she was having.

When the girls are school age, I might return to law enforcement full-time. My husband's schedule is very flexible right now. He's straight days and he can have any days off he wants in the week. Port Angeles had an opening and they were calling me, Would you please put in for it because we'd really like to have you on our side. But if this PI job takes off and I can still be a reserve or specially commissioned officer, I'll have the best of both worlds. A lot of PI work is done at home on your computer and the kids can be right there.

Leaving Blaine PD and sliding over my gun and my badge was one of the hardest days in my life. Letting it go after all the work that I went through to get there, all the struggles I went through to be seen as an equal by the department. Turning it over was very emotional. When COPS came on TV, I couldn't watch it. Seeing officers in uniform and not being able to do it was hard on me. When Wally Davis was shot, we went to the funeral and it hit me really hard when officers and reserves from all over the state were there. They were the brotherhood, all together out in the field, and I was not part of that anymore. I was there only because my husband was law enforcement but otherwise I would not have been able to join them to honor Wally. That was a hard day for me and that's when I told my husband, I'm going back into law enforcement. It was so surreal because here we were honoring an officer who had been killed and the same day I'm telling my husband I'm going back into it. Bless his heart, he said, I understand.

Community Policing

Patrol officers are at the heart of community-oriented policing (COP). When COP began, chiefs saw it as women's territory. Women could sit at the kitchen tables of lonely widows at three in the morning and chat. They could staff neighborhood sub-stations and supervise volunteers. Later you'll meet Deputy Detective Debbie Kronk who has been given an entire town to protect and serve, all by herself.

Little Rock, AR, PD Bicycle Patrol Officer Deborah Allen, born in 1969, is married to a narcotics detective and they have a son, age 10. Deborah is a member of the Fraternal Order of Police, the Black Police Officers Association, and Little Rock Association of Women Police, which meets in restaurants, takes trips together, and does projects such as putting together Thanksgiving baskets. Here is what she said.

What takes up the majority of my time is dealing with high school kids. Community police have a different enforcement than patrol officers. We're the kinder, gentler police, and communicate with the public on a different level than patrol officers. On a bike you're apt to find different solutions than patrol officers. In a patrol car when you run across a given situation, basically there is one way you're supposed to handle it and then you go to your next call. You can't sit there, be sensitive, and try to find the root of the problem.

I once stayed with three kids that I had to turn over to the Department of Social and Health Services for an entire day, trying to find a grandparent or somebody, because the mother was arrested, to take care of these kids before I had to turn them over. We're so free, we have minimal supervision, we don't have people calling us all the time for this call, that call. I do take calls, but I have the flexibility to spend more time on certain projects. For example, when I first started working in this neighborhood it was my everyday function to deal with kids who were smoking dope, breaking into houses, vandalizing the neighbors right behind their school. We videotaped for a month in a car where they could see us. Then we had meetings with school board directors, city board directors, the security people, and we put a fence around the high school so that they can't get out during the break.

At my Alert Center we work together, three officers, a facilitator, a secretary, two code enforcement officers, and our supervisor. We're all good friends and do things outside of work. Bicycle officers interact on a one-on-one basis with the public. We know where the trouble spots are. Right now the Center is working on a project in an apartment complex. We're going to meet with the management company and the tenants to take back the complex because it's out of control.

There are good tenants there. They're tired of the shootings, the drug selling, and we'll have a meeting and see who shows up to work on a crime prevention plan. We were there the other day for several hours and a few tenants approached us but didn't want it to be obvious that they were talking to the police. They won't come and tell us what's going on because they're scared of retaliation. One thing I'm going to stress is that they can phone us anonymously. If something's going on, call me and let me know. We had a homicide in a cul-de-sac there and everybody knows what happened, but nobody will talk.

Today I talked to a nineteen-year-old who dropped out of school in the eleventh grade. He had a warrant for a lousy ticket from two years ago. He's had two years to pay the fine. I talked to him. What are you going to do with your life? Why are you hanging out in the street? There's nothing but trouble in these streets. Find something constructive to do with your life. Well, he said, I'm going to GED school. I told him that in my opinion a GED is regarded differently than earning a diploma. I also talk to them about the pros and cons of becoming a police officer.

I love it. I don't want to work anywhere else. We go out to lunch together. I go to church with one of the other officers. We have birthday parties where we'll go out to eat, or we'll have a potluck. We have a Thanksgiving dinner and a Christmas dinner. We trade gifts. It's an extended family. If I have a problem, everybody knows something's wrong with me. They'll come into my office and ask, What's the matter? I also like having a woman partner. People refer to us as That Cagney and Lacey.

As far as my own family is concerned, when my work's done at 3:30, that's it. I go home and I don't think about it. What's been nice for the past month is I've been working what we call "Code 40," where we work off-duty for the City Parks and Recreation Department. My son plays football so I was able to be at the games to watch him play, at the same time providing security for it.

Conclusion

One's own kids and their need for Mom to participate in their lives sensitize women police officers to the needs of children in the broader community and they tend to channel themselves toward child-centered community policing.

Mel, Tania, and Deborah like interacting with children, at home and away from home. Readers can ask themselves, "Which of the three am I most like? Would I be satisfied with what they have chosen to do? If I were an officer, would community policing be my choice? Does bicycle patrol appeal? Does dispatching appeal? Does private investigative work appeal? How important to the act of balancing work and home is being married to men in firefighting and policing?"

4

Life as a Detective

While putting this book together I read a series of detective novels by Peter Robinson. His main character is Detective Chief Constable Alan Banks. A secondary character is a 27-year-old woman, Detective Constable Susan Gay. They work in a small town in Yorkshire. Are British women detectives much different from American women detectives?

Differences: British police women drink way more tea and way less coffee. They might drink beer at lunch. Do they work out? Exercise and gymnasiums were never mentioned nor was regular weapons qualification. Rank and file officers come from working-class backgrounds. Entering with a university degree means fast-tracking up the chain of command. Susan did not have a degree.

Similarities: Promoted to detective meant Susan no longer walked a beat or directed traffic. Nor was she expected anymore to make coffee and put out biscuits. Like American women officers, she comforted rape victims and fumed when she was overprotected by her bosses. Because she did not want to be talked about at the station, she didn't have relationships with men, neither cops nor civilians. She had a sense of determination and had been totally devoted to her career. Her parents disapproved of her choice of occupation, and she felt that even if she made chief constable they would still look down on her. Promotion meant Susan gradually became more balanced. She now had time for books and records and plants.

Detectives deserved a chapter all to themselves. What is it like to no longer be a uniformed officer? What do detectives do that is different from uniformed officers? What do readers think they would prefer, the uniform or civilian clothes?

You will now meet Detectives Jessica, Julia, and Debbie who could not be working in more different American departments. By virtue of being the only cop in town, Debbie is tiny Quilcene's de facto chief, while Jessica is tied to a computer overseeing a huge county workforce. And Julia? Well, what could be more unique than working in the Big Apple?

Taking the group of 53 as a whole, 11 women worked for small town departments, 12 for counties, seven for large suburban departments. Five worked in big city departments (Tulsa, Boca Raton, Seattle), five in medium-sized cities like Little Rock, and three worked for universities. Three women worked for the Port of Seattle, two for the state patrol (Washington, Alaska), two for NYPD, two for the Department of Justice, and one was a state academy trainer. The variety of their agencies was surpassed by even greater variety in their roles.

Jessica

Detective Jessica Belter was born in 1971 in Davenport, Iowa. She has two years of college core courses plus American Sign Language. Her partner is a restaurant server. They live with a dog that looked longingly through her kitchen window at our table and a very large cat that made it plain she also wanted to be interviewed. Jessica does hiring background investigations on people, commissioned and non-commissioned, being considered by the King County Sheriff's Office. She enlisted in the Air Force two weeks out of high school, hoping to do law enforcement. Instead, for four years she was a firefighter. After the Air Force she joined the Las Vegas, NV, PD, where she also spent four years.

I Rehearsed and Rehearsed

I quit smoking and I started running. It was the first time I did any physical training other than what I was required to do in the Air Force. I started getting in shape. I also prepared by having a mock oral board with some people who were already officers in the department. I made up flash cards with all the questions they could possibly ask with the answers on them and I rehearsed and rehearsed and I memorized. I made sure I had the perfect outfit. I practiced making eye contact with people, tried hard not to use hand gestures, tried hard not to say "Ummm" too much. The perfect outfit? I was told it needs to be a blue suit, it can be a skirt suit or a pant suit, and somewhere in there you have to have a hint of red because it shows power. How ridiculous is that?

A Field Training Low

I made a lateral move to King County in 1998 because I didn't like living in the desert and I knew that if I wanted a family someday, Las Vegas is not a place where I would want to raise a family. I went through two months of field training here, one month with a male officer, and two weeks with each of two female officers. I didn't get along with my first FTO. Looking at him objectively, he's a really good cop, a good investigator, a ton of knowledge, he's good with people, but I was the second recruit that he had ever trained so I don't think he'd honed his FTO skills yet. He's not a good listener and he had no idea when I got in his car the first day that I had any police experience and when I told him, he said, Well, how many years of that did you work in the jail? He was condescending, Okay, now, put the car in drive and step on the gas. He kept a tight rein on me; he didn't just let me be a cop.

He thought I didn't know anything because I was new. I didn't associate it as a male-female thing although knowing him now, I can see that it probably was. He wouldn't let me speak at a call. He would cut me off to explain to a citizen what was going on. I'm pretty assertive so my way of handling that situation was to tell him, not in a passive way and not in an aggressive way, but in a matter-of-fact way, what my feelings were about his behavior. But in the middle of that first month of my field training, I was so unhappy I was going to quit and go back to Las Vegas.

As a recruit I was expected to work a couple extra hours overtime at night and not put in for it. I felt like my rights were being infringed upon. A lot of what I was hearing about how things were was from this FTO who operates that way. He doesn't mind putting in three hours extra, that's him, but that's not me. That's not how everybody should be expected to work. He had a lot of views that I didn't agree with and the middle of my third week, I told him, Hey, I'm done.

At the point where I told him this department's not for me, he asked why. I said I don't want to tell you because you work here. I don't mean to sit here and degrade a place you like and where you work. But I started to tell him and he got pissed off. I said, Never mind. I was done. I knew I had choices in my life. I didn't have to be here. I went to change out of my uniform and by the time I got back, he said, Would you please wait because I called the FTO sergeant? She came screaming in on her day off and we had a really honest conversation. I said this is not the place for me and she said I want to hear about it, so we talked. At the end of the conversation I said, Tell me there's a light at the end of the tunnel and she said I promise there is. She said, Our department is not the way that it's being painted to you. Just give us a chance. Come to my home for Thanksgiving.

She asked me if I wanted to go to a new FTO. I said, No, there's no way I'm going to have that jacket of being a female cop, whining and complaining. I said, It's fine. I was pleased that it was his issues and it was not about me. In our final days of riding together, we were at each others' throats. But at that point I didn't care. He had called her because he thought, Oh, shit, I just screwed up, because the department wants this girl and she's leaving and I'm going to be in so much trouble. It wasn't for my sake.

From Patrol Burnout to Detective

I chose law enforcement because I wanted structure and stability. I wanted status and the feeling of accomplishment. I know how to talk to people, I have a lot of empathy and compassion for others. I'm intelligent, I know how to be physically fit and I know how to handle myself. Las Vegas PD is a very big agency combining city and county services. I didn't think there would be discrimination there and I knew that it paid well. I knew there were a lot of women in the department and I knew there were a lot of women in rank.

I have gone to detective because I wanted for the first time in my life not to wear a uniform. I wanted to feel what it was like to live a normal life, Monday through Friday, weekends off, not working evenings. I was burned out on shift work. I was burned out on patrol. I had been training back-to-back recruits. I was an FTO and also an MPO, master police officer, a corporal, so I had additional training responsibilities. It was time to expand my policing skills. When I'm not working I paint, run, spend a lot of time outdoors and with my friends. I go to Al-Anon a lot. It keeps me grounded.

I love my current job but I'm also testing for another position in the domestic violence unit. It's an oral board. I brought the books home this week. What I will do to prepare is read everything in our policy manual and training books on domestic violence and domestic violence laws. I will read up on what our department's vision, mission, goal statement, and core values are, because I'll want to plug them in there. I will review and write down, so I'll remember in the oral board, what training I've had. When it comes to domestic violence, I can speak from my heart. I'm one of those people who believes that if I don't get the job, then it wasn't meant to be at this time, and there's a reason for it. I have rehearsed in the past but I won't this time. As far as promotion goes, I don't know.

Travel is one of the best things about this job. Every time we have a lateral transfer from another agency, we go to their work site, we do a ride-along with them and meet with their supervisors. I've been to Austin and Wisconsin. I go to Hawaii in April.

I was so naïve when I began, if I experienced overprotection I didn't know that's what it was. I didn't notice things like that until later in my career after someone pointed out to me that a lot of times citizens will come up to a male officer before a female officer. Once I started to notice overprotection, then I did take it personally. How I've handled people's attempts to channel me was to say, No, that's not my interest. I don't want to be a community policing officer who hangs out. That's great and somebody should do that, but it's not me.

Background Investigating

I like the fact that I have a hand in choosing the future of the department. We're looking for maturity but we do end up hiring people who are 22 or 23. I don't automatically discount them because of their age and say they are too immature because if they are viable candidates, I'd rather have them come on now and grow. Are they able to do this job? Can they multi-task? Are they physically able to do this job? Are they intelligent enough? I also rank people who have some character, people who have had some life experience and maybe have been on the other side of the law a little bit. Not too extreme, but enough to understand a bit about the criminal mind. Sometimes we get lucky and get somebody who as a juvenile made poor choices but they've completely turned around and gone the other way. We want people who are all-round capable. We don't want somebody who's in it to drive fast, pull their gun, and chase bad guys.

We're currently doing a program called Hiring in the Spirit of Service. The federal government has given us a grant and we're in the middle of revamping what we're looking for. That's exciting to me. We're doing the first section of several sections of a long program. Because we're changing the way we hire people, we're going to have to retrain our trainers. We don't want to change the type of people we hire and have them all fail.

We don't investigate people until they've passed the testing process. We stay out of that so that there's no chance that we'll be subjective. We don't even do the oral boards. The candidates go through an interview at the beginning of their background investigation after we've gone through their criminal history, financial history, education, work history. We go through what we've compiled on them. We don't have a fixed set of questions. I might say something like, In 1988 you said that you did this. Can you tell me more about it? My favorite answers are to the question, Have you ever been detained or questioned for anything? For example, You have said no, however, the record shows that you were questioned about a burglary by Edmonds PD. He says, Well, I wasn't arrested. They play this semantics game and that tells me something about them.

Being Gay

I've never had a problem being gay. Gay women are more accepted than gay men, and if I were fired for something like that, I wouldn't want to work here anyway. There are people who are afraid they would be fired for being gay, afraid to be out in the department. I have heard improper comments about gay men, but do I think that in the Sheriff's Office that a man would not get a position because he's gay? No. Do I think he would be blatantly discriminated against? No, I don't. One of the things that attracted me to this Office is that they have domestic partnership for their insurance and sexual orientation is a protected class in the laws in Washington State against discrimination. It's not in Nevada. This is a more liberal, open-minded area and while I was comfortable in Las Vegas, I feel even more comfortable here.

Gay men have a harder time than gay women not just in the department but in life. In society in general straight men have a harder time accepting gay men, absolutely. It doesn't have anything to do with police work. Society is really slow to change. Sometimes it's because if straight men have ever thought about it themselves, they're terrified to admit it. It's going to take a lot of time for straight men to be okay with it. First and foremost, it has to do with being okay with who they are themselves. If a straight guy says it doesn't bother me that my male partner is gay, but are other men going to think that I'm gay, too? Even if men think it's okay and in their home they teach their kids acceptance of diversity, they may not feel it's okay at work.

Men and Women Working Together

My first mentor was a female sergeant in Las Vegas. She was a sergeant everybody wanted to work for, male, female, because she was so well respected. I learned integrity from her, to always do the right thing, choose your battles and sometimes accept that you just have to suck it up. I learned about tact from her, how to be assertive and have respect and not be considered a bitch because you're assertive. I tried to model myself after her. I picked her brain a lot and she helped me through the growing pains of being a brand new cop.

I'm currently working with someone who had been a cop for a lot of years. He's set in his ways and we disagree on just about every single candidate. But I am showing him a wider picture of what we should be looking at than what he's used to, for example, he's not interested in the Hiring in the Spirit of Service program. I have no idea what the man thinks of me. He probably views me as another person he simply has to deal with.

In general, male officers who are up and coming, being trained with and growing and learning with female officers, are exposed to different points of view about law enforcement. They don't realize that they are seeing things differently than they would be if it were an all-male job. I have heard several male cops say, Women make better cops than men. Because if women are intelligent, able to handle themselves, keep physically fit, and know defensive tactics, they are just as capable as men and add something to the job, good intuition and they're more mild-mannered and don't get upset and go overboard when they shouldn't. I teach everybody my way and two other FTOs teach them their ways and new officers start out a combination of the three people who train them.

Julia

Detective Julia Koniosis was born in 1956 in Brooklyn. Her husband manages a home improvement showroom. She has two daughters, 25 and 7. She is an assistant to the Chief of Brooklyn South detectives as well as President of the NYPD Policewomen's Endowment Association (PEA). Before joining, Julia had been a waitress and was attracted by the security and medical benefits of the police. She earned 32 college credits during her six months at the NYPD academy in 1984 and then went to a Neighborhood Stabilization Unit for further training. When she retires in two years' time, she plans to design kitchens in her husband's showroom.

A Trying Time at the Academy

I was 27 when I went to the academy. My parents were very proud of me. My father being Irish-Catholic from Ireland would have loved to have taken the job himself but he was too old when he got here. I went to a Catholic commercial high school and I was talking about going to college and my father said, Just learn to type and get a good job as a secretary. My mother went ballistic. Why does she have to be a secretary? Because she's a girl? Let her do whatever she feels she can do. I first thought about being a police woman when I was eight years old and watched a television show called Honey West, about a female detective. I even had a Honey West doll.

Two and a half weeks into the academy I had an emergency hysterectomy. I returned in 15 days, stayed out of gym for another five days, but then my department surgeon told me I could take gym. I ended up two years later with surgery for adhesions for I did too much too soon. I was determined to graduate with my class but it was catch-22. Because I left while the class was at the range, I didn't have a gun. I was always behind on the run and I was told I had to have an 85 on the first trimester exam to continue, which was ridiculous because other people got by with 65 and they'd been there the whole time. I got an 87, so that was good, but then they said I had to do just as well on the next exam, which I did.

When it came to Gun and Shield Day I was told I wasn't going to get a gun and shield because I hadn't qualified at the range. As a rookie the union delegates or representatives at the academy didn't do a whole lot for me until I made some noise. They then found there were other people who had missed academy days for reasons like a death in the family and hadn't qualified with the gun. To qualify you had to go to the exertion course.

But I had finally made the run. There was one woman, she's a captain now, I love her for this. She said, Run next to me. She controlled the run and she paced it for me. She'd say, Do you want to go faster? I said, Okay. She monitored my breathing, breathe this way, breathe that way, until we did the whole two miles. Everybody in my little squad cheered and clapped that day and it was really nice. I'd made the run, I'd passed the exams, but I'm not going to graduate because I don't have a gun because I didn't go through the exertion course.

Finally I and a group of people got to go to the range for the course. You run three miles with all your gear on. Then you get down in front of your target, do ten push-ups, get up and shoot your target. You continue doing this. If you drop anything, you're supposed to pick it up. I lost my flashlight. When I reached down to get it, I looked at my legs and I saw I was wet to the knees. I had residual problems with my bladder after the hysterectomy. I was mortified. A female instructor yelled, You keep going. I said, I can't, I can't, and I walked off the exertion course. Luckily there was one male who remembered me leaving for surgery and I told him, I have a problem here, I can't finish like this. He said, I remember you. You got sick and left. You know what? You do whatever you have to tomorrow and we'll give you this exertion course again.

I had called my boyfriend crying in a phone booth with my wet pants. I told him what happened and he said, But you have a chance, no? He said, Okay, we're going to do this. I'll get you diapers. He brought them to me. It was December, really cold and rainy at the range on top of everything else, and I'm leaving the house bound and determined I'm going to do this. I have my diaper on, my recruit pants, and my bologna sandwich. I asked my boyfriend on the way out, Can you tell? And he, of course, said, No, no. It's fine. You can't tell. I looked at my daughter and asked, Can you tell? She said, Yes, I can see it. I said, Oh, the hell with it, I'm going anyway. I went and passed. They took me by myself and redid it. I graduated with my class, which was a big accomplishment for me.

New York, New York

In December of '85, my first day out, I left the precinct and there were these two guys having an argument, but this one guy had cut up the other's taxi cab with a knife and had done about $700 worth of damage. The desk officer said, You have a collar, Officer. Put the cuffs on him.

Once you're in the Police Department, you're accepted. The NYPD is very understanding of people's foibles and that stretches as far as the civilians. We have people who are basically bug jobs, nuts. We have a civilian working for us now who drives people insane, but we're not going to get her fired, we're very protective of her.

When I was going for the job and we'd be called down for medical review and additional testing, I loved the antics of the guys who were talking to us and the jokes they made. I said to myself, I'm going to love this job if everybody has a sense of humor like that.

If You Are a Woman

When the men are in a car together and they have to pass gas, they do. But when they're in a car with a female, they don't. They stop the car and get out. So every time my partner had a wild meal it means lots of stops. I'd say to him, What would you do if a guy was here? He'd say, I can't do that. He was also always saying, Let me do that—climb the fence, go up on the roof, come down the fire escape. I'd protest, You don't have to do that and I would do it. He was one of my first partners. He got over it and most of them do get over it.

In my rank as a detective I'd love to get grade. I'm third grade and it can go as high as first grade, but because of my PEA work I haven't been very proactive in my job. So unless the department appreciates everything I've done for the Association, I'm not getting grade. Once January comes I won't be president any longer and I'll go back to a regular investigative squad.

Our department has excellent maternity benefits. From the moment you find out that you're pregnant, you go on restricted duty status. They find you an administrative or clerical position usually within the precinct, but I have a woman working for me who was sent from another precinct where they already have six pregnant women. With our jobs everybody has unlimited sick leave. But you can't abuse it. They stay on top of it. If you take sick leave more than three times in a one-year period, you're considered chronic and they start monitoring you and visiting your home. What happens with our maternity restriction is that if you are sick a number of times, they consolidate it into one sick leave. So if during that nine-month period, you're not feeling well, nauseous, vomiting, backaches, it all goes into one. Plus you get eight weeks' leave.

My second child is adopted and we adopted her when she was older. An infant is a whole different story. I cannot imagine raising an infant working full-time. Something has to give, you're juggling a lot of balls after that eight-week leave. When you have a two-cop family, sometimes it works out. The administration can say, Your husband's working nights, so you can work days. They go out of their way to accommodate you.

I joined when my first daughter was seven and my mother was well so my family helped. Now it's manageable because I'm a lot wealthier than I was then. My husband has a great job and the school that my daughter goes to is a private academy. I'm very lucky, but my heart breaks for all these young women who struggle to get baby-sitters and are away from the house for ten hours.

If only they could work out some way to subsidize daycare that would allow us to have it close to our commands. If I'm working in Staten Island, what's the point of my going to headquarters in Lower Manhattan to bring my child to daycare? It would be a three-hour back and forth commute. Daycare close to work would encourage women to stay, women who have one, two kids and say, I don't want to do this anymore.

Here I am, working at a job where I command the same salary as the guy sitting next to me. He goes home, his wife makes his dinner, irons his shirts, shops for his food, takes care of his babies. I go home, pick up my daughter from school, pick up whatever extra I need from the grocery store, make dinner, clean up after dinner. I have the luxury of having a cleaning lady who does my laundry and I'm able to pay for my dry cleaning. But childcare is my responsibility. We women allow this to happen. With my ex, it was the same thing. I made more money than he did and still had to take care of the house. So I have this great career and I'm killing myself. And there are always those times in a cop-non-cop marriage, where you're told to stop acting like a cop. Even your children say, You're always interrogating me. My older daughter says, Mom, I can't have a conversation with you. Every conversation is a battery of questions.

NYPD Policewomen's Endowment Association

The Association is about eighty years old. Women were matrons before they were switched to police officer status. The PEA was the union for the female police officers. When in 1973 we all became police officers, the Association was kept as a fraternal group and our monies for the union and benefits were turned over to the Patrolman's Benevolent Association. All these females paying into this union that is called the Patrolman's Benevolent Association! We've tried to get the name changed and there was a vote but we lost.

When I joined the PEA and went to meetings, I felt here is a place where I can talk and be myself and not worry about being judged. We were all equal and rank was left at the door. I get so much camaraderie and closeness through the Association.

It'll be four years this January that I have been president. We have a working fund, we have fees, dues, fund raisers. There are 6,000 women in the police department and 1,000 are PEA members. We have monthly meetings. We'll have a fund raiser like a dinner dance. We'll have a Spring Fling. We hadn't had a conference for five years, so I started a Women in Policing Conference that lasts three days and is a big networking situation. For the last two years we've had it at the police academy. Each conference has a different theme. We're late this year because of 9/11 but a committee of five women is currently planning one before December with a Recovery Theme. The week before there will be 15 of us getting everything together. We try to have give-aways because they encourage people to come back again. About 450 attended the last one.

We don't have a venue yet. If we can hold the next one at the academy as well—because the academy is full with 2,700 recruits—we could invite police officers from Westchester County, Nassau County, Suffolk County, and New Jersey.

What we are trying to teach women through group networking and training is how to play the game. I've been to conferences where there was nothing beneficial for the NYPD. It might work someplace in Idaho, but that doesn't mean it would work in our department. I would love to sit here and be anti-department—they don't do this and they don't do that—but for the most part when I compare our department to others, we do stick to the equal opportunity principle. What the PEA deals with are groups that do not make policy, like the police union with its traditional name.

Every time I go to some sort of training, I'll pick up a card if I like the speaker. I also work closely with the NYPD Assistant Commissioner of Community Affairs and she recommends people. She's a civilian, a wonderful person who has raised four girls on her own. She's always saying, What can I do to help you? Never, You should do this or you should do that. Police officers are used to handling everything themselves that when somebody says, What can I do to help, it takes you awhile to be able to delegate because you're so used to doing it all yourself. She's helped me in lots of different ways, for example, how not to be so gruff.

Debbie

Deputy Detective Debbie Kronk was born in 1956. She is married to a retired Seattle Police Department officer. She was in a community college administration of justice program when she was recruited by Seattle, WA, PD in 1977 and worked 23 years for Seattle. When we met she had only been in her current job in bucolic Quilcene, Washington (pop. 591) on the Olympic Peninsula for three weeks.

The new sheriff of Jefferson County (160 square miles, 18 deputies) believes Debbie is the answer to Quilcene's law enforcement problems. So she hangs out in this little old gray house across from the fire station. But "women's work" is never done and before Debbie could set up shop her job was to clean the place up and furnish it. She went out and asked for donations and the microwave ovens, crocheted afghans, and overstuffed armchairs poured in. First I admired the sparkling, polished wood-paneled reception area. Then we toured the kitchen with dining table, fridge, and toaster oven. She pointed out the contributed paint that kids with community service pending are going to use to brighten the walls. Women who work for the county stopped by for a tour and opined that they would borrow a floor polisher over the weekend and do her floors. I don't think she's spent a dime.

Living and Working in South County

I am so used to the quietness here that when I go to my mother's house in West Seattle, I spend the night listening to trains, sirens, car alarms going off. You don't hear that here. I go out on my Mom's deck and you can't see the stars as you can at my house. We have a Kubota tractor and I told my husband that we need to buy more property so I can dig some more because I love to do that. Anyway, I was sitting on the Kubota one day and I heard a flopping sound and I looked up and there was an eagle over my head, you could hear it flying. On the way to work I see eagles flying and deer at the side of the road. But in Seattle I would have been so busy and rushed, I wouldn't have had time to see eagles flying over if there were any.

I started out at the main office as a detective and then the sheriff asked me to move down here and network with the community. I still work cases of crime against children and child abuse, but in the meantime I jump in the marked unit and drive up and down the street. I say hi and wave. Once a week or so I'll put on my uniform and go out and stop people and tell them to slow down.

My job is to get out and go to community meetings to see what people's priorities are as far as crime is concerned and what's bothering them in general. Everyone is very excited that there is a deputy here. Right now the statistics don't show that there's a need for both a sergeant and a deputy here. I'm here to up the stats. I'm a firm believer of documentation for everything. I heard people talking throughout the last political campaign that crimes, like property damage, were never investigated. But when I arrived and looked into the stats, there wasn't a real call for it. I'm here to say, If you're going to talk about how somebody ran over all the mailboxes on Dosewallips Road, you'd better come in and report it so we can document the need for deputies in south county.

I gave a group of seniors cards with my number and told them I'd take their reports over the telephone. We have to do things differently here. We have to watch out for our neighbors. In the city you're used to police responding in five minutes. Here it is 45 minutes.

Traffic on Highway 101

Their number one problem is traffic. Highway 101 is a state highway so we share jurisdiction with Washington State Patrol. In the town and nearby Brinnon the speed limits are 30 and 40 miles an hour, but people don't pay attention and drive through at 50 miles an hour. The community wants people to slow down. I'll work with them, for example, maybe they need to write letters to the Department of Transportation to get some speed zone areas.

We can also do traffic emphasis. As a deterrent in different areas I'm going to set a little traffic radar trailer that shows your speed when you approach it. During lunch hour and when I know that the kids are out of school, I get in my car and hang out around 101. Just sitting there slows people down and makes them pay more attention to the speed signs.

Working with Community Groups

During winter the traffic offenders are local kids with beefed-up cars. There are a lot of retired people here and they take offense to the noise more than younger people. The other day all the kids were hanging out just off the school grounds so I drove my car up and said, Hey, guys, what's going on? They said, You're not in uniform. I said, I don't always have to be in uniform. I've got my car. You know who I am, don't you? They said, Yeah. I'm slowly building rapport with them. Twenty years ago police work was quite different but now you have to reach out and talk to people.

When I worked in Seattle, I was on a task force on Internet crimes against children so I have a good Internet background. Because everybody was getting computer labs here I visited these and gave the kids little pamphlets with personal safety tips from the Center for Missing and Exploited Children. I'm meeting with teachers and counselors, I've met with the superintendent. I also went down to Brinnon, which has an elementary school to let them know that I'm here. Two days later they called me to investigate child abuse and they didn't have to wait an hour as they would have in the past, which was one of their complaints. If a child discloses to a counselor, by law they have to notify CPS and then they call us and I can go down and make sure the child is safe. Sometimes the children are afraid to go home because of continuing abuse. I take them out of the home and put them in foster care.

I've been to the school and talked with the principal about their program for Future Farmers of America and I said I would like, if possible, to find a student who could come and answer the phones for me, because my assistant only comes on Tuesday and Thursday and I'm busy every day. I've gone to Chamber meetings, senior citizen meetings, school board meetings, 4-H, and now I'll get in touch with the garden club, the VFW and other organizations. I like talking to people, I'm a busybody, I'm very self-motivated. There are times in this job when you could do nothing if you wanted. It's not very often that I do nothing.

Reminiscing about Men and Women

I miss the camaraderie of working in a squad. I miss the city, the buzz, the hub-bub, you're going, going, and things are always happening. However, now that I'm older, it's very nice to sit back and look at things and be able to assess situations better. I had all this real busyness going on for 23 years, always working in a unit proactively like narcotics where I worked with informants and did search warrants.

Twenty-five years ago when I went into the police department men were very standoffish. There were times when they didn't back us on calls. I'll always remember two Black guys who worked together in a car who always backed me. It took me awhile to figure out that they'd understood discrimination forever and ever. If I was on a traffic stop at night, I'd take the license back to write it up and I'd look down the block and there they were. When I went to detectives there was a man there who has since retired who was very patient with me. For example, the first guy I went to talk to in the jail was crazy, stuttering, talking gibberish, and I didn't know what it all meant. This detective pointed things out to me. He'd helped me with report writing, how to be more specific. To this day I'm very specific in reports. I read some of these deputies' reports and think, Whoa, what really happened here? Who did what? When and where?

I didn't know what I was getting into. I was young, 21 years old. You get there and the men hate you and they don't back you and I'm going, What's this all about? I did what I had to do, got out and did the job. I remember working one night, which is, of course, scarier because you can't see things, and I was in the Arboretum and I had called in on a car and it came back stolen. I'm new, I don't know how these things work and I asked for backup. The sergeant gets there and he says, What do you need backup for? I said, Well, this is a stolen car. He said, If you'll look at the tires, that car hasn't been moved. See, the top of the tires isn't wet. You don't need backup. I said, Well, someone had to teach me that.

I have remained a detective because I like the action, I like the work. People who don't like it, get burned out. In many places I was an acting sergeant and it was way more work than work. I'd rather investigate a case and put the bad guy in jail than supervise whiny babies telling on each other. I went to some meetings for the lieutenant and he'd ask me what happened, and I'd say, Why did I even go? What did it accomplish? These people have been meeting on the same issue for two years and still don't have a goal or a mission.

Women have to be a lot more resourceful because we're not going to jump into the middle of a fight with muscle-bound 200-pound guys. We have to think of other things to do. One time I blew my whistle and it stopped a fight. That was all I had, my whistle, and I had to do something. I'm not going to get between two guys who both weigh 200 pounds. They'd crush me.

I remember a tea once at Seattle Police that a female captain organized for all the female officers to go to. We got so much flak from the guys. What are the women doing? Why are they getting together? They were very paranoid. What are you talking about? We're getting together to have tea and cookies. Why, do you want to come? They were very suspicious of our intentions. I never went to anything like that again.

I stay in touch with my friends, we send e-mail back and forth. My last assignment was in vice and I call over and talk to the sergeant and detectives. I'm always networking with Seattle PD. Today I was organizing things and sent over to Seattle for some line-up forms because I might have to do a line-up and we can't simply write things down. We have to have witnesses and pictures. I call over to Seattle quite often to get forms to copy and use here. You can make being a police officer what you want and, if you don't, then you need to go do something else. I don't want to be unhappy and being a detective here in this little town is making me happy.

Going That Extra Mile

There are lots of research studies that point to women's greater visibility in a department. Because there are so few women, they stand out. This visibility means they are watched more closely than men. This greater scrutiny, particularly if combined with expectations of failure, mean women have to work harder than men just to be considered minimally competent. Women feel this pressure to meet and exceed all standards of quality performance and go that extra mile. Here's a good example.

Bicycle Patrol Officer Tammy Nelsen: "We tend to work the problems out, help the citizens a little bit more, and take that extra step as far as law enforcement goes. I've been here 11 years, seven years on patrol, and I've wrestled people but I've never had to fight them. I'm a pretty good talker so I talk them out of it. I teach a class in community policing and I teach them to go outside the box. That's one thing about women, we're already outside the box. What I like best is meeting different people from all walks of life. From the richest rich to the poorest poor and being able to help them."

A 1994 survey by James Daum and Cindy Johns conducted with women police in a metropolitan department backs up everything I heard. Three-quarters said women were just as good on the job as men, while a quarter said women were better. Women had to do a lot more work to receive the same credit as men, that is, go that extra mile. However, this group also reported that the job had made them colder, less trusting, and less tolerant of others. These negative changes did not come through in my interviews.

Instead, I met warm, compassionate women holding strongly to a service-orientation toward the public and a nurturing attitude toward colleagues. These findings were what I reported in *Women Changing Work* (1990) and are not unlike a study published in 1992 (Bartol et al.) in rural Vermont comparing men and women officers' perceived stresses. The women were more stressed than men by worries about the safety of their colleagues, themselves, and the public. The women were also more sensitive and empathic and said that abused and dead children were perhaps the most stressful aspect of the job.

From Escape to Confrontation

A 1999 *Justice Quarterly* study by Robin Haarr and Merry Morash found that women officers more than men officers dealt with stress through "escape." This escape took several forms: just living with the situation, ignoring what was going on, suffering in silence, and avoiding superiors or other coworkers. The more stressful a woman's job, the more she relied on these tactics. The alternative to escape was confrontation, such as making a formal complaint to a superior or changing one's job assignment or saying as Jessica did, I'm out of here. I don't have to put up with this.

Campus Assistant Chief Annette Spicuzza dealt with being gay both ways, first escape, then confrontation: "The only time I experienced problems outwardly was in Chicago. I ignored it. I let it roll off my back. I just kept doing my job and I had my partner as support to deal with the men's harassment. However, I finally decided, there's got to be a better way to do policing. I am not going to put up with this anymore and I chose to leave. There were several gay officers at my last job here in Washington, we were open, the chief knew it, and the city accepted us. They had no program for us in terms of domestic partnerships and I tried to do something about that before I left."

Here's another example of escape followed by confrontation from an academy lieutenant: "My first year the men were waiting to see if I made it or not. But down the road, I was mentored by some good managers. As far as my being a mentor, thinking of the last department I was at, I tried to be available to listen to other women, and at one point I filed a lawsuit against the agency based on what they were doing to new women. This had happened to me and I hadn't done anything about it and I just couldn't let that happen again. We settled and the individual who was causing the problem was demoted and demoted until he went from captain back to patrolman. I started the ball rolling. The issue was not so much him as it was against the administration for allowing him to comment in inappropriate ways about women, openly, in public meetings."

For the Group as a Whole

There was very little use of escape. It tended to be used when they first started out. But by the time I met them, these officers were completely confrontational. The older the woman when she joined, the more she used confrontation, starting in the academy. The dancer, Judith Rock, told her instructors not to make jokes about spousal abuse. At the firing range the housewife, Jean VanLandingham, poured her dump bucket into which the male recruits had peed, into their buckets and walked out, shocking her instructor.

In addition to learning a bit about detective work, readers have been introduced to two important facets of women officers' lives—the need to go that extra mile to prove one's competence and that the most successful way of dealing with discrimination and sexual harassment is confrontation.

Readers making career decisions can consider, "Whose job is the most attractive to me, Jessica's or Julia's or Debbie's? Whose interests do I connect with the most? Am I already good at confrontation when I need to be? Am I willing to go that extra mile?"

5

Sergeants in the Field

I interviewed more sergeants than any other rank, 18 in all. Eleven women were patrol officers, five were detectives, and one was an intelligence analyst. Two were lieutenants, four were captains, two were assistant chiefs. I also interviewed two majors, one marshal, one commander, and lastly, six chiefs.

This chapter is devoted to the lives of women who supervise teams of women and men. Some women seek the promotion to change departmental policies and programs. Others see it as a way to continue patrol at a better salary. Still others enjoy the teaching and mentoring side of the job. We'll start with a woman for whom sitting behind a desk remains anathema to the freedom and independence of riding in a patrol car. My husband Cliff and I did a ride-along one evening with Sergeant Dianna Klineburger all around Sea-Tac Airport and it was clear that outdoors is where she wants to be. Dianna was born in 1945 in Phoenix, Arizona. She has two sons in their thirties, both of whom are nurses, and two grandchildren. She has a BA in criminal justice and had just finished a master's in organizational management. She joined the Port of Seattle, WA, PD in 1979 after a stint in the Army and a job milking cows and selling real estate for a commercial dairy. She was also in the Army reserves until 1984.

Why Don't You Check Us Out?

One of the people in my Army reserve unit worked for the Port of Seattle, and said, They're hiring. It's a good place. Why don't you try this? I had been looking everywhere for a viable job for women that had enough pay and benefits to raise two kids. They didn't exist. I said, Okay, I'll try it, not thinking of it as a career choice, quite frankly. I never expected to be hired but I was. Then I never expected to make it through the academy and I was good, so I thought, Okay, two years, that's all, but 23 years later I'm still here.

Right out of high school I went to Centralia College as a home economics student because that's what I was supposed to do. I didn't want to, but I didn't know there were options until later. Women today know theirs. Women who have been in sports, gone to college, and gotten some life experience, and learned how to play the game, come in and do well.

The Department hired six people when I came on, five guys and me, but I was the only one who had military experience. I had been married to an Army officer who encouraged me, otherwise I probably wouldn't have done it. I did two years active duty and six years in the reserves and it was a good thing. It was in the late '60s and I was in the last Women's Army Corps to go through basic training at Fort McClelland. I got an AA degree in Criminal Justice to get my credentials for criminal investigation when I shifted my reserve job status from clerical.

My family was so happy that I went into airport security. They were tremendously proud and thought it was very cool. Everyone was supportive. I was still living out in the country, so to get through the academy I stayed at my sister's house, and my ex facilitated the kids' care.

The Army Edge

The joke was that they needed a token Black and when they couldn't find a token Black, they took a female. When I applied I played the Army card. I play the Army card every time I have an opportunity to do so. You betcha. The Army card is very legitimate. Dealing with men, you know what the rules are, and you've learned how to deal with them. But I've never played the female card, ever.

I was physically fit and that gave me an edge. We had a long physical agility test that was eight hours' worth of running, going over the six-foot wall, the nine-foot fence, the balance beam, the dummy drag, we had it all and I did it with a broken toe. I understood the chain of command, how you either accept orders or you fight the orders in the appropriate manner. I'd learned how to pick the fight, and rule out the stuff that didn't matter. Army training plus my AA degree got me there.

The chief called me into his office and accused me of cheating because my academic work was so good and I almost reached across the table and choked him out. It's not the first time I've been accused of cheating because I go for excellence. Meeting the standard is never good enough for me. My master's degree GPA was 3.9. I'm proudest of the fact that my academic work was so good that they accused me of cheating, but they got over that real fast.

Resource Mom

What I learned from selling real estate fits perfectly with police work. I've got to be nice to people, I've got to cajole them. This is the way we're going to do it and we're going to do it now. I say it kindly and gently, but it's real clear. I also like mind games. How is this person thinking? What's his motive? Where's he coming from? I love murder mysteries. I read them all the time.

Currently I'm watch commander at night for a group of uniformed patrol officers, 23 in all, of whom five are women. I'm their Resource Mom. Whatever they need to get the job done, I help facilitate, including saying, No, you're not going to do that. This number of women is a change in the last couple of years and it makes supervising really different. Men are easier to deal with, they're very young and they haven't evolved as much so you can just tell them, Yes, No, but women are a whole different ballgame. A lot more verbal interaction, a lot more, Why? You can say to a guy, Sit down and shut up; you're not doing that. It doesn't work as well with women.

I'd rather appear before a promotion or hiring board of all men because women's standards can be so high for other women. They will forgive men, but if a woman screws up, all women screw up. That's why it's important to get high quality women. That works for Blacks, Asians, and Native Americans, too, not just women. So when women come before a hiring board, they're going to have to be a notch up, because on the job, they're going to have to do a better job. Being marginal is not going to work for you. You have to be better, work harder, be more careful, go for excellence.

The Port likes people from all over. The racial card is of value. We're an international airport so we've had an edge on diversity from the beginning. We're dealing with people from everywhere so if we've got someone in our department who speaks Russian or Japanese, we're happy. We want more Spanish speakers in our department because it makes our job easier.

There's a ten-hour makeup everybody has to do. During your cycle, which is roughly once a month, you have to do an extra ten hours to get your full complement of forty hours weekly for the year. So we schedule ten hours and then a two and a half hour overtime block to do the makeup. Sometimes we can let people go after ten hours if it's slow and there are enough resources. But when you've got a whole bunch of women all clamoring to leave, then I start complaining, You're not being team players, so, You know what? We don't really need you down here, but nobody's going home early.

I joined because I was looking for enough stability, pay, and benefits to get my kids raised. I had gotten nothing from my ex, except a lot of life experience. I've had an incredible career. The reason I didn't leave in two years is because this place has been fantastic. It's given me a whole life that I didn't know existed. It gave me personal power. I know who I am and I know how to ethically state my case, set my boundaries, and do the right thing. Whereas before the influence of my peer group might have come into play, not anymore. The department's rewarded me with many, many jobs. I could quit today and go out into the real world and have the skills to do something different.

Recruiting Through Personal Referral

We're hiring people with higher education now and the women tend to have more, most have a BA. We don't require higher education, but the people who are applying have it. A white male lieutenant got this up and running and, as he was diversity-oriented, he put a woman in charge of recruiting and hiring for the past five years. The whole department was willing to pick diversity up. One of the reasons I chose the Port of Seattle was that, even in the old days, the mindset was already there compared to other agencies. I didn't want to be a trailblazer; I wanted a job.

We all make an effort to talk to women. Most women get into law enforcement because of personal referral. One of the biggest reasons women go to a particular agency is that they know someone there who said, Why don't you check us out? I looked the Port over and found they were willing to support women, not as well as they do now, but at least they believed that women could do this job. When I got there, already there was a woman on the SWAT team. Some departments I investigated bluntly said, Women can't do police work. You can apply but we're not hiring you. I said, Fine. I don't want to work for you. Or they would say, We might hire you but women just can't do this job because they aren't big enough. Well, my mouth is big enough. Verbal skills go a long way.

The Dilemma of Promotion

I keep winding up on the lieutenant's list, but I don't do well at the assessment centers. I'm not trained for assessment centers, but I'm trained for a lieutenant's job because I've been an acting lieutenant over and over and over. At this last go-around, I didn't want to play the game. I told them what they needed to hear to get on the list, but afterward I looked at those guys and thought, I can't answer the way they want. I'm going to tell them what they need to hear, it's going to hurt me, but I don't care. That's exactly what I did. We all qualified. I ended up number four of five but I was proud of it. I could have notched up by playing the game differently. I was told to wear a skirt to up my chances, but I said, No, I don't own one. I'm not buying one. If that's what I have to do, I don't want the job.

I wanted two things, detective and sergeant. I want hands-on with the officers. The police department says that patrol people are the backbone of the department. But the patrol people are last on the list, over and over again, after detectives and special teams. Well, I like the backbone of the department. I'm a coach and a mentor. I ran the FTO program for four years. I could have run it at a less stressful level, but that's not me. They need someone to tell them what the right thing to do is and to help them out. I will take on the command staff when they need it or I'll take on the officer group when they need it. That middleman role, I'm good at it.

I could have retired three years ago. I'll take the bars if they give them to me but if they don't, I will be kind of relieved because it's all paper and staff. It's not where my heart is. However, people at the lieutenant level can facilitate the street. As a lieutenant I could continually make them shift their focus and run interference for the troops.

When I got promoted from detective to sergeant, they put me in charge of detectives. No woman had run detectives at that time as a sergeant. I found out I could do it well, but to start, I didn't think so. However, I'm more than willing to ask questions and to thank people when they tell me something I can use. I was never afraid to say, I'm a little confused here. Can you help me out? When you do it that way, people help you. One sergeant took me aside and said, There are rules here and they aren't stated and they aren't in the rule book. And he let me know what they were.

My Joy Is Watching Growth

What people find rewarding are little e-mails from a sergeant praising them. I need to do one right now. I went out on a traffic call last night. After the second officer got there, I stepped back and watched the tremendous way this young woman played this guy who was acting real hinky. He was crumped down in his car drinking a beer. Said he just bought the car, which was a beater but he had no paperwork. He didn't have any ID on him. He had three warrants out on him and one was fairly significant. An open container, a suspended license, no insurance, the list went on forever. He didn't want to identify himself and he's being real screwy and it easily could have turned into a fight. But she cajoled, joked, played the role really well. She's new, mid-twenties. This is her first police department job. She came through when I was the FTO and my joy was watching the growth from when she started, from new person to skilled person, that's payoff for me.

We have family-friendly policies. I couldn't even get time off when my kid had appendicitis. Now we've got family leave, bereavement leave, emergency leave, sick leave for your family's needs. You can call in sick days for your kids and not lie about it. We don't have part-time or flexi-time, but we accommodate people when we can on an informal, case by case basis. We have shared sick leave. One of our sergeants had lots of family health problems so we could all give him time.

Being a police officer is like being a parent. You treat people with respect. You get them to do what you want at the lowest level to get compliance. It works with teenage boys. My sons were my training ground for supervising guys at work. I wanted them to know what my job was all about because they were worried about my welfare. And I was worried about their welfare, so we shared stories. They talked about high school and the stupid things happening there, which were scarier than my job.

Most women police with successful marriages have husbands who are in emergency services jobs so the women's jobs make sense to them. But most women I know who are cops are single or become single. I don't even date. I had an 11-year relationship that broke up a year and a half ago. He was state patrol, retired, and went to Montana, but I was not ready to give up my career, so we did a long-distance relationship from Montana to Seattle and it didn't go anywhere. I hadn't had a date until two weeks ago, a real nice guy, but he wants to move to Florida. I play a dominant role and it's going to be an unusual man who's willing to deal with that. I heard a statistic yesterday on the radio that said relationships break up when women earn more. I don't earn that much but the men I meet don't earn more than me. It was also a problem in the 11-year relationship because his retirement income was considerably less than what I earn. Men are intimidated. I have met men in social gatherings who, when they find out what I do, turn and walk to the other side of the room, literally. They say, Oh. Turn around and leave. It's a big barrier, relationships come and go, but the payoff is worth it, the career.

Women's Organizations

I belong to the National Management Association. Women should join professional, rest-of-the-world organizations in addition to police organizations for balance. The International Police Women's Association is a good organization. I've been a member for a long, long time. But women shouldn't make that their only focus. If you're doing nothing but women's organizations, you're not learning about 90% of the people you're dealing with.

When I'd get to the point where the job was too overwhelming, too big of a battle, and I was sick of it, I'd go to an IAWP conference and hear other people's stories. I'd say, Oh, I got it really good, and came back refreshed to my agency. It's a balancing thing for me. A conference is exposure to different worlds. I went to Edmonton last year where they had a management-level program that was really good. How-to-manage by many women who have made it. Even if you're going to be a patrol officer for 30 years, which is a legitimate career path, you need to learn to manage, systems thinking, how teams work and how they have hierarchies and what the unstated rules are.

Detective Sergeant Susan Sill

How to have your cake and eat it too? Susan Sill still has patrol's freedom and lack of close supervision with her inside job, but what she really enjoys is getting calls from the field. Being supervisor of the King County, WA, Sheriff's Office Special Assault Unit works for her. Susan was born in 1958. She is married to a structural engineer who works from home. They have three boys, 3, 5, and 12. Susan majored in animal science and breeds golden retrievers.

My Last Day at the Academy

The day I had to pass the physical was extremely critical. I had knee surgery in 1981, so I worried about my knee. Would it make it? While I was at the academy I came in early every day and ran five miles. The physical test was pass or fail on the final day. You either graduate or you don't. The biggest thing was running around the track and getting over these two walls and it's timed. I had been doing it, no problem. The last day I had done everything else just fine but when we got to the run, my knee went out on me. It was so swollen I couldn't walk or even stand on it. A PT instructor iced it and iced it and he said, You're not going to be able to do the run. I said, Oh, yes, I am. He said, Okay, but the other PT instructor said, I'm not letting her do it.

We went to the track and they called out our names. Two people supported me and I was walking around. The one instructor said, She's not going to make it, but you can't not let her try. My knee hurt so bad. Finally, I was the last one. He said, All right, come on. I prayed and I prayed and I ran and I ran. I had no pain. I had no feeling. I dropped down from the first wall and that hurt. But I ran and I ran and by the time I got to the second wall the whole class was running with me and shouting me on. I finished with two seconds to spare and went straight to the doctor. I was on crutches for a month. But I made it over and to this day I don't know how.

The SAU

As supervisor of the Special Assault Unit, I'm completely in charge of my day and what I am going to get involved in. What I really enjoyed about patrol was being totally on my own in my car and handling everything by myself. But I still get to go on callouts although I couldn't possibly go out on all of them. I'm on call 24 hours a day. I only go when the detectives need my help, or if my supervisory decisions are necessary, or if there's a high risk callout or search warrant. I'll go if it's a high profile case and the media are involved. I go on about a fifth of my detectives' calls. On weekends I'm on standby for all the units, not just SAU.

It's not very different being a sergeant and being a mom. Who's got the better toys? Who is being treated better than the other person? Who got wronged by somebody? These are personnel issues moms deal with and sergeants deal with. To be a good supervisor you have to understand people and be good with people and being a mom really helps in that respect. The same theories that go with raising children go with supervising detectives. We could all use cookies and a nap.

Saving the World

Almost everybody who becomes a cop thinks they are going to save the world. I am no different. Right now I'm mostly trying to save the children's world. I've been able to do huge things not just in my job, but through the committees I belong to, to change how cases are investigated, to change protocols. I recently developed our Drug Endangered Children Program where I send a couple of detectives to every meth lab bust where there are kids. We go into a meth lab and my detectives' job is to document the living conditions and try to get, if possible and appropriate, a charge against the parents for criminal neglect or whatever charge is necessary for having put those children in that environment. What we do now is collect the children's urine immediately to show that they're poisoned because we had gotten virtually nowhere in showing how deplorable these living conditions are and how bad these chemicals are. They are dangerous because they can explode. They are dangerous to inhale. If it's in the children's urine, it's in their system. We are getting huge results. We're putting pads in babies' diapers, taking those pads to the toxicology lab, and there's methamphedimine, heroin, cocaine in those babies. It gets absorbed by their bodies in various ways. Their baby bottles are right there when they're cooking, they're breathing the air, and mom may be nursing them when she's doing cocaine. And we are going to change the lives of those kids because, You know what? You're not getting your kid back if you poison it.

There are lots of little things that make me feel I'm making a difference in the world. I like being on the street and being a detective more than being a sergeant, it's a lot more fun, but the tradeoff for that is I've been able to make much bigger differences for the children in King County. I wouldn't have been able to start the HIT program, the Highway Information Team. I have two detectives who go out once a month and do nothing but contact prostitutes. They contact them to take care of them, see how they're doing, and use them as informants and to find out if we've got a Green River coming up. We find out about the bad dates, and we search out the bad guys who are beating up on prostitutes. We find out who the pimps are, we find out about drugs, robberies, homicides, because these prostitutes know everything that is happening. And when they see these same detectives over and over again, the word is out that they can trust these detectives. Even if they have warrants, they won't arrest you. They take them to McDonald's, get them meals. If they have great gaping open sores all over their body because of their lifestyle, we take them to the hospital. We take care of them and we have developed them as confidential informants. Our main reason for being out there is to catch a serial rapist before he becomes a serial.

Another program I have implemented is suspect rape exams. Everybody's always done rape exams with victims. We send them up to the hospital for the exam, swabbing, DNA, etc. What's been sorely neglected in police departments and still is, is getting the guy swabbed down. He's got DNA all over him. We get a search warrant and take them to the hospital where my detectives do that. But that's not something I'd ask a female detective to do. I'm not going to have a woman swab a man's penis. Luckily I have enough men in my unit to call them in to do that. Similarly, if I have a rape victim in the hospital and she's got bruises and cuts on her breasts, I'm not going to ask a male detective to take those photographs.

Regarding Promotion

I got offered a captain's position and turned it down because the higher you go, the less you are a cop. Sergeant is removed enough. At least I get to go out on the street and deal with crime. If I went to captain, I'd be dealing with departmental issues. I have no interest in departmental issues. I only deal with them because I have to. Other than that I just want to be free to do my job. I have a job right now where I work four tens so I have three days a week home with my children. I pretty much come and go as I please. My husband takes care of the kids when I work and the minute I get home, he starts working and he works into the night. If I were working five days a week, that would be one day less for him to work. It really would have affected him if I had taken the captain's job, although he wanted me to. I felt it was a bad decision for my family and I wouldn't get the personal enjoyment out of my present job.

Outside of my job, my family takes all my time. I'm one of those lucky people that as soon as I finish a call, I go right back to sleep. When I'm at home I don't dwell on my job. Never have. If my phone rings and it's work, then it's work. But when I hang up the phone, I'm back to my three boys.

You Win More Fights with Your Mouth

Than with your hands, is what I tell all new people. However, I have been in some memorable fights. Years ago my partner, who was a real baby, and looked like he was 17, and I got called to a biker bar. Richy was young, buff, athletic, but a smoker. The bar seemed calm but there were these two drunk guys, would we please get them out? I told my partner to go talk to that guy and I'd talk to this guy. Mine had a knife on him. I decided I'm not going to talk to him with a knife on. He was this huge smelly guy. I said, I need to take your knife off. He said, Heck you are, bitch. And the fight was on. He grabbed for me and as we were going to the ground I yelled, Richy! I can remember him flying through the air, over the bar, and landing on him. This was the longest fight I was ever in. It lasted forever. We couldn't get to our radios to ask for help because this guy was tough and the people in the bar were screaming, Leave him alone, you fucking pigs.

Richy had him at the rear end and I had him at the top end and I am trying to do a hair hold and I am pulling hair out by the handfuls. Long red hair is flying all over the floor. At one point we could hear our radios ask if we're okay. We heard someone say, Okay, how many units? We're not getting beat up but we're not winning either. He wasn't getting away because we had him on the floor. At one point Richy had his handcuffs out but he couldn't cuff him, put them down, and those got stolen. I had my baton out at one point, put it down, and that got stolen.

Finally I'm holding his head and Richy is on his back with his hands behind him and I yell, Richy, cuff him. He just gasped, I can't. He was too tired. So I got on top of him and I cuffed him. Just as we finished cuffing him, the doors flew open and ten cops came running in. Now they show up! We got out as fast as we could because the crowd was so hostile. We moved to a gas station. I was feeling great, I was pumped up, full of energy, I had enjoyed that, and Richy is sitting on the curb puking his guts out. I said, Richy, you've got to give up those cigarettes.

Sergeant Jackie Hill

Jackie was born in 1962 and is married to a fire department captain. No children, just one elderly cat. Jackie loves to work nights and is a patrol sergeant for the night watch with Port of Seattle, WA, PD.

Continuing My Education

I finished my bachelor's with City University in criminal justice in 1999. I am now finishing up my first semester of an 18-month master's program in criminal justice through Boston University. This Internet course is an ass kicker, with homework every day, 24/7.

I have also been involved with a correspondence master's program at the University of Leicester, which meant I got three tax deductible trips to London. Leicester offers master's degrees in public order, police science, and crisis and disaster management, which is what I took. It's a two-year program and very intensive. What for me was difficult is that you'd send in your papers and wouldn't get any feedback for five weeks. They had weekend study schools during the spring and summer and I'd spend weekdays in London and then take the train up to Leicester. I met these wonderful criminal justice professionals from all over the world. I was impressed with how different the attitudes were between the

London police and the officers up in the Midlands. I probably won't get a degree out of it because I'm now focused on this other master's.

Dealing with Discrimination

I found an old academy book dating from 1984. It's amazing how much better the academy had gotten from 1984 to 1991 when I was there. I'm going through this old book and in the sex crimes section there was the usual perversion stuff and then it talked about homosexuality as a perversion. I couldn't believe it. You'd never see anything like that in a law enforcement book published now.

One my good friends is gay and we've both had our battles with the department over gender discrimination but for her it was worse. Because she's a lesbian, people harassed her. She had bullets put in her work mailbox, vague threats left in her mailbox. Based on her sexual orientation she was discriminated against when she tried to get on the canine unit. It was in the mid-'90s when I was trying to get on the SWAT team, so we banded together and tried to get the Port Authority to acknowledge that women were being kept out of special teams. If you'd look at the promotional exams and who was getting promoted, 99% of people with stripes and a bar had been on a special team and they were all men. The two of us went together to personnel with our research. It was a long fought battle, but eventually I became the first woman on SWAT and was there from 1996-1999 and my friend made the canine unit.

For SWAT, marksmanship is so important. When I first started, because we worked with submachine guns, the guys said, She doesn't know how to shoot that, when my clusters were so close. They simply couldn't believe that I could shoot that well. If you're on regular patrol you're issued single-stack bullet magazines for your sidearm. But when you go to a special team like SWAT, you're issued a double stack so the gun has a bigger grip. I had to ask, When am I going to get my M-13, which is the model that has the wider grip. They told me, Oh, those are too big for your hand. But there was a guy on the team who was my build and he had an M-13. They'd already made this assumption that I was too small to hold it. So I spent $1,200 and bought my own. I was so proud of graduating from basic SWAT, a week-long semi-military academy at Fort Lewis, PT at 6 in the morning and going to bed at midnight. It was a very long week.

The Quandary of Promotion

For so many years I was the only woman on patrol at nights. When this other woman got hired, we bonded immediately. When the two of us were together, the guys would get very nervous. What are you girls talking about? One of the biggest positives that has happened over the years is that there are more women to be friends with in law enforcement. Another positive is that we have more women leaders. The chief of Federal Way is one of the best in the state. She's very personable, she rides with her officers at least once a month, she probably knows all their names, whereas the running joke in our department was that our chief could never keep the Black officers straight. She's very approachable and takes the time to listen. She provides a lot of leadership. She told us of how she has these little revivals, these little come-to-Jesus meetings in the parking lot when she has an issue with one of her officers. What a great way of doing management.

As a patrol officer you are very autonomous. You work by yourself, you're on your own. Working on a special team is kind of foreign to police. It's a whole shift change, learning how to work as a team. When you're a supervisor, you actually have a team, a squad, that you're supposed to motivate or discipline or whatever you need to do to get the job done. It's more holistic, more big picture, and where you start to learn that is being on a team. In some ways I miss the individuality, being able to do what I want, and having to worry only about me instead of 15 other people.

One of our newer guys said something to me that got me thinking. He said, If you competent officers don't take those promotional exams, things aren't ever going to change. If you decide to stay doing what you're doing and you're happy with the status quo, then all we're going to have in senior management are, and here he rattled off the names of the most incompetent people. He's absolutely right. I should be thinking about the organization and be part of the change. So I have put in to take the lieutenant's exam. But to be honest, everybody hates lieutenants. Either you discipline, discipline, discipline or you're doing a project. It is also far removed from the heart of the department, which is the officers. As a sergeant, you're still kind of there, part of that larger peer group. But as you go to a lieutenant or a captain, your peer group keeps shrinking. And your whole focus is the organization, its stability, its integrity.

A Few Facts

The Winter 2001 issue of *Women Police* published an article my sister and I put together, "Fictional Women Police: How Close to the Facts?" Here are some facts to compare with the 20 fictional cops featured in *Food, Drink, and the Female Sleuth*.

Dianna has two children, Susan has three, Jackie has none. In the group of 53 women, 17 have no children, ten have one child, 16 have two children, eight have three children, and two have four children, whereas three-quarters of our fictional cops had no children. Real-life women cops seem to have more kids than their fictional counterparts.

Marital-status wise, the fictional cops were all unattached, i.e., single, divorced, widowed. Big contrast to our 53, only 14 of whom were single, divorced, or widowed. Three were happily partnered, while 36 or 68% of our group were happily married. My results also contrast with a study done in 1992 by Bartol et al. in which 91% of all full-time female municipal officers in rural Vermont were compared with a matching sample of male officers. Among women, 63% were never married or divorced, while 37% were married or remarried. Among men 27% had never married or were divorced, while 73% were married or remarried.

Physique-wise, the fictional women cops were strong and fit. So are the three sergeants you have met here and the rest of the real-life group. Five women of the 53 were somewhat overweight, but it wasn't interfering with the demands of patrol. Personality-wise, the fictional cops were feisty, stubborn, intrepid, and opinionated. I think that Dianna, Susan, and Jackie are also feisty, stubborn, intrepid, and opinionated, as well as achievement-oriented and ambitious. They had not shied away from testing and promotion, up to a point.

In fiction, the typical detective is a fast food junky. She doesn't do much cooking. Sometimes with all that running around, she forgets to eat. If she does cook, it is a good bet that she does it for her children. In contrast, real women police officers do not appear to be fast food junkies, although one major confessed, "Cooking has never been a strong point of mine. Too many years working swing shift. Give me a good bowl of popcorn and parmesan cheese for dinner any night of the week." It should be noted that many women had husbands who are very good cooks, so their wives were eating healthy.

Readers checking out career possibilities can ask, "How good a supervisor am I? Would I be comfortable supervising male officers? Am I willing to possibly jeopardize my personal relationships with men? Do I like teaching and mentoring? How do I feel about continuing my education? How important is it to me that women go after supervisory positions?"

6

Sergeants in the Office

The focus now will be on what sergeants can accomplish at a desk. How do job satisfactions differ from those derived in the field? What talents and skills are a good fit for office work? How much variety is there in assignments?

SgtMom is Sergeant Joy Mundy's e-mail name. Joy was born in 1948 and has a 30-year-old daughter and a granddaughter. She is married to a reserve officer for a rural county. She studied history in college and left a job with a construction supply company when she joined up. Joy is from Watkins Glen, New York, moved to Seattle when she was 29, and joined Seattle, WA, PD at the age of 32.

There Was This Party

I worked as a secretary during college in a theology department where I learned a lot about what I didn't want to do. While I was still in New York, before I turned 27, I applied for the state patrol. When you turned 27, you were too old. On my twenty-seventh birthday, they sent me the application. That's how they kept women out back then.

In Seattle I was at a party when the company I worked for was going out of business. I talked to a woman deputy about her job and I said, Unfortunately, I'm too old. She goes, No, no. A Seattle police officer said, Come on, Joy, try for it. I kept thinking this is a very young person's job, which in many ways it is, physically. This officer showed up at work the next week and said he was taking me to lunch. Instead he drove me to the Seattle Police Department to apply. On the way over he said, If we've got to have women, we might as well have someone smart and tall. This happened in January 1980 and in May I was in the academy.

My mother cried but my father said he wished he could be here for my graduation. After that he was silent until ten years ago when he had a heart attack and had to have a valve replaced. I flew back to New York and was walking him into the operating room when he said, I need to tell you, I've always been so proud of you and what you do. I tell your sister that. I said, Well, Dad, it's time to tell me now.

Young People Pushed Me

I had not been doing very much physically. I began working out and running. I hurt myself and had to go to a doctor and get special shoes. The best thing was that when I finally had to test, I was up against younger people who pushed me to run faster and work harder. Among the men testing us was an African American male who also supported me. I have repeatedly said we need mentors for women the minute they come in. They used to say, Here's the name of a mentor, but that doesn't work. New people don't know who we are or who to trust. We've got to go to them.

An African American friend explained that they were so glad when women came along and white males had us to pick on instead. African Americans understand team and togetherness. Women still have not been oriented towards team mentality so we're dependent on males to get us into a job somewhere else.

Since we're talking about physical fitness, five years ago the union agreed to physical testing only if it was positive. They didn't want people hurt by the program. The department agreed to pay 1.5% more in salary every year if you passed these physical exams. The department did so well the city didn't want to pay out all that money. The union said again, We're not going to punish people for not being in shape. That was the end of the physical fitness program.

Working in an Office?

I joined in 1980 and was on patrol until 1983. I was injured pretty badly and got a desk job as a crime analysis officer. It was day shift, which was great because I had a child. I did that until 1989 when I was promoted. I was the first woman to spend eight years as a patrol sergeant, from 1989 to 1998, and I did it because I wanted women to have a role model.

When I began there were old guys who had been here a long time and they would tell you right up front what they thought of you. I've got to work with you but I don't want you here. However, after some time those older gentlemen treated you with respect. It's gotten more subtle over the years because the men are afraid of harassment charges. I would rather have the old days where the men were overt and outright.

I never liked the idea of working in an office. The police gave me the freedom to get out and work with the public. Being involved, working with the community was totally something I could see myself doing. Coming from a small town I never thought of the other side of it, the horrors you're going to see.

My Partner Went into Protection Mode

Normally in my patrol shift I worked with a partner, but one day we were short of people and we all got put out in individual cars. I got called to an incident where there was a man at a transient service center where they wash their clothes and play cards and this guy was creating a ruckus. You had to go downstairs. They sent my backup, a little Filipino guy who weighed 125 pounds soaking wet. This problem guy had just got out of prison, was 6'2" and he had muscles that he had been popping up in Walla Walla Prison for five years. I talked him into coming upstairs and got him outside. He started to pump up again and you could tell he was on drugs. I kept saying, Kenneth, you need to calm down. He kept saying, I'm going back down and what are you going to do about it? I advised him that they didn't want him there and that he'd be trespassing. Finally I said, Okay, Kenneth, I'm calling my army. He said, Oh, yeah? But he totally calmed down.

I never asked for extras unless I really needed it. They come rolling in and my partner, who would normally be with me, rolls up to the guy. Before he even spoke to me to find out what the situation was, he went into protection mode. He said, What are you doing to her? What have you done to her? And the fight was on then. This guy picked me up and threw me on a car, he was so strong. We had ten officers there getting their clothes ripped off and everything's flying. They're trying to get him off me and they used nightsticks until he's not moving. When it was all through I said to my partner, if you had just talked to me. He said, Well, I thought he was going to hurt you.

The Home-Job Switch

When I was first in police work I was totally engulfed in it and didn't manage the home-job switch very well. My daughter was eight years old and I never realized until she was much older that she was afraid for me every day. When I became a sergeant, even though on ride-alongs kids are supposed to ride with somebody else, I told my lieutenant, I'm bringing my daughter down and she's riding with me. By this time she was 18 years old. At the end of the night, she said, Mom, if

I had known this was what it was like, I wouldn't have been afraid every day. So police officers need to have their children do that.

I was also tougher on my daughter than I should have been, wanting to keep her out of trouble. Because she was an only child, she was very overprotected. I made sure when I had my days off, they were spent with her. When she was in high school, something I didn't realize was when she had a boyfriend, she wouldn't introduce me right away. She knew he'd get the third degree. It was always, what do your parents do? Because if I knew what the parents did, it gave me a good impression of this child.

I Am Kind of a Mom

I didn't always have a partner, because the department doesn't work like that, but when I did, my partners learned the benefits of my approach. I would walk into a bar fight and go up to a guy and say, Hey, talk to me. Most people I meet on the job are bigger than I am so I don't put my ego out there because I can't back it up. My daughter calls me Sergeant Mom and the guys call me Mom Mundy. Whenever I talk to an officer, I usually put my hand on his arm because police officers need touch. They live in a world of negativity and feel isolated much of the time. I feel like I have a ton of sons and daughters in this department that I've talked to over the years and helped raise from student officers to adult officers. So I am kind of a mom.

When I came into this office, I watched how the other detectives treated the administrative specialists/secretaries. My attitude is we all need each other, and the secretary is our backbone. Rank doesn't mean a thing to me. Respect and dignity and how you treat people are what matters. I used to get laughed at on patrol. The guys would say, Oh, here we go again. Sergeant's going to read us the oath of office. Once a month they were reminded that we are public servants.

One of my favorite projects was with street kids. We kept getting complaints that the officers were too tough on them so a community service officer and I did a tape called "Cops and Kids." We wanted to show it at roll call. But the men saw it as some soft woman thing and said they didn't have time. It's a 15-minute tape. We went up to a youth center where the street kids take GED training. We talked with them and we talked with cops. Then we brought the kids and cops together to do this video. Both sides talked about respect. What the cops learned was that the majority of these kids were out on the streets not because they wanted to be, but because it was safer than home. Some had two jobs, were going to school, and trying to find a place to sleep. They came from alcoholic parents, abusive parents and were hanging out on the street because it was the safest place to be.

The kids wrote incredible poetry. One poem was titled "Sofa Surfing," how this gal went from one sofa to another. We framed their artwork and put it on a precinct's walls and the chief came and we brought the kids in and did a presentation. They were so proud. We were trying to give them some recognition of who they were and what their life was about.

Diversity Changes People

Our new chief is trying to send a strong message because for the first time in the history of the department our assistant chiefs show diversity. We have five assistant chiefs and a deputy chief, which include two African American males, a Hispanic male, and two females. He understands the need for the top to show diversity to get it to happen at the bottom.

I supervise six detectives and one administrative specialist in the Auto Theft Squad. I have one female detective and my administrative specialist is female. I have a very diverse squad. When we finally get our secretarial position opened up, the secretary will be a male. I have a detective who was born in Vietnam, a detective who is Japanese, a detective who is Puerto Rican. It's wonderful to see how diversity changes people, how having people with a second language changes others. I love my job and I have to keep focused on the fact that there are incredible human beings who work this job. I have male detectives working for me who are like brothers and they would go to the wall for me.

I had an argument with another sergeant the other day. One of his officers was moving up to detective and he was carrying on. I finally said, You know, my biggest accomplishment is when people leave my squad. It means I have succeeded and they have succeeded in moving on to a better job. He said, But everything changes. I said, Well, that's it. I get somebody new to work on and, true, everybody's got to adjust, but that's life.

The Biggest Retention Issue

A big retention issue is childcare. What we have wanted is a childcare center because women who work in many different city services have nontraditional hours. A lieutenant in Portland accomplished it there.

We deal with the notion of extended leave this way. A mother has to have a doctor say that she can't return to work yet because, for example, her back hurts from the pregnancy. Our insurance policy will cover 50% of our salary for anything that's not duty-related. Women I've talked to have said you have to make sure you have a physical problem to stay away. Still, you never know from one time to the next how the department will handle it. It depends on who you are and who you know. From a union perspective you'll never see part-time or job-share happening. But what you do see now is men in court with their backpacks on and their babies in them. Judges allow them in court as long as the babies are quiet. Even the men are now calling for daycare.

Another retention problem I helped with was to get an insurance policy in the union that assured that women would be paid for their pregnancy. It used to be you had to report you were pregnant by five months and they just said you had to go home and you wouldn't be paid. The department wouldn't guarantee them a desk job or anything. The firefighting women, who were more impacted than anybody with the issue of breathing smoke, fought the policy with a lawsuit because they had no desk jobs to go to. The police department followed suit and the administration had to at least find us desk jobs at the point where the doctor said you could no longer do physical work. I then worked to see that this policy was available to all women in Washington. It's a disability policy that is for both men and women.

Promotion Hurdles

I joined when I was 32 years old and a single mom. This job was going to be my livelihood, so I didn't let people roll over me and I set my course from the beginning. Back then we had older-style chiefs who went through the motions of affirmative action. It created a lot of resentment in the patrol among men who were trying to get promoted. What the chief should have done is call everybody together and say, This is the law. These officers said to me, How could you possibly get on the list? And be willing to take a promotion you know you don't earn? I would say, You've been here 15 years. You've got fifteen service points that they attach to your test score. If you'd be willing to take off those points, I could compete fairly. Because I could not be hired 15 years ago. That's why we have affirmative action. With service points behind you, it's not going to be equal. Until civil service is willing to take them off, there's no way for women to compete.

Today we're more on equal footing, we have equal points and so you see women and minorities at the top of the list. But it created a lot of animosity because the men believed that we were taking their promotions. Affirmative action is virtually gone—it was voted out in this state—but there is still backlash.

When I Retire

In two years we're going to move to Lake Havasu City, Arizona. My husband says I won't be able to stay away from law enforcement so I might work for the private sector, work for an insurance company as a fraud investigator. If I had my druthers and could do it financially, I'd work with kids. Another woman community service officer and I attempted to follow a program here that they had in San Francisco, which was to set up a safe house for young female prostitutes. She and I worked very hard and got things to the point where our prosecutors went to San Francisco to look at the program. But they didn't see female prostitution as a big issue. However, we did write a manual and other police departments, like Las Vegas, adopted it and set up programs in their area, so we did bring awareness in other cities.

The majority of teenage prostitutes are there because somebody in their family has done them emotional or physical abuse. They've lost their self-esteem and it takes a family atmosphere and strong support to get them off the street. I always say, But for the grace of God that could be me because my family split up. I was five years old and I was sent to grandmothers, aunts, uncles. I was never in the same school for over a year until I was 13. I was moved from place to place, but at least my parents kept me with other family members. If it had been a foster situation, I could have gone sideways. Feeling abandoned, a girl could easily choose prostitution to find some kind of comfort and acceptance.

IAWP and Other Women's Organizations

When I go to the conferences, it's the one place where I'm no longer in the minority. There's this indescribable feeling of sisterhood. I've met incredible women who were the first women out there. The IAWP honors women for what they do. They reward us. I received a mentoring award in 1999 in Philadelphia and it was the pinnacle of my career to be honored by those women, because I know that their accomplishments have taken twice as much work. Most have given their own time and money to get to the conferences. Only through sheer determination have they gotten to those meetings to offer help to women who need it. Here's what you do if you are in this situation. These are the laws that cover you. Go do this, go do that. It's still a long road, but I have bonded with women from all over the world. These organizations let women know that there's somebody else out there who has walked that path.

The last time I attended I had just had a mastectomy and I dragged myself there. My chief paid for everything for the first time in the history of this department. I had told him I was a Vice-President of the IAWP and that I represent the department every day around the world. I need that bond every year to keep me fired up and there's more stuff to do.

Joy has been in touch since our interview. She is also very proud to be the first woman elected to the Seattle Police Guild's Board of Directors. She was the editor of a Historical Yearbook of SPD in the mid '80s, the first editor of the guild's monthly newspaper, and also the State Chairperson for four years for the Police Pension Committee of the Washington State Council of Police Officers. She served as the IAWP Regional 9 Coordinator for Oregon, Washington, Alaska and Idaho from 1998-2000, from 2000 to present as Second Vice President, for which she has been reelected for another three years.

Her e-mail message of October 2003 said: "I am proud to say we now have LoJack in Western WA as a result of my work. It's a stolen vehicle recovery system. If it were not for my office taking on the work to get it done, contracts, tracking equipment installed in patrol vehicles, training, etc., it would not have happened. I am now trying to start up a Decoy Vehicle program so if a bad guy takes our electronically equipped decoy car, we can shut it down by satellite and not have to have cops standing by watching it."

Sergeant Lisbeth Eddy

I sought Lis out because she had made the list of Seattle's most outstanding citizens for the year 2001. She was born in Oakland, California, in 1954, received a degree in speech communication in 1976, and is married to a retired electrical engineer. She's thinking about getting a master's in psychology when she retires. Lisbeth begins by describing her unique role with the Seattle, WA, PD.

My Officers Have a Heart

My title is Crisis Intervention Team Coordinator. I'm responsible for training officers to deal better with the mentally ill. I liaise with mental health providers to provide better policing services for them and their clients. I also liaise with family members of mentally ill persons, and I'm a team leader for the hostage negotiation unit. I do administrative work and respond to callouts based on all that. I review police reports every day and work with the mental health court. I do threat assessment analysis. We read reports where individuals appear to family members to be decompensating, but they haven't yet committed a crime. The family is often anxious to intervene before the person breaks the law, threatens or injures somebody. We try to problem-solve these situations and get things resolved before there's an actual crisis.

I only supervise one officer directly who does a lot of hands-on, out-in-the-field arrests and meetings with county-designated mental health professionals to do pickups and serve warrants. Indirectly I supervise 200 commissioned patrol officers and am responsible for training and follow-up on cases involving mentally ill people. A third or more of these officers are women. It's a volunteer program so they have a heart for people who suffer from mental illness and who are going through emotional crises. As a result of their training, they have techniques to better communicate with the mentally ill and know how to better utilize the county's resources.

Officers have joined the unit with just one year on, while others have had 20 years on. Some veterans have said it was the best police training they ever had. I tend to get newer people because that's where your patrol officers are.

I Like Making My Own Decisions

I also took the test for the Seattle Fire Department so I had a choice of which way I wanted to go. Police work is a lot more independent. You go to roll call, collect your stuff, go out to your car and you're on your own. You make your own decisions, who you're going to stop, what you write them up for. In the fire department you're more like a soldier. You respond to a fire and wait for your orders. You go do battle with the fire and then it's all cleanup and hauling dirty stuff around. But the choice came down to, I like to make my own decisions.

I knew in high school that I did not want a traditional woman's job. I didn't want to work in a typing pool all day. Back then, there weren't a lot of women's jobs that were any good. There were no women executives or airline pilots. My Dad was a Navy pilot but when I talked to a recruiter the jobs available as a female naval officer weren't that swell. I wanted to be in a jet plane. I wanted to fire a gun. Like most police officers, I am a bit of an adrenaline junkie. I need that fear factor every now and again to charge me up. I wanted a job that offered excitement and the chance to work with people. My first goal was to be a doctor but my aptitude was not in chemistry and calculus, at all.

I shifted to the drama department, but it was full of strange folks. So I transferred to the speech department where I got to work with people, got to perform a little bit, and the people weren't weird. I had a very good aptitude for speech. I thought I'd probably end up in customer relations.

After college I was an ad courier for a newspaper and a volunteer firefighter. In 1976 the newspaper announced that Seattle PD had just hired six women to be street patrol officers. They were the first who went through the academy and were commissioned. I remember thinking that that was pretty neat, but I also knew there was a height requirement, so at 5'1" I dismissed it.

Being a volunteer firefighter was an eye opener for me in terms of what I wanted to do. I realized I loved public safety. The chief of public safety asked me, When are you going to take the test to be a police officer for me? I asked him, Don't you think I'm too short? He said, No, I think being a good police officer takes attitude more than height. You have the right attitude and I want you to take the test. I checked around and found out that nobody had a height requirement anymore so I tested for many departments and Seattle was the first one that called me. I joined the police in 1979.

Parental Reactions

My Dad thought it would never happen. I was the youngest daughter and the shortest in the family, but my Mom was a pioneer herself. She was a WASP in WWII. She has an adventurous spirit, so she was very supportive. However, she wanted me to work for the department where they live, a smaller community, where it would be safer. But Seattle hired me first and I was at the academy for two weeks when the director of public safety in my hometown called me and said I want to interview you. You're in the top five. But when I had that interview he said, Well, if you were my daughter, I'd tell you to stay in Seattle. You'll never get that experience here. If you ever get tired of Seattle and want to come over here, I'll always take you. He's still there. He's a wonderful guy. I give him credit him for encouraging me because I had thought that being a small woman, they would never take me.

My Dad flew props and then jet planes. They transitioned to jets about the time I was born and he was flying jets off of aircraft carriers. My Mom flew P-51s escorting bombers over Europe. When I graduated from the academy and my Dad saw me with a gun on my hip for the first time, it began to dawn on him that I'd made it. I asked him if he wanted to ride with me and he did. He was still into denial, not wanting to think of his daughter going into a bar fight or pulling a gun on a bank robber. But when he rode with me that day, he got to see that I could do it. We went to a shooting and we arrested a suspect. He got to see a big police response to a situation. We went to a burglar alarm and caught a burglar inside the house. Oh, yes, he stayed in the car.

There's also a little bit of law enforcement in my family. My Mom's brother was sheriff of Orange County, California, for some time. He started the Orange County Crime Lab and my cousin, his son, is a sheriff with the Los Angeles Department.

Eddy Packs Some Sand

I was a swimmer, and my work as a firefighter maintained my upper body strength. I did push-ups and sit-ups to prepare and I was very glad I did because they'd have us all in a row and you'd have to do as many push-ups or sit-ups as you could in one minute. I often did more than many of the men. I felt good about that because I didn't want to go into the academy at my size and be at the bottom of the list physically. I was probably in the top third in terms of my performance so that surprised my academy mates.

I was number two academically, but it was expected that the women would do fine academically. What I was proudest of was the way I played basketball. Academy staff members came up to me years later and said, Do you know what I remember the most about you? It was the way you would get out there playing basketball and you'd get knocked on your ass, head over heels, and you'd just get up and keep running. We could tell you were tough as nails. I might have been short but they said, At least Eddy packs some sand. What they fully expected twenty-three years ago was for women to get poked in the eye and crumble in a heap and cry. That if a woman officer got in a fight and someone smacked her, she'd be worthless.

Handling Discrimination

When I graduated from the academy, I met the chief of police and my tactical officer who said, This is where you report tomorrow. I showed up at the precinct not even knowing who my FTO was. Here I am brand new, a short woman, and when I walked into that roll call, all heads turned and you could see the hostility everywhere. I thought, I'm here and I'm going to do the very best job I can. It was very uncomfortable.

An incident happened when I only had a year and a half on that was significant. I had to take a gun away from a guy, shots were fired, and it was very scary. I came out the victor, took the man into custody. That got all over the department and it helped my reputation a lot. After that the guys in my precinct had no problem with what I was capable of.

But when I transferred to another precinct I was the new kid in class again. They had what's called "the prisoner wagon" for transporting prisoners down to the county jail for booking. I was part of a relief squad so when a squad was off, my squad worked that sector and we had the duties for those two nights of being the prisoners' driver. My first night on the acting sergeant gave me prison wagon duty. I was willing to accept it because he told me, This duty falls to the newest member in the squad. Everyone, including myself, would rather be in a patrol car.

Eventually we got a new guy with less time in the department than I had and yet I got assigned to the wagon. The first week I didn't say anything. The next week this acting sergeant said, Eddy, you got the wagon. I said, I've got a question for you. I've been on that stupid wagon since I got here. How come, now that Dude is the new guy? He said, I didn't know it was that big of a deal. I said, Yes, it is. I had the wagon that night, but I never had it again.

When spots were opening up at the basic academy I applied. I was selected to take the place of a female staff who was teaching Crisis Intervention when she transferred. On my own time I went out and sat in on her classes. But when the transfer came through, the job was given to another woman who had not been preparing. I was livid and the captain said, I will get you out here, and two months later he arranged for me to be on loan though there were no openings yet. I was an extra body and assisted in classes, particularly in the Criminal Law class. It was expected that this instructor would be the first to be promoted out and that I'd take his class. Or I could also teach the other class in Communications.

Then at a staff meeting it was announced that both classes would be taken over by instructors from outside. I went to the Criminal Law instructor and said, What's going on? He said, Do you want to teach Criminal Law? Well, yeah. He said, We've never had a woman teach Criminal Law. I said, Do you have a problem with me teaching it? He said, Not me. Why don't you talk to the sergeant?

I had some time to think and finally the light came on—Crisis Intervention is a women's course but a woman teaching Criminal Law? It had never been done and they couldn't handle it, even though the captain had brought me out here for that very reason. I went to the sergeant's office and asked, Why am I not being considered for the Criminal Law course? He said, I didn't know you wanted it. I said I did and asked why I wasn't being considered for it or Communications. He was baffled. He did not have an answer for me. At the next staff meeting it was announced that I'd take over Criminal Law.

How I Came to Create My Job

In 1997 I was a team leader for the hostage negotiators. Reviewing some statistics I realized we had a whole bunch of calls involving mentally ill people. Luckily most were being resolved in a peaceful way but some were not. I felt my team didn't have enough training. I went to an assistant chief with a proposal that we establish a new unit. Certainly the hostage negotiators needed more training with the mentally ill. The chief had, in fact, said to this same assistant chief that he wanted him to look for a better response to dealing with mentally ill people. So when I came up with my proposal, he said, That's very good. I'm going to make you part of the committee because we need to do something about this.

I was part of a committee that involved the police department, community providers, legislators, advocates for the mentally ill, and other concerned community members. We reviewed different programs in the United States, and one of them was the CIT (crisis intervention team) program, which originated in Memphis, Tennessee, where they had success with it. Portland had recently copied it. The whole committee went down and got a firsthand look at Portland's program and decided they liked the model. It was the easiest to create because you just took a cadre of first responders, patrol officers, and instructed them in how to deal better with these calls. But they are patrol officers first, responding to radio calls, dealing with drunks on the street and bar fights, writing tickets, going to accidents, standing in the rain directing traffic.

I worked with the assistant chief on the job description and the city council approved a new sergeant's position to coordinate this function. The chief said we have this job now if you want it. I was invested in some things I was doing in the domestic violence unit and as much as I wanted this job I had pretty much created for myself, I had too many things hanging in domestic violence. An officer who had helped in the committee search was very high on the sergeant's list. I said, Why don't you promote him and let him get it started and when he's tired of it, I'll take it over. I worked closely with him getting it put together. Two years ago, he said, I'm kind of tired of this. Do you want to come over now? And I said yes.

Telling It Like It Is

I'm in the process of doing a survey that the chief and an assistant chief want done. They thought our attrition rate for women in the department was high. I don't think police work is as financially attractive as it was shortly after I hired on. In the '80s and '90s it was a good paying job and a job where women got equal pay. Now there are much better paying jobs in computers in the private sector and law enforcement everywhere is suffering in recruitment.

Over the years at golf events I have encouraged women who had all the characteristics I love to see. I remember one flight attendant. She was a very tall, very stout woman, certainly assertive, and I imagine an excellent flight attendant. I thought she would make a great police officer. But she said, No way. I don't want to carry a gun. Now flight attendants are basically the law enforcement on airplanes. They tell people, Don't smoke. Go sit in your seat. Put your seat belt on. They're protecting other people and themselves. But the thought of carrying a gun, absolutely not.

When I was an instructor in basic training, women came to talk to me because I was a female staff member. At the end of the third day this 21-year-old gal stopped to ask how often we encountered someone who had a weapon. I told her that depending on where you worked, every day. Her eyes got huge and she said, You're kidding. I said, No, in certain parts of town, I probably took a gun off of somebody every single day.

It appalled me that she had gotten this far before that light came on. She ended up resigning. Fellows do the same thing. One came up the first day and said I don't think I should be here. I said, What makes you say that? He said, I could die out there. I could get shot or killed. Now, applying to be a police officer is not like walking into Burger King where you fill out the application form and start in an hour. Instead, you fill out your forms and then it is months of backgrounding, psychological tests, physical tests, written tests, before someone offers you a job.

My personal opinion is that recruiting should change in several ways. First, raise the hiring age to at least 25. We get recruits who have never left home. They haven't graduated from college, never purchased a house or dealt with a landlord. They haven't experienced independent living. And we're giving them the authority to use deadly force, the authority to make decisions concerning people's liberty? We need to extend the preparation process for entering law enforcement to move it into the profession that it is. Second, require certification via a two-year or four-year degree.

Third, recruiters should not avoid talking about the inconveniences and dangers inherent in the job and weed out the people who are merely attracted to the money and how people react when they announce, I'm going to be a police officer. Discuss family issues with women who want to have a family. One option is to have the family first and start the career later, because the job's going to be here when it's easier for them to do both.

Retention and Rehiring

When I talk to my friends about why women leave the department, the overwhelming reason is family. But the department is good about hiring women back who left to have a child. The most important factor in being rehired is being a productive employee when you're here. When someone reapplies, personnel can make some phone calls to prior supervisors. If supervisors say, Oh, yeah, I'd take her back in a minute, then the odds are in favor of her coming back.

An incentive for women who decide to have a family and announce they are going to quit could be job-sharing. If you asked them, Would you be willing to work two days a week, a lot of them would say yes. Right now our patrol officers work a four-day workweek. Two women could work the same car, this person has it these two days, this person has it these two days, and then they're off two days. But it must be available to everybody and, of course, you'd have to offer half-time benefits. The other thing is that the city should offer on-site childcare. Just where is a two-police officer family going to find childcare when they both have to work the Fourth of July?

Rewarding outstanding performance also aids retention. There's Officer of the Year for each precinct, which is based largely on supervisors' nominations but anybody can make a nomination. We also have employee recognition awards which come with a day off which is a real incentive that doesn't cost the city very much. But the basic, day-to-day commendations we use are called "Atta boys." It could be a commendation from a citizen who writes a letter to the chief. That letter goes in your file, your chain of command gets it, everyone's notified that you did good work out there and a citizen felt obligated to thank you. This is the most important thanks that we can get.

The Jefferson Award is named after Thomas Jefferson. It is a national award that was started in 1977 by Jackie Onassis to recognize outstanding community service. Here in Washington State the award is sponsored by the Seattle PI. They do all the legwork. They solicit nominations and put together the panel of judges. This year over 200 people were nominated and they weeded it down to six finalists. I was one of the six. One of the six gets selected to represent Washington State in Washington, D.C., and has a shot at getting the national Jefferson Award.

Women Police Organizations

I joined the IAWP when I became an officer. The first conference I attended was in 1983 in Vancouver, British Columbia. There were over 200 of us and it was a very powerful experience for me. They had one day when we wore our uniforms and here were these Mounties in their red jackets and tall boots who looked so cool. Then there were the East Coast women and the West Coast women, and their uniforms were different and the way they talked was different. I felt very included. I felt very powerful to be with this huge body of women police, this organization that was there to help us. I learned a lot, it was a very informative conference. I've since gone to a number of conferences. I went to the one in Birmingham, England, and I'm certainly taking advantage of the one in Australia.

There is also the Washington Association of Women Police and for awhile we had some good trainings. Many national conferences now are geared to management, which is fine for women who want to do that, but I do not. I'm in a job that I generated where I'm very happy. I'm looking at retirement in maybe three years, and in the meantime I like the hands-on level of supervision that I have. I get to go out and make arrests, and do street work with people. Connecting with patrol officers is where my life is.

Retirement Plans

People tell me I have public speaking ability. I can make lessons interesting. I think I'm a good trainer but I'm not good at marketing myself. If the contacts I make through the training commission were to recommend me to other departments or if the commission wanted to retain me as a part-time instructor, I would like to do that kind of consulting. But I'm not about to generate my own work. Also I'll probably volunteer more in training than I do now at the Crisis Clinic.

Sergeant Frances Carlson

Frances was born in 1953 in Albuquerque. She is married to a civil engineer. She has an AA degree in criminal justice and is 18 hours away from a BA in business management. She worked as a general office worker and in store security before joining the King County, WA, Sheriff's Office in 1981, where she now sits behind a desk in the Internal Investigations Unit.

A Trying Time at the Academy

When I failed this horrible oral interview with King County I decided, I'm not doing this right. So I began my community college education in criminal justice. I also became an intern, got to ride with different deputies and got familiar with patrol. All this prepared me for the next time I tested and the next time there was no oral board so I was able to get in.

My husband and I would go to the track and he would watch me run. I was already physically fit because of karate. I didn't prepare book-wise. I wasn't a very good student and I never worked so hard in my life. They were three of the longest months I ever lived. I was 21 of 21 and totally stressed out, but in defensive tactics they could see that I could take care of myself. I grew up with a bunch of brothers who took care of that. I would not hold back and I did not want the men to hold back because I was a female. I'd already had the crap kicked out of me in karate, what more could they do? The men encouraged me in every kind of physical training and they knew I didn't take tests well so they also studied with me and helped me get through that part of it.

I had a lot of support at home. My husband did all my uniforms and shined my shoes so I could focus on the notebook we had to present with typed notes. You had to take notes, transcribe them every night, thank God for my office experience, I could type, and then turn the notebook in at the end of the week for the tac officer to read and review.

What I Like Best

I'm where I am now as preparation for promotion at some future time. I now work closer to the sheriff and the different chiefs. There is a lot of confidential information coming through and here I am, a talker who can't talk about it, which was a real adjustment. I also had to adjust from having a very flexible schedule to working Monday through Friday, 8:30 to 4:30. My boss understands that I'm not a morning person so she lets me flex my schedule. The best part of being here is her. She doesn't hold back and I appreciate honesty above all else. We have a good working relationship. I'm pretty much left alone to focus on my job.

It's interesting to hear and see all the different things that our deputies get up to. We had an individual who was finally terminated because he claimed to take military leave but he wasn't on military duty. Or he'd take sick leave and he wasn't sick. We've had to let deputies go because there have been domestic orders against them, restraining orders, with a clause checked that they are not supposed to have a weapon. If you live with someone who has filed any type of no contact or restraining order with that clause, if they are in law enforcement or they get convicted of domestic violence, they can no longer carry a gun, they can't do their job, they can't be a police officer. We have individuals, who every once in awhile get very relaxed and forget to wear their uniforms or they wear their uniform shirt with jeans. We get people who don't want to work next to each other because each one thinks the other is an idiot. We used to have the code of silence, what's said in a car, stays in the car. If you're going to confide in someone, you want to be able to trust them. So it used to be that if a certain behavior was in violation of the manual policy or just plain wrong, nobody would say anything. Today, if you don't tell somebody what is going on, you can be held accountable. Not telling is not doing the right thing, especially if it's a blatant violation of the manual policy. People are more comfortable coming forward with a wrong because they are not ostracized as they once were.

The Complaining Younger Generation

Only a few people coming into the department now have military experience while years ago practically all the men had military experience. The climate has changed. We're getting people who don't have any life experience. In the first year and a half we figure out which individuals, for whatever reason, don't get it. We tell them there's no shame if this is not the right job for you. What causes me concern are people who think we owe this to them. Well, yes, some of the tools of the trade like our laptops could be better, but wake up, this is a government agency, not Nordstrom's or Burger King where we do it your way.

Because of our size and temperament, women use other options, like reasoning, while these young men would sooner get in there and duke it out because that's what they think the job is. We get these 21-year-olds who haven't quite lived a life yet, it's brand new to them, it's exciting and there's a testing ground that they go through. I see all the use-of-force reports and I see the same names. But at least these young men are more accepting of women because morals have changed and the higher divorce rate means that a lot of them have had single mothers.

Educational Rundown

Joy has three years of college, majoring in history, Lis has a degree in speech communication, and Frances almost has a degree in business management. What about the group as a whole? What were their college majors? In particular, how many majored in criminal justice? The answer to that last question is 15. The next most popular major was business administration, in all its various forms, with 14 takers, the same number majoring in social sciences, primarily psychology and sociology. The humanities drew 12 bodies; the most interest was in English. One person each majored in American studies, animal science, flying, and education. It won't add up to 53 because of double majors.

Only five women had gone no further than high school. In terms of years of education for the rest, 14 had 13-15 years, 21 had 16 years, eight had 17-18 years, and five had 19-20 years education. Degrees? No degree for 17 women and an AA degree for five. Nineteen had a BA or BS, 10 had an MA or MS, and two had a doctorate degree. Four of the "no degree" women had 15 or more years of college but for different reasons never got a bachelor's degree. Once immersed in police work, it no longer seemed important.

Readers interested in law enforcement are now in a better position to answer, "Am I more attracted to a job in the field or the office? Could I create an office job for myself based on my special interests? What are the advantages and disadvantages of a job in the field versus a job in the office? What is more appealing, supervising a team as Joy does, or working independently at a desk like Frances?"

7

Sergeants and Family Life

There are several ways to solve the job-family dilemma. All of them need to be mentioned in this book. Perhaps the most important is to research and compare departments' family-friendly policies before choosing where to go.

Monroe, WA, PD Sergeant Cherie Harris

Sometimes, I was told, a new woman will get no help from women already in the department. The explanation is, "No one stepped forward to help me, so you can just figure everything out by yourself like I had to." Sometimes, I was told, the women who have been in the department for years act like Queen Bees and are threatened by new women eager to make their mark. But Cherie very candidly recounted a third dynamic. When her department was hiring and women were applying, she and two other women felt threatened, the reason being that these three had very strongly bonded. Cherie had watched while the other two women were given matching tattoos of a Japanese symbol that means female warrior. All three wondered, what would another woman do to our friendship? She opined that they all were a little more mature now and beyond that kind of thinking.

Born in 1972, Cherie has an unusual job history. In her senior year at Washington State University, majoring in political science and public administration, WSU PD offered her a job. She had worked for them as a student employee and had tested with them in the summer, just for the experience, and came in number three on their list. Her husband also worked for WSU PD before transferring to Seattle PD where he is a sergeant. They have a girl, age 7, and a boy age 5. Cherie has a semester left to finish her bachelor's degree.

Why I Joined When I Did

I had friends who had graduated and were living with their parents, looking for jobs. I was very much motivated by security. My parents offered to pay my tuition, rent, everything, if I stayed in school. Looking back, maybe it wasn't the best decision. However, I was worried about getting out of school and being on this testing circuit that so many folks were on, where they went from department to department to department. I had worked with all the people at WSU for years as a student and knew them, liked them.

Dealing with Stereotypes

I got hired in January and worked with a uniformed officer that month before going to the academy in February, so I only had a month to prepare. We did a lot of boxing where we did one-minute drills with boxing gloves and head gear. It was to demonstrate how fast you tire if you are fighting someone. They partnered everyone up. They put me with a partner and then they gave him another partner because I was a woman.

This pissed me off. When our little one-minute drill began, I started punching him as hard as I could on the corner of his head, over and over and over until his head split open even though he had protection. They stopped the fight and I was pretty proud until this instructor said, This is a good demonstration that you shouldn't underestimate a woman. Which I thought was ridiculous. I was also annoyed that I spent more time at the range than was necessary because the range master kept talking to me, over and over and over, Stand like this. Hold your hand like this. I'm a very good shot so I finally said, Would you please look at my target?

Because I was a student in the college police department I knew a lot of officers who had moved on and gotten jobs elsewhere. So when we moved here I researched departments through the people I knew. I did ride-alongs all over the Seattle area. I had two job offers and when I did a ride-along at the other department this officer told me they went out after work a lot and partied together. I had my little girl by then and when I did a ride-along here, I found it was a family-centered department. If your child has a baseball game, you're encouraged to go. If you've got shopping to do on your way home, you're encouraged get to the businesses before they close. I decided Monroe had a small town atmosphere that was better for raising kids and I've been very happy with my choice.

Some Days I Do It Very Well

I supervise a patrol squad of four guys. Some days I do it very well, and some days I have the title of Queen Bitch. But for the most part we get along well and I've been able to talk through issues I've had with the men.

My most recent issue was last week. We are devising our patrol schedule for 2003, and we're forming squads that stay together for a year. In 2002 we did it this new way and everyone is very much in favor of officers staying with the same folks for a whole year. We sergeants consider seniority first. Then we see if performance ratings meet standards. If you had a bad evaluation you stay with the supervisor who gave you that evaluation until you have corrected your deficiencies. Then we looked at the new guys. Those with no seniority get day shift. In other departments people probably prefer day shift, but people here want to work nights.

We had to move people around, and one of the officers who worked for me this year will have to work on another rotation with a different sergeant. He has strong relationships with the people he works with so he's very upset that he's leaving his friends. That required a sit-down, two-hour talk that started in the parking lot between our cars. He had taken the decision personally and felt I didn't like him. My husband works in a huge department where if you get transferred to another squad, so what? You get transferred.

But relationships in a small department are important. We do run into some strong personalities who have bonded with other strong personalities and they will challenge me and other sergeants. This often happens in briefings when you're trying to relay information. For example, our new chief doesn't want us to wear a long-sleeved shirt with an open collar. He wants us to wear our tie. At a briefing I might say to somebody, Hey, I see that you've got a long-sleeved shirt on with an open collar. I don't know if you saw that order that came down that we have to wear ties now. I try not to single people out when we're meeting in a group because they get defensive and their buddies come to their aid.

Doing It My Way

I have gotten into very few fights in my career and have been able to de-escalate situations where male officers were escalating. I was the sergeant one time when we had to deal with a subject in town who is deaf. When he gets intoxicated, he gets out of control. I got there late. He was handcuffed, on the ground with guys on top of him. He was yelling, not coherently, but yelling. His sister was there. I said, Guys, get off of him, get him up. He's cuffed, he's not a threat. His sister asked, Can I talk to him? The male officers said, No! I said, Well, why not? She can sign so she's the only one here who can communicate with him. So his sister told him, They'll take the handcuffs off so you can communicate, but you had better relax or you'll be back on the ground. He relaxed and ended up going home instead of getting thrown in jail. Using the sister seemed to me just common sense. But I was not the men's favorite that day.

Sometimes I take things personally and my husband all the time says, Get over it. When I first got promoted, I had disciplinary assignments that were uncomfortable, but I did them. I had taken all these supervisory classes and heard, You must deliver the message as if it were your own. You don't say, The chief told me to tell you this. When I first got promoted, I thought the men were calling me a hardass. I thought, That's not fair. I'm getting a bad rap. I've got much thicker skin now. And everything looks better after a good night's sleep or a day off.

How High Up Are You Aiming For?

Our new chief has opened the commanders' positions. We currently have two commanders. They are exempt, they do not have civil service protection. The chief wants to add a third. I told him that I was not going to apply but he encouraged me to and said he would consider me for it. That's not what I had in mind, but I thought about it and put in an application. If you're not changing, you're not growing.

Right now I can balance administrative work with getting out on the street, writing traffic tickets and being out with the officers. But a commander's position is basically administration. A lot of policy decisions are made at that level. Obviously the commanders have more influence on the chief as far as what happens. The commanders are responsible for motivating the troops. It could be an interesting job. A commander out working the street, however, is not a very good use of resources considering the hourly wage of a commander and the hourly wage of an officer.

Family Issues

This department is across the board fantastic on family life for both men and women. When I had my son I took three months off. We live in town so my husband would bring the baby to work and the chief let me breastfeed him in the rocking chair in her office. I would feel very protective of that practice if another female officer were hired and wanted to have children. I would very much encourage her. I'm sure there were some people who were very uncomfortable, but the administration was incredible. That is certainly not something that would be okay where my husband works.

When I get home, my husband's on his way to work because we work opposite shifts. I've tried to get involved in activities that my kids enjoy. They love soccer. I'm coaching my little boy skiing. We're very active in our church. Even though I'd much rather be a police officer than a teacher, I've done Sunday school kindergarten teaching. My children really care about how much time I spend with them so I try to be with them whenever I can.

My daughter is very mature for her age and will look at me and say, Mom, you've had a hard day. I have to be very careful talking to my husband about work because she knows who everyone is and what I'm saying. Her principal told me that my daughter told her that I wasn't going to be a sergeant anymore. She said, Mommie said she doesn't like this job and wants to be an officer again. The principal laughed because her daughter is in the same school where she's a principal, so she could relate to having to be careful with what you say.

It's also difficult when there are two police officers in the household. Who's in charge? During the day we have a second grader in school all day but a pre-kindergartner who just goes a couple of hours a week. My husband's in charge at home during the day. When I get home, I'm in charge. When we have weekends together, we have to get back into a compromising mode because we can't both be in charge. The kids get very confused at that point. It takes about a day to get back into swing of sharing.

Little Rock, Arkansas

Sergeant Jennifer Bartsch was born in 1965. When we met in autumn 2001 she had been married six years to her husband who is a police captain. She enlisted in the Army to take advantage of the GI Bill, but left after several months to become a police cadet with Little Rock, AR, PD in 1985.

I've Always Lived on the Edge

I like this type of work, I always have. It's exciting to me. Never a dull moment. I don't mind being in a man's world. You probably hear this over and over, but I wanted to make a difference in people's lives. If I'm out on a hostage negotiation situation, when I leave, in 99 percent of our cases, I know I've made some sort of a positive impact in those people's lives regardless of who they are, or where they came from.

I've always been very athletic, a tomboy. My family was used to me riding horses or riding motorcycles. I've always lived on the edge. All of them have been supportive, even my grandfather. My mother never realized how responsible I was until she went on a ride-along with me one night. I got involved in a pursuit, I had two radios going, I was talking on one of them, listening to the other, and trying to catch up with the officer I was going to back up, and at the time we weren't required to wear seatbelts, and I looked over and said, Mom, put your seatbelt on. She was a little afraid but she told me later that she felt completely safe with me and she said, I have to admit that was the first time I've actually seen you as an adult.

I happen to be a person who has the upper body strength but a lot of women need to get ready, run, do push-ups, sit-ups. Now with our pre-employment agility test, you have to bench press 80% of your body weight. You get in even better shape when you go through the academy, but we won't hire you unless you pass the physical agility test, which means you have to be in good shape to begin with.

Oh, Lord, I was a great shot. I could shoot the pistol. In that particular class I had the best time on shooting moving targets. It was a great time to bond with those people. I went to the academy in south Arkansas, which is the state law enforcement training academy. Now in Little Rock we have our own. I had just come out of basic training. So the physical side of it was fun. When the guys played basketball they always asked me to play with them. I was well accepted.

Recruiting Strategies

You need good, strong women recruiters. You also need women in key positions in the agency as examples of what women can get to. But we need an open-minded administration to allow that to happen. There's lots of room for improvement but it's come some way. I've been in this department 16 years and I've seen change in people's perception of the way women can do this job. You have to earn it, you have to get in there and prove yourself.

I started a program here in the early '80s, the Citizen Police Academy. It runs for 8 or 12 weeks, depending on which department is putting it on. A cross-section of the population, just everyday people, comes one or two nights a week to learn the inner workings of the police department. They have to be 21. We always had a year's waiting list. Then we do teen academies for the underage kids in the summer. It's a great recruiting tool. We just had a lady graduate from the police academy who went to the Citizens Police Academy when I was there several years ago. She was in the military, got out, and now she's here.

Women's Ways of Doing Things

We don't have a problem with female officers leaving. The women have just as much incentive to stay here as the guys do. I should be completely burnt out with the place, given the difficulties I've had, but I'm not. You've got a lot of men down here who are single dads raising their kids. When I adopted my son, I could have taken a leave of absence. If I could have got maternity leave with pay and used my sick leave, as if I had actually given birth to a child, that would have helped a lot. But these were not options. I depleted every bit of my vacation time to take care of my son. Somehow or other we should all be able to work together to have some sort of established paid maternity/paternity leave.

Women have different interests than the men. We would like to start 24-hour daycare for law enforcement officers. It would be beneficial to more men than to women. But we haven't gotten enough interest in the department to help us do that.

Every mentor I've had has been a man. I wouldn't call them mentors if they weren't exactly that, because a mentor is somebody you have the utmost respect for. I've been a mentor for the male officers who work for me judging from the little things they do for me. The plants they give me. That squad of officers there, that picture hanging on the wall? They made that picture especially for me and had it put on a plaque, in appreciation of the things that I do for them. I mentor mainly by teaching them that to give is good, and to receive is good, and they need to accept both. I take them out to eat once in awhile, and they take me out to eat. When I go to do my physical fitness test, I am as equally good as they are.

I've had a special relationship with 98% of the people I work with, although they actually work for me. I write them up. I just finished writing up four of my officers, three of them for police commendation bars, and one for civic achievement award. He does so much work in the community he lives in. People look up to him and come to him because he is a police officer, not just because he's a good person. He has a degree in education and he tutors kids in the afternoon. He works a lot with the elderly and kids and now he's developed this program to combine the two. He's got the retired teachers who live in his area to help with this after-school program. He does this on his own time and he's been doing it for years.

A civic award was given to Tammy Nelsen who spent time with an elderly gentleman in her neighborhood. She would go by on weekends and bring him groceries. She'd say, Mr. P, get all your bills together and she would help him balance his checkbook. Some of it was done while she was working, some of it on her days off. He had a son who had a mental disease so they'd have disturbances at the house and she'd go over there and try to help him. She went through all the proper avenues to get the son moved, but he had nowhere else to go. All he had was his elderly father who wasn't able to take care of himself much less this guy. So she told the father, he could do what he wanted to do, but she'd found him a place to stay in the Veterans Administration retirement center. He said, yeah, he wanted to go, but when they got over there that morning, two of the officers on her squad were going to help him move, she found him in a back bedroom and he shot himself in front of her. They had a bond together and we believe that he did that, not necessarily meaning to do it in front of her, so that she could take care of his body. She did all that, arranged for the funeral. When she got her award, the men were all crying and they called her an angel.

I don't see gay women officers having anything to deal with. Trust me, I'm close to female officers who are gay and they just don't have a problem with it. However, I have not seen a successful case of a male police officer who was gay openly. It's the South. We just haven't got that part of it down yet. When we've had male officers here who were openly gay, you would hear comments that weren't favorable.

I did the Citizen Police Academy, crime prevention, and community-related work for a long time. A couple times I tried to transfer out but I didn't get to. Four years ago the lieutenant of the SWAT team asked if I'd like to come over and be one of the supervisors, because they had an opening. I was very flattered. Other SWAT team members talked to me about it. I thought for sure that I was finally going to get out of the division I was in. I requested the transfer but the chief wasn't ready to let me go completely to that end of the spectrum. He wanted me to stay with the community policing aspects of the job. So I came over to the special operations division, doing what I'm doing now. I don't know if I'll ever get to join the SWAT team but I'm satisfied with what I'm doing because it's very convenient with my two-year-old.

I like the fact that you don't know from one day to the next what's going to happen. Some people complain about presidential or dignitary visits, but I like them. If I go on a hostage negotiation callout, I don't care if it's one o'clock in the morning, I'm going to wake up when I get there because it's exciting to me. It's why cop shows are so big on television.

The other aspect is that I love being able to take care of people. I like the fact that when people see me, they look at this uniform and they see a person who can somehow or other counsel them on a problem or talk to someone else in the city who can help them. I appreciate that I can wear so many hats.

Sergeant Cindy Chessie

Cindy was born in 1958. She is married to a data analyst at Microsoft and has two boys, ages 21 and 18. She has two years of college study in early childhood education and psychology. She has 11 years in law enforcement, having left the department of a small mountain town for the fast-growing town of Monroe, WA, closer to the big city.

The Moms Took Care of the Boys

I wanted to be home with my kids until they went to school. But when my youngest went to kindergarten I said, I can't stay at home. It's driving me crazy. I answered an ad in the paper for a part-time police clerk, which was perfect because I could be there when my son got home from school. I did that a couple of years and it became full-time. I met a lot of officers who told me, You should go to the reserve academy and see how you like it. Okay, so I did.

I wasn't going to pursue it any further but there was an opening and I thought if I am going to be a police officer, I should do it now because I'm 31. I tested and I came out number one on the list and was offered the job. I went to the academy in 1991. My Mom stayed with my kids half the time and my mother-in-law stayed with them the other half. The Moms took care of the boys, who were seven and nine. I lived in the city for four months during the week and was home only on weekends. I couldn't have done it if I didn't have the help of the grandmas.

To prepare for the academy physically I did more push-ups and sit-ups. I always did run. I was in pretty good shape. Mentally, I had just been to the reserve academy so I knew what to expect. I didn't have a ton of time to prepare because I was a working mom right up to the time I went. I was proud just to make it through and graduate.

What Significant Others Thought About It

When I was a reserve officer, my husband thought I was just dabbling and I'd get over it. So he didn't like it when I decided to be a police officer full-time. We fought about it and actually separated for a little while. We finally came to an understanding and got back together and he's been very supportive of my career and me ever since. That was 12 years ago and we've been together 24 years now. What made a big difference was moving to a big enough agency with a great reputation, and he knew I was going to get proper training.

Neither of the Moms said too much about my decision. But my grandmother read me up one side and down the other. Why do you want to do that? It's man's work. It's dangerous. She was very much against it but eventually she got used to it too. My Dad never said anything. Now my Mom and Dad think it's the greatest thing in the world that their daughter is a police sergeant. My Mom and Dad and mother-in-law were all here for my promotion to sergeant last August. My mother cried through the whole thing. People said to me afterward, Oh, your Mom is the sweetest thing.

A Little Job History

I got into police work when I was older, 33, and set in my ways. I believe you should do what is right, no matter what, and if that conflicts with other people's views, too bad, because I usually voice mine. I started on patrol in that little town where I'd been a police clerk. They had advertised the wage in the newspaper, but when I got hired they didn't want to pay me that anymore. Monroe was testing and I said, I'll test and see what happens. I came in number four, and was hired right away. I hadn't mapped out a career plan. I simply thought I'll give it a try and see if I like it. I've liked it well enough to stay 11 years.

I was a patrol officer for several years. There was this elderly woman who would get up at night and wander around her house. She was experiencing dementia and she would call the police at three in the morning saying there was a burglar in her house. I would respond and she'd be out in her yard or down in her basement or somewhere that wasn't safe with her flashlight. I would take her back in the house and she'd want to make me coffee and visit. Ten years ago there wasn't that much policing to do here at that hour so I would sit with her and she'd tell stories about the town, her late husband, her life. I'll always remember sitting at her kitchen table when I was working graveyard.

Before I was promoted, for four years I was a detective. I love detective work, putting all the pieces of the puzzle together. One case we had recently, and you may have read about it in the paper, was The Starbucks Robbery. A former employee and her boyfriend concocted this scheme to rob Starbucks. They went in at 5:50 in the morning when they first open up to use the bathroom. Each pulled a gun and told the employees to lock the front door. The former employee was immediately recognized by one of the baristas. The safe was on a time release and it was going to take 15 minutes for it to open so during those 15 minutes, because they wanted everything to look normal, one of the robbers served coffee out the drive-through window. The female half of the pair told customers who came to the front door that they were remodeling and to use the drive-through.

Finally the safe opened and they took all the money. They tied the three employees to the racks in the back room. They took some merchandise and the money out of the till. One of the employees' ties weren't very tight and she got loose and got on her cell phone right away.

We started by knowing the former employee's name and she had applied at a nearby Starbucks within the last month so we got her application which had very current information on it. We had officers sitting on their apartment while we wrote the warrants, but then this couple left, so the team went into motion and arrested them on a traffic stop. We secured their apartment until the warrants were written and we executed the warrants the next morning. All the merchandise and the money bags, all the evidence was there. I was the supervising sergeant so my role was to oversee the tasks each person was doing. It was a great job of teamwork. We had both robbers in custody within 14 hours.

The chief has been my primary mentor. Even when I was a police clerk up in this other little town, we both served on a child protection team and she taught me a lot about investigating child abuse and domestic violence cases. Her knowledge in those two areas is incredible. One of our newer officers who is a sergeant has helped me a lot now in this role. As far as mentoring others, I have a girlfriend who is an officer up in Arlington, and she started five years ago and she always says, I went into law enforcement because you did. I've known her since junior high school. We're really good friends and we see each other a lot. Our families even vacation together.

This fall I'm going to take Spanish because there are many people in our community now that speak Spanish. Through a drug interdiction program I took a crash course, two weeks of long, eight-hour days, so it was really crammed down your throat. After the first two days we didn't speak English any longer. But if you don't stick with it, you lose it quickly, so this time I want to go and keep going. Also, for the last five years, our family has traveled extensively in Mexico so it's been a place where we could practice.

Family-Friendly Practices

All department members have a flag that they created hanging off the beams in the main room of the police department, which has really high ceilings and looked very bare. A banner can be anything that you want it to be. Most people pick the family theme, but they're all unique. The banners are given to the officers and they can add whatever they want. The chief started it, maybe seven years ago, to brighten the place up. On the bottom of my banner is a replica of the house we used to live in which was in the mountains, then there is a baseball, basketball, and football because my children helped me make it and they are very active in sports. There's a CD and musical notes on ours because our family's very much into music. Then there are little stick people representing my husband, me, the two boys, and our dog. And the peace sign because that's me.

Our chief was very flexible and if you needed to be somewhere for one of your kids, you went. She always encouraged family to be a priority. If you had sick kids or a recital, that's what was important. We had one female officer who was nursing her child and her baby would be brought down here during her breaks and she would sit in the chief's office because it was private and she could close the door and she'd nurse her baby. The chief's philosophy was you can't have a good work life if you don't have a good home life.

Another of our officers adopted a child two years ago and full-time work she decided was too much because she really wanted to be home with her child, but she didn't want to give up her job completely. So the chief assisted in opening up a part-time position for her. She comes in and works half-day on a patrol shift and then goes home to her child. In fact, this part-time position is a shared position because they're looking to hire that other half. They're looking for a lateral position, someone in a similar position as our officer, someone who wants to be at home and has children. A retired officer has already put in a resume for that position. Other folks, men and women, have been given more than the standard six weeks' family leave when they had children.

I can't say that every day when I left work, I left the job here. There were times when I worked some cases that I took home and I still do, the ones that get you, right in the heart. They were hard cases where children died. At times when I couldn't switch it off, I would go home and my kids would be asleep and I'd just sit in their room and be grateful that I had what I had. I've seen a lot of children beat up and hurt and sexually abused and bitten, horrible things that shouldn't be happening to kids.

Another Woman with Two Boys

Sequim, WA, PD Sergeant Sheri Crain said that what she liked best about her job was the ability to have input and make changes: "In police work you have a great deal of discretion. You have the ability to use all the resources you can muster to solve a problem. That kind of freedom doesn't happen with a lot of jobs. I have the ability to plan my own day. I have a lot of responsibility on my plate. In talking with women in high schools and colleges, I emphasize that this is one job where you get paid for doing the job. They can't base your pay on your gender so I make as much as the guy next to me. Growing up, I always thought that was the way it should be. In this job, it has to be that way because everything is set by the union, including benefits. I've been the shop steward for several years. When you work the graveyard shift you get used to using a lot of plain language, it's hard to pull yourself back, but I've always been pretty diplomatic at expressing what I think should happen.

I have been promoted and anything that I've ever wanted to do, I've been able to. This is a good department to work for. I say, I'd like to go to that class. Or I'd like to do this or go there. I have a really good chance of getting whatever I ask for. Then six months later, the guys will say, How come you got to do that? There are a couple of reasons why I would want to be a chief. With this small department, that's really the only place to go up. Secondly, I have a lot of ideas that I would eventually like to express and see what happens.

The fact that I've been here awhile makes it easier for other women to come in. The guys spent a good four months before I got here worrying about what I would be like. We have a large reserve organization and if we're able to hire somebody from our reserve program, we've worked with them and we know who they are. But anybody from the outside, they always wonder, who is this person? But with the last woman we hired, there wasn't that old, Oh, my gosh, a woman can't do this job. We're all going downhill now."

Conclusion

I had not expected that researching different departments before making a choice was so important for women's success. Do men research different departments beforehand? Minority men might, but it's probably an unknown concept for the majority of Caucasian males who simply want to know, "Who's hiring?"

Not all the solutions to the childcare dilemma have been spelled out yet. However, readers can probably ask themselves at this point, "Am I willing to not have children so I can succeed at the job? If I do want children, which solution to the childcare problem would work for me? What resources do I have? Do I believe fathers should be just as involved and spend just as much time with their children as mothers? If I were a single parent, would I handle childcare differently?"

8

Starting Early

First a Word about Balance

My book, *Women Changing Work* (1990), was based on interviews with women in nontraditional jobs—electricians, carpenters, engineers, firefighters, police officers, to name a few. Regardless of their occupations, the women shared (1) a service orientation to clients, (2) a nurturing approach to coworkers, (3) an insistence upon a balanced lifestyle, and (4) an attraction to managing others using power differently than men did.

What I reported back then was that typically a new police officer would put the rest of her life on hold and postpone balancing until she had proven herself. I noted that this temporary work centeredness was hard on civilian husbands and that a lot of relationships didn't survive. I quoted a sergeant who said trying to constantly have perfect balance would drive you nuts, and that sometimes she compromised her family for her job and sometimes the job when the family needed her.

So the women worked long hours when starting their careers but didn't think of themselves as workaholics for doing this. It was just the right thing to do at that moment in their lives. Later, when they were established, balance surfaced. They could now afford to see work as just one of several important things in life, instead of *the* thing. What they now wanted more time for were family relationships, community activities, hobbies, personal growth, and recreation.

What I found in the present group was that whenever a woman began a new role in the police, particularly if it involved a promotion, she lost her balance again and threw herself wholeheartedly into the job—long hours, coming in on weekends, taking work home—until she realized that if she kept it up, she was going to burn out. She had to make time for vacations, continuing education, sports, cultural events, significant others, if she was going to be good at her job. She had to get balanced again.

An academy lieutenant at Oregon's Department of Public Standards and Training said the transition between work and home for her was physical: "I lived, still live, in a very rural area. I commuted 30 minutes to get to town. There was this mountain to go over. This side of the mountain was home, that side of the mountain was work. So when I got to a certain point in the road, if I was going to work, I would pull the switch, and I would be at work. When I was driving home I would get to that same point in the road, pull the switch, and be at home. I didn't think the transition was that tough, but my kids say I always interrogated them when I got home. And it's true that consciously I would make an effort to talk about things that bothered me when I was at work. I can't talk with my husband, I never have. We've always had a line between my work and other stuff."

Now you'll meet some early starters like Detroit's Police Chief, Ella Bully-Cummings, who says she was 16 and a ticket cashier at a movie theater when she first saw a woman in full police uniform. That was in 1974 and three years later she joined the Detroit, MI, PD (Leinwand, 2004).

In the spring of 2003 I met Detective Kathleen Larson at the Northwest Women's Fair where she was setting up a recruiting booth, selling T-shirts to benefit the Special Olympics, and handing out King County Sheriff's Office Junior Deputy badges. Katie was born in 1961 in Seattle. Her husband works in the radio/electrical field and they have two youngsters, a boy and a girl. Katie has a BS in criminal justice. Her business card says Green River Homicides Investigation. Not long after our interview Katie was being featured daily in newspaper articles and on TV newscasts. The remains of more victims were being uncovered, young women murdered so many years ago, and it is Katie's job to tell the public what's happening.

Training Experiences

I did my internship with the King County, WA, Sheriff's Office and I was very impressed with how they handled themselves. We are single deputies in our cars. I liked the fact that we cover rural areas and urban areas and that you're very independent. It was my patrol car, my district, my responsibility, and I had to think on my feet. The southwest precinct is our busiest precinct and we were in the throes of Green River when I got hired.

During my internship they put me with a number of units so I was exposed to many different activities. This was great because if you got bored somewhere, you could move on. At the academy I was 22 years old, very young, very quiet, and not as outgoing as I am now. But I had had a great educational experience and a great family experience. All four of us kids got jobs when we were 16. We all earned our own cars. As far as careers, our parents just wanted us to be happy. They were fine with my internship at the precinct. I told them I'll take the test with the county. If I do well, I'll proceed and see how far I go. If I don't do well, that's a sign and I'll go to law school. I came out number four on the test and I thought, I'll do it for ten years.

The second week I was in the academy we had to box the academy instructor. He was 6'4" and 230 pounds of solid rock. Only the women had to box him. If you cried, you were out. If you got hit and went down, you were done. The guys boxed one another but they didn't have to box the PT instructor. I thought, I'm very athletic, I played basketball and volleyball, ran track, played tennis and floor hockey, but obviously at 115 pounds I'm not of big stature. First I boxed another academy female who had just got out of the army. One of my arms was in a sling because I'd separated a muscle. We were wearing 14-ounce boxing gloves. The entire class surrounded the mat watching us as we boxed for two minutes. That was fine. But I knew what was coming when I saw the entire academy staff file in and stand at parade rest to watch.

We started boxing. The rules were, he could hit me anywhere, but I could not hit him in the face or groin. I knew that this was a training exercise and I did not feel threatened. In my head, I'm thinking, This is just silly. You don't know me from Adam, you don't know anything about me, but you're looking at me and making an assumption. And that's the first thing they teach you, Don't make assumptions about people. It can be very dangerous. He'd hit me and I'd fall and go to get up and get a kick in the ribs and go flying. After two minutes they said, Time, but he said, No, she needs a little bit more. We boxed for another minute and as we were boxing, he said, You're going to be fine. You're all right. I thought, Well, I can sleep at night now knowing you said that.

The next week we did wrestling. Wrestling you start back to back on the mat. I'm quicker and more agile than others, so I excelled there. I thought, If this is how it's going to be, I am going to get so physically fit. Every day I ran four or five miles and lifted weights. The PT final was the day before graduation and if you didn't pass it you had 30 days to retake it and then you were finished. I had an A average when I left the academy and I was determined to excel in all ways and I did. I worked out. I ran the 440 over a six-foot solid wall and then a 12-foot chain link fence. I did the 180-pound dummy drag. I did the whole thing.

Afterward I said to the PT instructor, in a professional way, You have to understand that times are changing. People don't go out and get in physical fights anymore. I'd like you to ask the men in this room, how many have been in fights? It's not just the women who haven't been in fights. I said, Also if you know a person has been involved in sports, you know that that's a competitive person. He said, You're right, so after that he started boxing some of the men. My whole class did well academically, we were very competitive and we wanted everyone to do well. I went to the academy incredibly naïve but left knowing I could do the job.

Starting Out

My first four years were spent on reactive patrol at the southwest precinct. My first two days were free days, I wasn't in the field training program yet, and my first day a guy blew his brains out and my second day I had a burglary in progress and a bar fight. I thought, Oh, my God, this is like a Wild West show. One thing after the other makes your day fly, because you're so busy. I talked with another female I graduated with and I told her what I had handled in my first year, suicides, homicides, burglaries in progress. She had not been exposed to any of that. Later on when you apply for other positions, that experience really counts.

Naïveté is very different from common sense and good judgment. The men said they knew I was going to be okay because of what they call "officer presence." Even though I was quiet and young, when I got into a room, people knew I was there. I would take control. It felt better being away from the precinct and away from the other deputies and out on my own because then I could be myself. Safety is tantamount in this job so all of us were cognizant of where the adjoining district cars were and are listening, Oh, oh, that person's voice doesn't sound right. Everybody knew that the quieter my voice got, that meant I was in trouble.

I learned a lesson early on from a woman who called that her house had been egged and TPed, toilet-papered. I thought in my little snotty mind, And you're calling 911? I went out and she said, This has been happening to me for two years, every weekend. I can't take it anymore. I still thought, Oh, brother. I asked her, Who do you think did it? She said she thought it was the kids at the end of the block. I walked to the end of the block, knocked on the door, they see me, I say, The house that you egg and toilet-paper, you got to knock it off. Get brooms, buckets, mops, you're going to clean it up. We come walking down the street. She's in tears and I'm still thinking, This is such not a big deal. I'm a police officer, for Pete's sake. She wrote a two-page letter to the sheriff. Reading that letter humbled me because what I thought was so insignificant and ridiculous to her was a big deal and I needed to get my attitude squared away. It taught me at 23 years old that when somebody calls 911, for them, it is significant.

You Need to Step Back

I always said to people coming into the background investigation unit, You are responsible for your career, you will make or break it, and the most important thing is to identify those people who are excellent and let them be your mentors. My captain here I worked with on patrol. He is technically incredible, and I said, I want that. He is so well-respected. I want that. Other people are incredible at interviewing, so I watch them. I look at other people's work ethic. You need to take a little of this, a little of that, and put it all together. Figure out your style and if it works, go with it. If it doesn't work, change it. Another thing I learned when I was young is that this job is a job. It is not who you are. If it ever begins to take over, you need to step back and take a look, because this job can eat you alive.

I like arresting people and investigating crimes. I took the test for promotion when I was six years on and was offered the rank of sergeant and turned it down. I had just been asked to go into the drug enforcement unit. I thought, I'm so young and I know I have such a long career. Do I really want to get into administrative work? Some people love it, that's what they were born to do. After patrol I went into crime analysis and the major at that time said, Just go. I would bring him ideas and he'd say, Write it up. I'd put it all together and show him a proposal and he'd say, Go girl. I'd say, All right, we're going. He trusted me because he knew I did my homework. It gave me such confidence. I worked the drug abatement program for King County for about a year. The gang problem was starting to rear up so let's get educated and find out what this is all about. I left the crime analysis unit in 1990 and went back to patrol for a short time and worked at the county's first contract city. It was just the lieutenant and myself so we split up all of the duties as far as working with the city government that was being set up at the time.

I've had incredible opportunities. In the drug enforcement unit, my partner and I for two years followed a group of Mexican heroin traffickers and worked it up to the point where we did a federally-authorized wiretap. I wrote all the affidavits so on them is my name, Janet Reno's name, and the federal judge's. I ran the wire room with all the interpreters and developed the code book so I could send out the teams to do X, Y, and Z. That's why this department is wonderful because the administration often has afforded us the opportunity to follow our cases to their logical conclusions as opposed to saying, Whoops, that's outside our boundaries. It was so rewarding, I got all the grand jury, all the debriefs of suspects. We had multiple warrants both here and in San Jose. My partner flew to San Jose and I ran everything up here. We were working in partnership with the DEA and the FBI. We worked it all the way up from very small profiteers to the top, to the source of supply in Michocan, Mexico.

Community Policing

At the same time I was still involved doing drug abatements. For example, there was a nearby apartment complex of 30, 40 apartments that had always been a source of irritation. It was so out of control that the person who owned that apartment complex couldn't even collect rent. He was threatened off the property. Gang activity, multiple shootings, stabbings, stolen cars showing up there, and prostitution were having a very adverse impact on the surrounding neighborhood. A drug abatement is a civil remedy. You take all of the information that we gather at the Sheriff's Office and put it together in some kind of order. Then you go out and take declarations from the community as to the adverse impact this property has on their lives. They can't go out at night. They can't let their kids walk down the street because people might think they're prostitutes. A lot of drug use.

We put all that information together in affidavit form with declarations from citizens. For all intents and purposes we file a lawsuit against the property owner. What we ended up doing in this case was I met with the owner. He was in arrears in his taxes, being fined, he said, I don't know what to do. We said, Why don't we work cooperatively then? We'll abate your property but with your blessing. It will be an agreed abatement, and we will close the property for a period of up to one year, get everybody out, and start over. We identified those families that were not involved in any criminal activities and moved them to different Section 8 housing, a safer environment, and they were very happy.

The bad people hadn't been paying rent, had chopped down walls and intimated families out of their apartments so they could take over. We posted a 72-hour injunction and said, We're going to be back in 72 hours. Anybody who isn't gone will get kicked out and their property out on the curb. They knew their free ride was gone. Early in the morning we showed up en masse and there were two families still there that had to go. We boarded up the building and that evening, because these people had lived in this situation for so many years, we gave an awesome block party at the storefront substation with cake and punch.

My Current Role

I was working in the background investigations unit when I was selected for my current assignment. Four of the Green River victims are assigned to me for review and follow-up. I am also one of three assigned to the Gary Ridgway portion of the investigation, things physically associated with Gary Ridgway. I also handle all of the press for the Green River Task Force, press releases and currently we're working with Curtis Productions from A&E television. They want to do a piece on the Green River story. Because this is an open investigation, it's not been formally adjudicated, we have to be very careful because we're preparing for the trial in July 2004.

We have seven charged cases, 42 remaining, 49 in all we attribute to this Green River piece. Is Ridgway specifically the Green River killer? We can't say that because we don't know. What we can say is that we believe he is responsible for seven of the homicides currently, for which he's been charged. We go through our cases with the mindset of looking for evidence that either will include him or exclude him and put us on a different track.

This case is based a lot on forensics and we have well over 10,000 pieces of physical evidence that have to all be looked at and reviewed for forensic purposes, and forensic includes trace evidence, dirt, paint, fibers, hairs. You're also looking at the DNA piece as well. It's a very time-consuming, methodical process that we have to go through, as well as interviewing many people. The Green River investigation never stopped but in 1990 it was down to one detective, and he has carried this through himself, right up to 2001 when we got the DNA evidence. He retired as a deputy after 30 some years and has come back as an administrative specialist and consultant with us. So he still works full-time.

Having a Family

I didn't get married until I was 31. We had our son a year after we got married and my husband was a stay-at-home dad because I was in the drug enforcement unit which is 24/7. We were in the middle of our Mexican drug investigation and we had surveillance at five different locations. I worked right up to the birth. I did paperwork in the office, followed up cases, and I sat and watched the videos which ran 24 hours on time-lapse and I could tell from watching those videos when the drop days were, when a load car came in. It was a job that had to be done but what a perfect one for me, to sit there and still be part of the investigation. Then I had so much sick time accrued that I took five months off, paid, after my son was born.

My husband stayed at home with our son and he did a great job. We had our daughter two years later, so he was taking care of both of them. Then he went back to work part-time on weekends. I had weekends off. Then we started them in pre-school. This last year he went back to work full-time and he works from 5 in the morning until 1 in the afternoon. I take the kids to school, he picks them up, and then he has a full day. Our daughter has ballet and gymnastics, they both have swimming lessons, and he coaches our son's Little League team. As a mom, I'm on the safety commission at our kids' school, I have to put in so many hours of volunteer time at the school, I work in their tea room. I'm still on callout, though, like when we were on our way to a movie and they found some bones somewhere.

Making Changes

I was placed on temporary loan from the drug unit to the background investigation unit. I was working with a detective who had been there nine years. He had his way of doing things. I was processing people but thinking, These people will never make it, their scores are very low, and taking everything cumulatively, I know they're not going to make it. He'd say, It doesn't matter. Hire them anyway. They've passed all the tests. I said, Wait a minute. A, that's not fair to that person. B, it's not fair to the FTOs. Our FTOs were having a 60% retention rate. That's not good for entry-level deputies. I said, What's the bigger picture? Why are we hiring people we know aren't going to succeed? It's not fair to that person and it's not fair to the department. And fiscally, financially, it makes no sense whatever. Why do we do this? Because that's the way it's done.

But why? Let's look at the bigger picture so we can make improvements. We know typically that people who get these scores do not do well in our department. We have a very heavy emphasis on writing ability and that's where people usually don't make it, their inability to write timely, well-written, grammatically correct reports. I also got together with the psychologist, What do these things mean in your reports? They started to educate me. This is what we look for.

The other detective left and I became the head background detective and we revamped everything. We went to civil service and said, Anybody who scores under an 80, we're not going to process because typically they have problems and they don't succeed. We looked at the different psychological instruments that we used for testing. We used the MMPI and now there's an MMPI structured for law enforcement, so why weren't we using it? In the oral board why are we asking people situational questions? They don't have any training. They aren't police officers yet. It's more important to ask, What have you done to prepare? We now ask more background questions in our oral boards and they are not adversarial. I never understood the point of that.

For the deputies sitting on the oral boards I asked them on the forms they complete to write down any concerns. I put boxes on the side for them to check if they had a concern, because as a background detective I'll go right there. You have drawn my attention. Something didn't feel right. Write No. Write a lot of Nos. Write a gut feeling. Write that he wouldn't make eye contact. Write all these things down for me. We totally redid the background questionnaire, much more in detail, much more in depth. Then, I'd give the whole package to the psychologists. They'd get to see everything. And I'd get to see everything. So we just fine-tuned the process.

The final interview is called the captain's interview. It's myself, the background investigator, the captain of internal affairs, and the candidate. It's basically between the captain and me to make the recommendation to the chief. In King County, if you disqualify someone through civil service, they have a right to appeal with an arbiter there and the unit was going through a lot of these appeals. I didn't understand why. Why don't we tell the candidate ahead of time, these are your issues. This is what you can do to improve, but these issues are so significant for our department, we don't think you can overcome them. Be honest with the candidates. By changing that process, I had one appeal in two years.

Katie loves to cook, she cooks "voraciously" and bakes a lot. She loves to give parties and do the food. She's catered for a couple of friends' weddings. When she retires she's going enroll in Edmonds Community College cooking program, become a chef, and start a catering business. What a change from sifting through dirt for bones.

There is this little nondescript storefront caddy-corner from a movie theater we attend frequently, because admission is only $3 and once a movie gets there, you know it is on its way out of town. The little nondescript storefront, on the other hand, is very much in town to stay and represents community policing at its best. It was there I met Michelle who depends heavily on a cadre of volunteers from a nearby senior center.

Sergeant Michelle Bennett

Michelle was born in 1969 and is one of 13 women in her suburban department of 43. She has a bachelor's degree in criminal justice, a master's in psychology, and just finished her first year in an education doctorate program. She has taught extensively at the academy and at community colleges. She is partnered with another law enforcement officer. Michelle is day shift-, school resource-, Explorer-, and storefront-sergeant at two suburban neighborhood police offices, for Shoreline, WA, PD. She somehow balances these duties with studying for yet another degree and teaching yet another class.

My Interest Started in the Ninth Grade

I was 21 when I joined the police. My parents reacted differently. My mother simply said to be careful, but my dad said, I was hoping you'd do something professional, like become a doctor or attorney. At family gatherings now, though, he'll say, My one son is a lawyer, my other son is at West Point, and my daughter is a cop and do you want to hear her latest story? So whatever he says, his actions are completely different. I have three brothers who have been supportive. We all went into service-related fields. The West Point grad went back to teach there, one's an attorney, one's a teacher.

My interest in policing began when I sat behind this girl in U. S. history in ninth grade who was an Explorer and she was always talking about we went and did this, we went and did that. I also watched all the TV cop shows and it looked exciting. Cagney and Lacey. Hill Street Blues. Wow, it sounded so cool to be part of the Explorer program. This early desire got realized as a cadet when I was 20. My duties included such exciting things as matching pawn tickets with stolen property.

The two-year degree I had in criminal justice meant at the academy I was number one academically. I had studied everything we were given. Physically I prepared by running. I've always worked out and played soccer, indoor and outdoor softball. I bike. We didn't have push-ups or sit-ups when I went through so I got ready for the obstacle course, a dummy drag, a wall and a fence. We lived out in the boonies when I was growing up and I shot my first shot when I was seven. I went duck hunting, pheasant hunting, rabbit hunting with my dad and brothers so I was comfortable with guns.

I Want to Make A Difference

I can remember being on patrol and having this 6'5" huge guy, biker, tattoos, long hair, totally drunk when I arrive. He's been in an accident and he's out of the car, being aggressive. I start talking to him, soft and kind. What happened? How'd you get here? Are you hurt? Do we need to get somebody to come look at you? Before he knew it, he was in the back seat of my car handcuffed. All of a sudden he says, Hey, wait a minute. What's going on here? Am I in custody? Women have to use their mouth a lot more because not all the time do we have the same stature or physical size.

I joined because I have a lot of energy, and I wanted a job with diversity, a job where I would not have to do the same thing every day. I couldn't stand the thought of being behind a desk. I wanted to help people, to make a difference, and I enjoy going into situations and controlling them. As an example, last Monday we went to the suicide of a young mother, she was 35, she'd found out her husband was cheating on her. They got in a big fight, he left, she swallowed all the prescription pills in the house. He finally came in after hours of more drinking, didn't realize she was in distress, found her in the bathroom in the morning and by then she was deceased.

She had a large extended family and a child who was staying with relatives. I had him come home and then I coordinated between assistance personnel, the extended family, the child. Everyone wanted information, what happened, she was so young, how, what, why? So on my day off I answered the messages from the family and talked to them explaining that it wasn't anybody's fault. They were trying to blame different people in the family. I said the most important thing is the child. How are you going to take care of the child? Where's the child going to go to school? Pointing fingers won't solve anything. It'll just mean more anger and discontent.

That was why I went into policing, to be able to control, organize, and go about things in an orderly fashion so that everyone has their needs met in the best possible way. We had trauma intervention come out, they're a volunteer group that works with families for grief counseling. I referred one relative to a counseling program that could also provide family counseling. I called out the student's school resource officer and he contacted the student. If you handle things the best way you can, it reduces the trauma for everyone because these are events people remember for their whole life, life-altering events. A major accident or a death or a robbery or being exposed to at the bus stop or an assault, these are things a victim remembers forever.

It makes me feel good personally to make a positive impact. Every once in awhile you'll get a letter five or ten years later saying, You don't remember me but you helped me. That's the whole reason right there for me. I made a difference. That's the bottom line, why I got into it. Most officers get a sense of family and brotherhood on the job but people also stay for the pay, benefits, and retirement system.

Recruiting and Retaining Women

When I came to this department there were seven fewer females than there are now. I lobbied hard to get two of them. We'd worked together at another precinct and they are both very good officers. Other women came because they heard it was a great place to work, with a female chief who is awesome. The atmosphere is supportive and it's a fun place to work. Everyone gets along and there's lots of camaraderie. I've been at three of the four precincts and this is definitely the best place to work.

My chief mentors us all the time. I can go in to talk to her about some issue or what's happening. Today I bounced ideas off her as to how I would like to reorganize the school resource officer program. We need more accountability for the officers, statistics kept so they can analyze and evaluate the program later. These officers go into schools and act as counselors, mentors, class instructors, curriculum specialists, and they ensure campus safety and security.

I'm 33 now and in the last four years I've mellowed a lot as far as how I look at things. When I came here I was burned out and asking myself why have I been giving so much time to this job? For what purpose? My attitude was, I'm not giving one minute more of my time than my eight-hour shift. But my new chief changed that attitude for me. Now I spend my time off coordinating projects but not to where it's all-consuming and out of bounds.

For example, DARE was never evaluated properly so when they finally did evaluate it, it didn't show any appreciable effect. My goal is to evaluate and assess this school resource officer program. I also self-designated myself to be the controller of all the curricula in the county and wrote an SOP for the department. I gathered and then wrote a list of appendices with the help of another officer of all the programs that we have. I've offered to write the curriculum since my doctorate is in curriculum and instruction. But somebody has yet to say, Yeah, do it.

It's difficult to see the difference good supervision makes when you're within a bureaucracy where, This is how we've always done things so this is how we're going to do things. I've seen so many people turned around by just one person mentoring or coaching them. When supervisors take officers under their wing, give them positive reinforcement, praise the good things they do, and let the officers explain to them why a certain way of doing things isn't good, you can turn probably 80% of people around 180 degrees and make them productive, happy employees who get fewer complaints.

The Down Side of Promotion

My captain's currently trying to get me to take the captain's test. I had six and a half years on when I got promoted to sergeant and sometimes I wish I had waited longer because I missed out on things by being promoted, other units I could have gone into. Everyone has their own gifts and specialties. I'm very organized, a good program manager, while other people are talented in SWAT or radar or computers. Some people are good with youth while others excel at technology. I'd like to see a department cultivate those talents and get everyone in positions where they are most beneficial not only to the department but to the individuals, making them happy with what they're doing for a living.

When you are a police officer, you can't always choose what department you are going to work for. This is part of why I don't have a huge ambition to get promoted. I would trust working for my current chief because I know what her priorities are and I know she's always acting for the good of the department. I'm a senior sergeant now and as long as I remain a sergeant I can stay where I am.

Future Plans

I've thought about taking two years off, finishing my doctorate and traveling, because a lot of the work that I do is international, but I don't want to risk losing my job. In November I was in China. In May I was in Russia. In October I'll be in New Zealand. Part of what I'm doing with my doctorate is International Comparative Education. When I go to New Zealand I will be studying what they're doing in the area of youth violence and bullying. Part of my job is to set up anti-bullying programs. I pay for all this travel myself and do it on vacation and comp time. I'll be going to the IAWP conference in Canberra, be in Australia a total of two weeks, and then on to New Zealand for two weeks where I'll try to set up a sister school for Seattle Pacific University.

After my doctorate, I need to finish this anti-bullying initiative, do a research program in the schools based on that, and I'll continue with law enforcement for three to eight years more. I'll have 20 years in eight more years. I don't know if I want to stay until 20, it depends on what comes up. After policing I'll most likely teach full-time at a college or university. And I love writing. My last article on bullying was published in a Russian journal.

The Major and Mr. Mom

Major Robin Fenton's husband retired from the Washington State Patrol in 1993 when their little boy was born and has been "Mr. Mom" ever since. Born in 1959 Robin has a two-year degree in criminal justice and 145 credits at City University where she studies weekends and evenings for a bachelor's degree in business.

Robin is a King County, WA, Sheriff's Office precinct commander. She has 129 people under her, working for six contract cities, an area of 500 square miles. She herself is chief in one small town, while the other five towns have sergeants as chiefs. She and her two captains work hard to constantly communicate issues that arise and make sure they are dealt with. She says that the smaller the town, the more difficult it is to operate because everybody knows everybody. All of her "cities" have unique situations that she plays a role in.

Getting to the Academy

When I was in high school I wanted to be a dispatcher. First, I thought I would get a criminal justice degree and learn more about the police. The county came to my community college and recruited, saying they were looking for women. A girlfriend said, Come on, take the test with me. I said, I want to get my degree first. Oh, come on, she said, It's good practice.

I took the test and ended up doing well and they offered me a job in June of 1980, but I wasn't going to be old enough until October. I was 21 for a month and 10 days when they hired me. I was one of eight kids, wonderful mother and father, very protected home environment. It was like lifting me out of a shell, and saying, Okay, Robin, here's the real world. I was the last person in my high school class you would ever have expected to go into law enforcement. My Dad was very proud but it scared Mom. Here was her little 21-year-old carrying a gun. Fortunately when I came out of the academy, they sent me to the South End Precinct because it kept me out of my mother's north end neighborhood. Every time she heard a siren, she didn't have to think maybe it was me.

I prepared for the academy by running, doing push-ups and sit-ups. The obstacle for most females was the six-foot wooden wall. You had to have the upper body strength to throw yourself over. The first week you meet your tac officer and weigh in. He'd say, Okay, you need to lose so much weight. I was the only one who was told to gain weight. I was proudest of my pursuit driving. Because I had played basketball, baseball, volleyball, soccer, I didn't have to struggle in the athletic area. During the second week they had us all lined up to run that track and do that six-foot wall for the first time. I was the only female in the class that went over, first time out. It was pure adrenaline. The tac officer said, Well, there's one I won't have to worry about.

On-the-Job Relationships

I was told at the academy that I'd be assigned to a precinct where I'd work for a sergeant. I walked into my precinct and at the time this precinct had a captain who had the same position that I have now, and he walked up to me in full uniform and said, Oh, so you're my new one. I said, Are you my sergeant? And he had maple leaves, oak leaves, all this stuff on his collar and he turned to the trainer and said, You tell her.

People bent over backwards to help me. They didn't want me to fail. A female captain asked me once if I would sit down with a group of women and talk to them about my first year. Why had I had been so fortunate? Because I did not come in, acting like a man or trying to be like a man. I didn't have the foul mouth. I kept my femininity to the degree where they treated me like a lady. I'll never forget going into my first roll call with a new squad and there was another female officer in the room and the sergeant said, Oh, I don't know what we're going to do. We've never had a lady in roll call before. I thought, What a slap in the face for her. But, in fact, she was rough-tough and foul-mouthed. Also, I didn't date the men. I didn't have relationships with them.

At the beginning I was very naïve and saw it as a compliment when people said, Be careful, Robin. When I had my first transfer my sergeant called me in, shut the door, and said, Now Robin, there are people who will hurt you there. He was like a father talking to his daughter. He would never have done that with any of the guys. With me, he had to make sure I understood the dangers of my next assignment.

Even female dispatchers would warn me. We had a guy who was wanted, armed and dangerous, and we believed we had spotted his van. I remember one woman taking me to a separate channel and saying, Please be careful. People treated me like their little sister and it started when I was halfway through my criminal justice program. One of the instructors came up to me and said, Robin, they're hiring meter maids for Seattle. I said, Well, thank you, I appreciate that. But I was devastated that he thought I should be a meter maid.

Early Experiences

My academy class was a mixed group from several counties. Some members came in very familiar with police policies, having shot guns for years. It was all brand new to me. The first time I ever fired a weapon was at the academy. I was assigned to by far the most active precinct, which was the best thing they ever did for me. Within the first year I'd been to five homicides and handled numerous rape cases. I had to learn fast.

I was there three and a half years and during my first year I was dressed up as a decoy walking the highway as a prostitute. I did that 50 times, right through the Green River days, when girls who were prostitutes would be spotted and two weeks later would be on the missing list. I really enjoyed the decoying. After that I was Officer Friendly where I would go out and do all the little safety talks to the kids in schools. I also did crime prevention, house checks, block watches. I also was an FTO to new people.

From 1983 to 1988, I was a detective in major crimes in what's now the Special Assault Unit. I handled all the abuses cases involving children. At one point for some presentation I gave I said we had handled over a thousand such cases during that period. I was single and didn't have children at the time but still it was hard to see bad things happen to children that were going to affect them for the rest of their lives.

Mentoring Experiences

I have one woman who struggles in the interpersonal area. We all know she does, she knows she does. I'm probably the only one who would have given her corporal stripes when I did. But she had reached the point where she thought she was never going to get ahead. I gave her the promotion thinking that this will show her that she has a lot of great skills, but we have to work on her lack of interpersonal skill. If she talks to somebody and it sounds rude, I call her on it. I'll say, I know what you're trying to say, but here's how it came across. I've got male officers, too, who don't realize how they come across and I bring it to their attention constantly. It's tough to do but if I don't bring it to their attention, there's no way they can improve.

An important mentoring relationship for me started when a friend and I were both promoted to lieutenant. We were sent to different precincts, but every month, like clockwork, we would meet and talk about what was going on. We have issues that are similar, and we help each other work it out. We've stuck together, just the two of us, we communicate in an environment that is comfortable. We always part saying, Okay, I'm ready for another month.

I'm Just Like My Mom

My prior chief told me he didn't see any difference between his role when he was a major at a precinct and mine. I said, You don't have to go home and on your way there decide what you're making for dinner. Your dinner's sitting on the table ready for you. You don't have to worry at night whether or not your little guy needs to take a bath. You don't have to make his lunch in the morning. I'm 100% convinced there's a difference between what I do in my role and what he did and other guys do.

Fortunately, I have a one-hour commute. That one-hour commute gives me a chance to unwind from the workday, handle any phone calls that I need to make, wrap up my day. Then halfway there I think, What do I have in the freezer? My husband has been terrific watching over our son. I don't worry about him if he's sick. I don't have to miss work. But my husband is not the wash-the-windows or have-dinner-ready-for-me kind of guy. I wouldn't expect it of him. I come home and it's like a totally different job. I start with dinner, pick up the house if it needs to be picked up, see if there are clothes needing to be washed.

I grew up in a family where Mom did everything. She used to say, Don't start something, Robin, you're not ready and willing to do for the rest of your life. Well, I started something. I wanted to show my husband that, Look, I'm just like my Mom. I'll do all these things for you at home because that's my role, housewife.

Life Has Been Good to Me

I was very shy early on but patrol brought out a side of me that is a more confident, more comfortable. I always used my verbal skills to keep out of fights, not that I didn't have to fight because there were times my interpersonal skills didn't work. But I got out of more fights by the ability to talk rather than use physical force.

It's okay to be emotional after the fact. You can cry all the way home if you want, but you can't cry at the scene. You're supposed to be making decisions and helping these people. I remember a gal in the Special Assault Unit on the phone with the mother of a victim and the detective was crying and the mother was trying to calm the detective. You can't do that.

People see that I'm happy and enjoying life. If you talked to the 129 people in this precinct and asked them if they'd ever seen me mad—I'm not saying there aren't things that make me mad—but if I'm unhappy or upset, it doesn't come out on my people or come out in a way that makes people back off. If I get upset, they're not going to come back. I need to have that open door. The only way to know what's going on is if people feel comfortable coming to me and telling me.

When I retire, I'll leave the criminal justice field. I see it as a time to do other things I'm interested in, horticulture and more training in the computer field. I can retire at 53. I will have 32 years in. I see us traveling. I'm going to find a job whether it's working at a nursery or a bookstore, doing something that I enjoy. I have always said I will stay in the job as long as I enjoy what I'm doing. If it gets to the point where I dread coming to work, which I've never had so far, I will quit. I don't believe I should be here if I'm not happy.

I Was Supposed to Go to Law School

Detective Anne Malins was born in 1969 in Seattle. She is married to a police officer and has a 4-year-old son. She has a BA in sociology and considered getting an MA in social work or a law degree. Instead she joined the Redmond, WA, PD in 1992, fresh out of college. She is currently attending an evening court reporting school. I first encountered Anne when she stuck her head in the door as I was interviewing her boss and shouted, We got him, we got him, him being a guy just out of prison who ignored a restraining order and threatened his wife, again.

Anne was supposed to go after the guy the week before, but the case got put on the back burner when she got called out to a homicide and the endangered wife put in a hotel for her protection. Ironically, when I was first scheduled to interview Anne many months later, she had to cancel because of an emergency surveillance, keeping tabs on the apartment of the chief suspect in the homicide the year before. Here's Anne.

I had applied to law school and got in. And I said, I'm not doing it. I had been in school for 16 years and was asking, Do I want to go anymore? I had taken one of those tests in the ninth grade that said you'd be good at this, you'd be good at that. Law enforcement was one of them. I said, Maybe I'll do that, and the other kids laughed and thought it was hilarious.

When I graduated my parents asked, What are you going to do? If you're not going to law school, you need to move out and have your life. My attitude was, I like living here, I can play. They said, You need to get a job. It takes forever to become a cop and that way I could live at home and play while I'm at the academy. And they train you, show you what to do, and pay you while you do it, of course.

I've always loved food and was never much interested in working out. So how was I going to pass the physical agility test? My Dad put up a wall and I practiced every day getting over that wall. I went to the junior high school and ran the track and had my parents time me. We did sit-ups and push-ups. Well, the academy didn't take forever and soon I had several choices. I chose between Skagit County where all my distant relatives live and Redmond because it is close to where my parents live.

Redmond had a fabulous reputation, they pay very well, there are lots of benefits, they're always on the cutting edge of everything. At Skagit County you had to work at the jail before you could get out on road. I did ride-alongs everywhere to help decide where to go. One of my big questions was, How many women do you have? Because if the department has no women or can't keep women, don't go there. When I got hired here one of the gals said she had lasted two weeks at one agency that didn't have any women. I was careful. I talked to lots of people including hiring officers who referred to different standards. A higher standards agency was the place to be.

When I hired on they asked a lot of very strange questions, like was I a cop groupie, a female who dated a lot of cops? Knowing what I know now, I should have said, None of your business. I almost didn't get hired because I lived at home. They asked me if I would move out if they hired me. Yes, when I have the money, I'll leave.

I was really proud that I was number two in my class academically. I'd never been dumb as a stump but when I was testing I would go to a test and there would be 500 people there. I was always afraid someone would come up who was a part-timer or reservist and brag about what he'd done the night before. And I would think, Why am I here? At the academy these people who had been in the military or reserves knew everything. I felt like a moron.

I don't have anything psychological about guns but I'd never shot before. At the academy there was this older instructor from Seattle who didn't call me by name. He called me Redmond. Redmond, you're not getting it. Please shoot your own target, Redmond. To this day I am not a great shot. They qualify us four times a year. Well, if you only shoot four times a year, guess what, you're not going to be very good at it. I don't shoot much off duty but this is the premier training police department in the state. They will give you time during the day to train and I make a point of going downstairs to the range and shooting a couple hundred rounds once a month.

DARE Is Hands Down the Hardest

I started on nighttime patrol from 5 p.m. until 5 a.m., 12-hour days, three on, three off, rotating days off. I worked with a patrol officer who preyed on people he perceived as weak. I was the only female on nights on my squad. I was so young when I started, only 22, and I am not exactly big and beefy and male-looking. I wanted people to like me, I wanted to fit in. I was the worst possible personality type for a person who likes to pick on vulnerable people. He picks on men, too, anybody he thinks is weak. But at some point later in my career I was like, Hey, guy, that doesn't work anymore, and we get along fine now.

After three and a half years I was ready to do something else. I tested for DARE and went into that unit for two years. It was the best thing I ever did because it opened my eyes to, You're not the only female here and there's a lot more to policing than nighttime patrol. I got to know other people and got interested in the Family Violence Unit through answering assault calls and getting to deal with the people.

I went to days and I went to DARE and it was great. Hands down, that's the hardest, most exhausting job I've ever had in my life, working in the schools, working with kids. Because it's constant show time, you're always on duty, no matter where you are, because the people in the community know exactly who you are. It made me realize that as talkative and outgoing as I am, that's not who I am on my off time. I can be at home and the phone will ring and I say to myself, Don't answer it.

Moving On

After a couple of years I became the family violence coordinator, coordinating all the cases. Then we realized that this was too big for one person and we needed another investigator. They brought a guy in to help but he didn't stay. For him it was too much work, too much paper, he'd rather work the street where the cases are done at the end of the day, you go home, you play, there's nothing hanging over your head.

I like working with women. I have access to a part of society that a police officer doesn't ordinarily get access to, legal advocates, grassroots organizations, agencies devoted to combating domestic violence. Working nighttime patrol, you work around men, all the time, and I missed working with women.

Redmond is one of the only agencies in the state that has a body fat requirement. We take physical fitness tests and if we do well, we get a percentage of our annual salary as a bonus. Other agencies have standards, too, but usually body fat is not part of it. Part of our contract says our fitness will be judged as competent, distinguished, or unsatisfactory, and if you are distinguished in all the categories, you get 2% of your salary in a bonus check. Mine comes tomorrow. I'm very thrilled. In addition to that, as part of our contract, we get to work out three hours a week on duty. It totally benefits the department. It means less sick leave and we don't have the obesity issue you see in many other police departments across the state.

You can choose to work out every day if you want, so I take part of my lunch and part of my PT time and work out an hour a day when I'm on duty and two on my days off. My husband is very buff, which is extra incentive for me to stay in shape. But eating is my hobby so in order to fit into my uniform and to keep my body fat down, I have to work out. And when I got into police work I realized I really love running.

I would like to incorporate my court recording into my police work because, for example, right now the homicide team tape-records statements. Then it takes a transcriptionist with a typewriter all day to do an interview whereas for a court reporter it takes as long as the interview takes. I haven't been in school that long and already I can transcribe at 140 words a minute.

When There Are Children

If you ask the department who has a child, it's me. My husband and I both work there, but I'm the one with the kid. I'm the one who loses 15 minutes in the morning and has to make up 15 minutes at the end of the day. It's not official; it's an arrangement that my very nice boss and I have. Who takes the sick leave when the child is sick? I do.

Fortunately, my parents are very helpful with my little boy. They're constantly taking him in at night when I get called out. I phone and say, Hey, I got called out, gotta go, I'll meet you at the door. He has bedrooms at my sister's house and my parents' house. He doesn't do daycare at all. But I'd love to do part-time. I am constantly saying to my buddy that we should do a proposal. She says, They're not ready yet. But she's going to have another baby in a year and she's going to say, I'm leaving or you're going to give me part-time.

Police work can become your whole life if you're not careful. My husband and I are careful about spending only so many minutes at work talk. I'll call him on my cell phone on the way home and we'll talk and by the time I get home, we're done. We try to compartmentalize because my son is very aware when the police car is in the driveway, Oh, Mom, you might have to go to work.

As far as promotion is concerned, I've noticed that as women go up the chain, women do most of the work up the chain. We have a female commander who does the accreditation every year even though it's been assigned to one of the male commanders. Last year I was voted Officer of the Year and the reason I didn't like it was, again, Congratulations, you're doing a great job, now let us heap thousands of more responsibilities on you. The longer you're here, the more they know they can rely on you. So I don't want to promote.

My buddy came from another department and hadn't experienced any harassment and said she never would have put up with it. She says exactly what she thinks. She has definitely helped me in that area. When the environment on patrol changed I wasn't part of it anymore. I was in DARE working by myself in the schools. I'd go home and turn on the news and say, Is that what happened today? She was still in patrol and let me know how things were changing. She helped me realize that there's no going back and that I'm not that same patrol officer. I have expertise now. People call me and ask me questions and I know how things work.

Early Overprotection

One of the other detectives and I are like brother and sister. We work the same way, we get into sibling rivalry. We were talking about this brand new 22-year-old officer. He said, She did a really good job on this case. I said, Why are you surprised? He said, But she's so little, she's not like you, you can take a beating. I said, What? He said, You can take a beating. I said, I know you haven't looked lately, but I'm not exactly 200 pounds and six feet tall. He said, But you're tough. We don't worry about you anymore.

I had just gotten off training. We hadn't had anything big happen. During training it's hit and miss. You may get five burglaries or five robberies or nothing. The other women told me, The men are concerned about how you're going to do, your first fight, just so you know what's going on. I got in trouble in the academy for skipping. The whole class was told that police officers have dignity, they need to have officer presence, and today an officer was seen skipping down the hall. I thought, Who did that? I got called in. No skipping. I was young, hyper, funny, so they were worried about me.

One night we got a call. Another officer was arresting a drunk. I backed him up. He said I'm fine, you can go. I left and he called, Officer, I need assistance. I hit my siren and went back up there. We're grabbing the guy and he threw me off and flung me underneath the patrol car. I hit my head on a tire but I got back up and fought him and we got him into custody, put him in the car. To me it wasn't a big deal, but I got a letter in my file from this officer saying I'd done a wonderful job.

Ideas about Retaining Women

Port of Seattle Lieutenant Myra Harmon said regarding retention: "One of the keys to keeping women, because you can attract them all you want, but to keep them a lot of women want contact and mentoring. I routinely have women I have brought into the department call me at home for advice. They feel that they can trust me and can talk to me as a peer instead of a supervisor. They look at me as their buffer.

Women need mentors, one-on-one during the testing process, and after they're hired. One thing I always did with the women was check in on them at the academy to make sure they knew I was available. One woman called me the day she was supposed to go through the testing with pepper spray. She was starting to panic so I went over to make sure I was there for her and helped her wash the stuff off. I knew she could do it, but she needed someone there.

Sometimes the most helpful thing is knowing you are not alone, that someone else went through, or is going through, the same issues. It's not you; it's a problem within law enforcement in general. One woman is in litigation with her agency right now. It's been ongoing for about a year. She's needed someone consistent to listen and give her suggestions and ideas. We talk weekly. She needs to know that there's someone there who (a) knows what's going on, (b) supports her, and (c) knows what an incredible asset she is to her agency.

Sometimes minorities struggle with the nuances of the English language, and law enforcement does have its own vocabulary. Sometimes there are cultural issues, such as having to take an enforcement role against people of their own ethnicity. A cop in the Chinese culture is not necessarily thought of as a positive thing. And if you're female, you are regarded even less. But a good thing is that minority officers recognize that women are in somewhat the same position they're in, they're different, so most of them are supportive of women."

Retention Tally and Early Starting Questions

Tallying up what these 53 women had to say about retaining more women, the number one way was flexible scheduling, tailored shift work. What schedule works best for you? Number two was 24-hour daycare for all emergency personnel. Number three was a good maternity/paternity or disability policy for men and women with light duty and leaves. After that came constant mentoring by the chief, followed by job-sharing and part-time work. There should be lots of rewarding people publicly for a good job, little e-mails of praise, "atta gals" on the bulletin board. There should also be lots of opportunities for working in a variety of units.

Younger readers after information about policing can ask themselves, "Who do I most identify with, Katie, Michelle, Robin, or Anne? Why is that? What advantages are there to starting early? Am I already prepared mentally and physically for the academy? What changes in my lifestyle will have to be made if I apply now? How do I feel about carrying and using a gun? Do I know how to find support and mentors?"

9

Starting Late

Because a sizeable number of my interviewees began police work "late," i.e., at 27 or older, they deserved a chapter all to themselves. If law enforcement is going to recruit women in their '30s and '40s, there needs to be information out there about how this plays out. What are the experiences of older women like as they progress through the academy, FTO training, and the first years on the job? Do their job satisfactions match those of younger women? What are their strengths for policing?

Nine of my interviewees joined at ages 27-30, and seven at ages 31-36. There were five really late starters, one at age 39, two at 41, one at 43, and one at 44. Over half of the group began policing in young adulthood—18 women between the ages of 21 and 23, 14 between 24 and 26.

How many years had this group been police officers? Six for 6 or fewer years, eight for 7-10 years, and eight for 11-15 years. Ten had been with the police 16-20 years, 14 for 21-25 years, and seven had between 26 and 29 years of service behind them.

I met Retired Deputy Constable Sarah Cortez (who joined when she was 43) in Reno, Nevada, at a Police Writers Association conference where she taught memoir writing. Born in 1950, she is divorced and has three degrees—BA in psychology and religion, MA in classical studies (Greek and Latin), MS in accounting. She now writes poetry full-time. In 1993, after 14 years in accounting and employee benefits consulting, tired of sitting at a desk all day pushing paper, she paid for her own police academy and joined the University of Houston, TX, PD. When we met she was working part-time unpaid as a senior reserve officer for Harris County, Texas.

A Bit of Memoir

I should have been a boy. Everything I liked to do my whole life for the time period in which I was born, only boys could do. I couldn't get a gun and charge up hills and be a soldier. That's what I wanted to do as a child. For better or worse, I have a pretty high IQ. I was always on the honor role and was a national merit semi-finalist. I got accepted at Rice University, which is a very prestigious private university. I went off in an intellectual direction because I couldn't do what I wanted to do in the '50s and '60s as a female, which was be a soldier.

Being a cop is the ultimate boy thing. Any roll call, every roll call, is a cross between deer hunting, fishing camp, boy scout meeting, and poker game. And that's not a negative to me. Being a cop for me is as close as I can get to being a boy. I like action, danger, risk, guns. I'm an extremely good shot although I'd never shot a handgun until the police academy. My Dad, in spite of being a good Dad, didn't allow females to go on hunting trips. So this is my world of action even though it's often boring and dirty and sometimes people treat you like shit.

My memoir of being a cop would relate to my living out that childhood dream as best I could, the dream of being a soldier, the dream of standing up for what's right, the dream of being a service to my country, or in this case, my state. I take my oath to the State of Texas very seriously. It means a lot to me.

Recapturing the Dream

I was very involved in civic work in my neighborhood. For 11 years I was on the board of the civic association, which represented 30,000 people. I held many positions including president of the association. We had intense problems, very typical of old American inner-city neighborhoods—prostitution, muggings, a lot of cruising because it was a gay neighborhood. In trying to help the neighborhood solve those problems, I met many police personnel. They were smart, responsible, creative. They followed through on projects. They wanted to help us save our neighborhood and indeed they did. They got things done and this was very impressive to me. I thought I possessed qualities that would be useful on the street, but it was very hard, coming from a civilian perspective, to look at becoming a cop at my age with my background.

However, in 1991-2, with only three agencies in and around Texas who would hire me at the age of 41, I paid for my own academy. My parents accepted my decision with a lot of equanimity. They said, If it's going to make you happy, do it. Sometimes I think I was in my adolescence in my mid-forties but they always supported me. Both had a very strong sense of public duty. My father volunteered to fight in World War II the minute he could after Pearl Harbor happened. My mother was a renown bilingual educator in Texas. Until her dying day, she was always volunteering to be part of medical studies.

I worked my butt off preparing for the academy. When I started preparing, something was wrong with my pelvis. I couldn't run. I would run half a block and be in a lot of pain. I went to all kinds of doctors and exercise therapists. I finally got that sorted out. I lifted weights and did pilates, it is a system of exercise developed for professional ballet dancers. It makes you strong and flexible. I lost a lot of weight in the police academy, I went from 135 down to 113, but even at 113 I could pick up my boyfriend who weighed 170 and carry him over my shoulder. Pilates got me through. I did a lot of very high-level physical exercise for eight months.

Realizing the Dream

I graduated from the academy and passed my TCLEOSE test from the Texas Commission on Law Enforcement. It is a state-wide test that you have to pass after you go through the academy and have the hours of training they mandate. Then, in 1993, I tested for my first job and started working full-time as an officer for the University of Houston PD where I got promoted to corporal. Corporals basically were trainers. I was trained as an FTO and when I wasn't training a rookie or doing a special assignment, like writing training materials, I did patrol duty. I was there until January 1998. Then I went to work as a deputy constable full-time for Harris County, which meant I was on patrol, answering calls for service, and fixing problems when I got there. When someone needed to go to jail, I'd take him. I was looking for a place with more danger, more risk, like domestic violence.

Two years ago I received a visiting scholar position at the University of Houston, which allowed me to pass from full- to part-time police work and full-time writing and teaching. My part-time position is called a senior reserve officer but in Texas it's not legal to get paid for that. I work a shift and a half a week. It's exactly the same as regular policing. You're in a patrol car, you're alone. I went to part-time policing because my writing career took off. I couldn't meet the deadlines I had on contracts and other assignments and still be a patrol officer.

My personality fits with police work because I was brought up in a household where there were a lot of rules and a lot of respect for elders, principally my Mom and Dad. It was not permitted to transgress. No one ever did. I never did. I was a very good kid. So taking an oath to defend Texas and enforce the law and do anything that entails including getting killed fit with the way I was brought up. This respect for rules is mitigated by how many generations a Mexican American family has been in the U. S. Once a family has been here six generations, the respect may be gone and in its place there may be drugs, gangs, etc.

I also like the physical challenge of police work, not chasing people or climbing fences, but needing the ability to concentrate and focus on work when you're exhausted, pissed off, need to pee, haven't eaten in 12 hours. It's very physically taxing but in a non-athletic way. It's simply, can you keep up your stamina, your concentration?

Every Scene Is Different

It's the hardest job I've ever encountered. I've had lots of jobs, I've taught school, I've been in retail, in hotel-restaurant management. I was earning over $70,000 a year in the job I left to go into police work where my first pay was $14,000. For me, what I love about policing is, you have to go into situations you know relatively little about and deal with people who are always wishing you weren't there. Even if you just saved their life, they don't want you there. You have to read their emotions, listen to all their stories, memorize everything everybody says, figure out who is lying big and who is lying small, because everybody lies a little bit to cops. You have to keep the scene safe and legal for everybody, including yourself and your backup. You have to keep everybody safe, even the people who hate you and you've got to take the right people to jail if somebody needs to go to jail.

Every scene is different. One minute you're a hero, the next minute they're trying to stick a knife in your back. People act crazy in the height of emotions, drunk, on drugs, and you've got to figure that all out, keep it safe and legal. To me that's the ultimate challenge, bringing order out of chaos. My style? Hardass.

Women on the Scene

A big help was finding another woman to talk to. She worked the shift after mine out of our small substation. For example, there was a guy in my department who hated all women. He would go around telling lies about what I did on scenes, which infuriated me. And she said, Oh, him, yeah. He's an asshole. Just laugh the little prick off. She could see it from another perspective but still a woman's perspective. We would have long talks about what was going on in our personal lives, and I've told her how much I appreciate being able to talk to her. She would come into her shift early and I'd stay late and we'd talk in the station house when nobody else was there. It's wonderful to be able to talk with another woman cop because there is so much stuff civilians don't understand, can't understand, and never will understand.

One reason men have a hard time relating to me as a female officer is that I'm all business. I'm not there to flirt with them, I'm not there to sleep with them, I just want to do my job. I often make one to three arrests every shift and a lot of our men, if somebody cries, they feel sorry for them and make excuses for them. They're pushovers, which I don't understand and they don't understand me being a hardass.

For example, I'm not the kind of woman who has always wanted kids. I don't have kids. I don't know anything about babies. We were on a call one time, we had multiple arrests and one of the arrestees had a small baby, and one of the other officers said, You hold the baby. I said, Eddie, I don't want to hold it. He said, It? It's not an it. I said, Eddie, a baby is an it to me. You have three kids, you change diapers, you've done all that shit at home, I've never changed a diaper. So he held the baby. But four years later he's still kidding me, I can't believe you called a baby an it!

The University of Houston was a tough department for many reasons, but they put a lot of emphasis on extremely detailed report writing so I got very good at that. I wrote very, very detailed reports and never lost a case. You investigated all your own cases. At both agencies where I worked you were responsible for all aspects of the investigation, filing charges, booking. You did everything. You became very good as an investigator if you cared about it.

The Quest for a Mentor

I have a mentor who has been in police work two years longer than I've been. She's a very decorated cop on the East Coast. She was my student when I taught high school back in the late '70s. She was on my soccer team, in my honors psychology class. A brilliant young woman, and a good, strong athlete. Both she and her mother are close friends of mine. When she graduated from Sam Houston State in Huntsville, she could have gone to law school, she could have gone anywhere, but she wanted to be a cop.

They were initially from the New York area, so after she finished college they moved back. She went to an academy and got hired immediately, even though in Texas you can't get hired if you tell them you're gay. It's illegal, so they find other reasons not to hire you. But on the East Coast she took her exam and they asked her, when was the last time you had such and such experience? She said, Oh, a week ago. They hired her anyway.

We keep in touch usually by phone, especially when I was in my first policing job. I had just come out of an intellectual world, a world of computer programming and being a consultant, where part of your intrinsic value as a consultant is to ask questions to solve a problem. In police work they don't want anybody to ask questions. They want people who follow orders. It was a rough adjustment for me. I finally learned to keep my mouth shut. I used to call her a lot and say, God, what do I do?

For example, before I hired on at the University of Houston I worked for a small jurisdiction as a reserve officer. They started all new people out in dispatch so I was dispatch and running plates. It was a dirt-poor community, very out in the sticks, they didn't have any other females. I was really excited but also scared about being in this environment, scared about the social dynamics. I called her and her advice was, Keep your mouth shut. Don't talk about yourself. Don't talk about anything. Everybody will be dying to find out about you, because you're female. But don't tell them shit. Instead, listen to them talk. You'll figure out who are the fools, who are the liars. Just listen.

Talking from the Heart

One case that sticks in my mind at the University that I felt very good about was a telephone harassment case. She was a graduate student, she was Asian, she was in her dorm room, she was one of these intense scientists, hyper graduate student, and she was there studying and this male person called her and started making the typical sexual remarks, but he also got off on a whole lesbian accusation against her. It totally freaked her out so when I got there, she wouldn't even answer the door.

She said she was scared to go out so I spent a long time reassuring her and trying to help her out emotionally. She came months later to me, when I was walking into the station, and said, I want to thank you so much for helping me. I recommended that she go to the counseling service, and she did and spent some time in therapy and made some kind of miraculous transformation in her own life about dealing with her passiveness, claiming her own identity. She became this new person that she liked very much. That made me feel good. You owe it to people who make a call for service to look them in the eye and be honest, and, if it's legal to, say the right thing. In my heart of hearts what I told her was what I thought was the best thing to do.

When I worked full-time for the county we had an assault case between a teenage boy and a guy in his thirties who was upset because teens were always racing up and down his street and he had three small kids. This kid was racing and the man yelled at him, so the kid went home and got a hammer and came back. Anyway, it was one of those crazy situations. The kid's mom was there and the homeowner's wife and kids and everybody's upset. The man could have filed aggravated assault charges on this kid but he decided not to. I spent a long time talking to that kid and his mom because, not surprisingly, the kid's dad handled his anger in similarly inappropriate ways. I talked about how our culture doesn't teach us appropriate ways to handle anger but you have to learn how through a therapist, minister, classes. I always say those things, Go to a therapist. Do this. Do that. I say them because I believe it is the right thing to say but I have no hope ever that people will transform themselves because I've been at police work too long. But the mom wrote in to my supervisor later that this had really made a difference in this young man's life.

My Writing Life

I wrote when I got home at night. My first book was written in ten to twenty minute spurts at night after my shift. I wrote when I was on hold on the phone. I rarely wrote in the police department because both places I worked we were incredibly busy. My first writing as a child was letters. I had a very dear aunt who wrote letters to me and I would write back. One time when we visited her up in Washington, D.C., she showed me a special box that she kept all my letters in, tied up with blue satin ribbon. She loved children although she got married late and was childless. She let me know how special all my letters were to her. I wrote about school, my pets, what I was reading, simple household events.

I wrote my first poem in 1992. The classes I took starting in 1987 were all in fiction because the short story is my first love, and the novel. In 1992 my marriage was falling apart because my husband didn't want me to become a cop. We had been in therapy a year and a half; it didn't help. It was a bad situation. And every time I would sit down to write, what started coming out was poetry. I had no idea this was going to happen. I had one dear girlfriend who knew a lot about poetry, so she would send me books and Xeroxes of poems she liked and tell me to read certain authors. She was my writing mentor for a long time.

I met her through a mutual friend in Houston, she was the ex-lover of a girlfriend of mine. She was an engineer living in the Washington, D.C. area and when she visited Houston they invited us to a dinner party and we just clicked.

We had a voluminous correspondence. We wrote pages and pages of letters, two or three times a week, for years. I have volumes of them now donated to the Mexican American archives of the city of Houston. They wanted all my literary papers.

The City of Houston got grant money ten years ago to start Mexican American archives. This young archivist for the Houston Public Library started joking around with me, When are you going to donate your literary papers? I said, On the totem pole, I'm on the bottom. I'm nothing. And she's, No, no. But finally I needed to clean out my office and I said, Either I give them to you or I throw them away because I can't keep them.

In 1995 I attended a poetry workshop in Oregon that made a major difference in my life. People in the class bonded and we started sending poems to other people in the class to critique so I have piles and piles of comments that I have written on other people's poems and vice versa. Every poem that I have comments on I look at all the comments before I revise it. I have a folder set up for each public appearance. I used to have as many as five public appearances a week, every week, in Texas mostly. I have folders on my other projects and all the original versions of my poems. I'll also give them my Dad's extensive scrapbooks that mother kept for him. All the countries he was in in the Second World War. I want to give them to this collection so others can see them.

I had been taking writing workshops all along because I wanted to be a fiction writer, but then I took a week-long poetry workshop with this incredible poet, incredible person. She was very magical and it was my first experience with a teacher who encouraged each individual voice for what it was. I was scared because I had had only one poem published at that point. I didn't consider myself a real poet. I wrote a newsletter for that group every six months for several years. We kept in touch for quite awhile. If I hadn't had that experience, I don't know that I ever would have published a book. Now I teach poetry workshops so I'm the person who is commenting on each poet's work. I wouldn't be able to do that if I hadn't spent all those years writing comments and getting comments from other people through the mail to people in that class.

From Editor to Cop

Sergeant Robin Biffle was born in 1951. She was the news editor for the weekly *Port Townsend Leader*. In 1986 her "Cops and Courts" reporter became ill and she couldn't find anyone to cover the beat. So on New Year's Eve she rode along with two officers. By the end of the evening, she was hooked. She continued doing ride-alongs, took college law enforcement classes, and tested for both the city police and sheriff's office. She was hired by the sheriff's office in corrections and dispatch in 1988, was on the road as a deputy sheriff in 1990, and joined the Port Townsend, WA, PD in 1992. Here's what Robin had to say.

That ride-along evening I saw that most fieldwork is crisis intervention, mediation, conversation, comforting someone, all skills that I was good at. The other component that is often overlooked is writing ability, and, by interest and trade, writing is very comfortable for me. I also liked the physical challenge since I've always been physically active.

Ideas about Recruitment

Each department offers different things so there have to be individual recruiting strategies. But overall, they should reflect the career and the profession as one to which women are uniquely suited by virtue of our flexibility, intuitiveness, expression of empathy, and response to challenge. Recruiters and departments need to put out a real image of police work, not driving cars fast and chasing bad guys. COPS shows crisis after crisis after crisis, pursuing somebody who refuses to stop, then a foot pursuit, then handcuffing him. To make policing look like that's all there is—very few women are going to be interested in a career that's so one-dimensional. In fact, in the course of a year in this community our officers are involved in fewer than five pursuits.

In this community we recruit simply through interaction with folks, that is, talking to high school classes and younger classes, and being involved and visible in the community as women in police work. When women in other professions get to know us, across the board, they're surprised because their perception of us was that we had to be macho women, very narrowly focused on this male-oriented and -dominated track. I work with the head of the Port Townsend branch of Peninsula College. She refers women to me who have come into the criminal justice program to work one-on-one with them. We offer a ride-along program, a cadet program, and an Explorer post.

I'm Going to Show You

Our defensive tactics and physical training instructor was from the Seattle Police Department. He was an ex-Marine, he'd been to Vietnam, and he had a very militaristic attitude. When we first got to academy and were doing runs and push-ups, we had several people who were not strong performers, the majority of whom were women. He made that a gender issue, instead of a strength or endurance issue. And my response was, Okay, bud, I'm going to show you. I don't know why I adopted that attitude, but I did. I weighed 120 pounds when I went into the academy and could bench press 65 pounds. And when I left the academy I could bench my body weight. That accomplishment meant a lot to me. I earned his respect and showed him there is a place for us here. If I can bench my body weight at 120 and he can bench his body weight at 220, clearly he's stronger. But it's the same accomplishment.

Drunk drivers are often resistive—I don't want to go, you're ruining my life. I was, and still am, happy to engage them, listen, talk with them. We end up getting the handcuffs on them and getting them in the back of the car. But this one guy called me a name and the officer who responded with me lost patience—You don't call her that—and he used more force than he needed getting the guy into the car. I didn't like that because 30 seconds later I would have been able to do the same thing. I didn't respond at the time. I was very new, I went on with my day. The same officer did a similar thing a few months later and this time, I said, I'll take care of this. He backed off and didn't try again.

Ideas about Retention

I came to policing later, but if women come into it earlier, they need to have a sense that there's going to be a place for them during pregnancy. But in a department this size, we don't have a desk job, every officer is a field officer, so what do you do when she's six months and can't work in the field? But we do need to accommodate women who want a family but don't want to lose their job, skills, track. We've had injured male officers and we've done make-work situations in the front office. I'm sure that's what we'd do for a pregnant woman but there is no union job description for that. We made special accommodations for injured men, with everybody agreeing that it's fine, but there are problems that could arise. I can hear guys saying, She got light duty longer than I did. Accommodating women's family needs is the way we would best retain them. Flex-time can be doable. We had an officer, a single man who had a child, who asked for and got a particular schedule in order to accommodate his daycare provisions. So we do these things on a case-by-case basis. Again, civil service and unions could get in the way.

Attaining supervisory positions in law enforcement is very important for women. I took my promotion, this job, because I wanted the men in patrol, most of whom I deeply respect, to have the opportunity to answer to a woman supervisor. The other reason was the chief said, You have these skills and these are the skills I need. But the job puts me way out of my comfort area. I believe it's good for anybody to move out of one's comfort area. It's good for us to push there. But for many women, a supervisory position where most of the people one is supervising are men is outside that comfort area.

One officer ignored the fact that I was a woman. He thought it was good that I was smart, willing, enthusiastic, a quick learn, steady, he liked those things so he spent time with me. When we'd be on a call together, he would watch me, and after the call he would make observations—I really liked what you did there. This was really good, were you aware that you did that? Or, when you did this, you put this person in jeopardy. He was able to show me places to learn without making me feel like, Oh, boy, I really blew that. He also said things like, I would never have thought of doing that. So he made me feel like I was helping him learn too, even though he had years of experience. And now I have that rare opportunity to have a mentor who is a woman. Her skills in administration and management are exceptional.

What I like best about my job is the ability to have a meaningful impact in somebody's life, usually at a very difficult time, whether they are a suspect, victim, or witness. Mentally ill people are, all the time, so disoriented and afraid and I like being able to give them reassurance. One woman had tried to commit suicide, and I had to sit with her because she had done harm to herself, until the mental health professional arrived and I could turn her into his custody. It was some number of hours by virtue of his distance from us. But by the time he came, she had gone from the point where she wanted not to be alive to the point that she had recognized a number of reasons why she wanted to be alive. There was also a woman whose husband had died, the aides had come and taken off with her husband's body. She was there by herself. I couldn't even imagine how difficult it was for her, but I was able to be there for her, stay with her and then get some folks to be with her.

Women from the beginning, as young girls, are always trained to be aware. Watch out. Keep your eye on that guy. Don't go out after dark. As a result we're constantly more aware of our surroundings. Whereas the big, muscular men you find in police work have been physically dominant much of their lives in whatever situation they have been in. So when confronted with a situation that involves deadly force, or force that is greater than their own, they freeze. While women are so accustomed to that sense of physical threat, we have a number of different responses, and we can continue to think in those situations.

Women are not afraid to ask questions. If they don't understand something or they want to know more, they'll ask, How do you do that? Whereas men often are afraid to admit they don't know something. They'll give incorrect and wrong answers rather than say, I don't know. Women see it of value to say, I'm doing this differently today than yesterday because I know more today.

Officer Sherry Erickson

Sherry was born in 1957 in Antioch, California. She has four children, ages 26, 23, 17, and 16, and has been happily remarried for two years. She was a dental assistant for 18 years before working part-time in parking enforcement for the Port Townsend, WA, PD. In 1998 she graduated first from the reserve academy and then the full-time academy. Her dad was a police officer for 22 years and is now the coordinator of her department's volunteer program. She has a son who said from the age of three that he wanted to be a cop and will be as soon as he finishes a degree in criminal justice.

Why I Did It

My very first scary encounter was when I was doing parking enforcement. I ran into a character known to the other officers as one who did not like law enforcement and had been in trouble before. I didn't know this guy from Adam. He had pulled into a red zone right in front of me. When I said, Sir, hello, this guy came right at me. I didn't even have a radio at the time, just a ballpoint pen. I thought, He's going to hit me. I stood my ground and kept talking. That's all I had, my mouth. He did listen and got back in the car and after some name-calling, he spun out and took off. I went into the nearest shop and called an officer. They found him later and cited him for intimidation. After it was over, I was shaking. It finally dawned on me what can happen to you out there. I had had no training up to that point. I wanted to be able to yell for help so I got a radio after that.

The draw was, at the time, when I separated from my husband, that I had a newfound attitude of now I can do what I want to do. My ex was not supportive, whatsoever. I think he was afraid I would succeed. My divorce was finalized in 1996. Here I was, single with no real benefits or retirement from dental assistance. I wanted to be more independent all the way around. I was looking for a change. What are my interests? What do I want to see myself doing? That's when I took a good hard look at my life and law enforcement appealed to me in every way. I could give back to the community, hopefully be an asset to the department, and be financially secure, because I'm not getting any younger.

I was running and exercising anyway so the physical part was fine. I had gone out and done what I needed to do. A couple of weeks before the academy started you had to take the Cooper's test, sit-ups and push-ups, run, and a flex test. I did all that five times a week. I made sure I was ready mentally and physically. I thought, When I get in I'm not going to have any problems and, surprisingly, there were people who did have problems and got washed out that day. I thought, I'm taking a chance here. I'm 41 years old, I have kids, I'm letting go of a full-time job that pays well, for around here anyway. I'm gambling that I can make it through and I wanted to give myself every shot for completing it. I knew what I wanted, I'd done my research, I'd prepped myself. It is a whole different mindset when you're entering law enforcement.

Where I Am Today

My goal at the time was to get hired, do patrol, be a police officer. But now I'm gearing myself up for a sergeant position. From there we'll see. When I got out of the academy, being 5'4" and a hundred and nothing pounds, I wanted to work on defensive tactics because I didn't feel strong in it. Right away I started campaigning for a defensive tactics program and after two years of whining, they said, Sherry, here take it. So in addition to patrol work, I help train our officers in defensive tactics. They sent me to a controlled force class in which we learned new hands-on techniques. I brought that back to the department and introduced it to the officers.

I'm struck by a sense that I've accomplished much more than I had set out to do. I'm helping to instruct our officers in defensive tactics, I'm an FTO with people looking to me for guidance and direction. I got handed being coordinator of that as well and now we have a manual and a pretty good program going. But I'm probably proudest of my reputation with the kids in the community. I've been a cheerleading advisor. I enjoy hanging out at the high school talking to the students. I'm strict but I'm fair and I treat them with respect and I get that back. We were doing community-oriented policing here before we even understood what we were doing, before it became PC.

This department is unique. Everyone gets along, everyone likes each other, everybody looks after each other and I like being a part of that. I also wanted the FTO program to be less stressful, and more organized and consistent. We haven't achieved that yet but we're getting there. We meet, we talk, we want to be on the same page so that we all have the same expectations of a new officer. He has a schedule for the three months so he knows who he's going to be with and what is expected of him. We do daily reports. We jot down good things, bad things, and go over them with the new officer. We're going to have weekly and monthly meetings so that a new officer has every opportunity to succeed. I want them to critique us as well. What are the good things, the bad things? What can we do to improve?

I know from talking to people who graduated in my class that I get much more training here than they're getting. We all wear many hats here. We don't have special teams. We don't have an office full of detectives willing to step in and take over your cases. We're there start to finish, so we have to be well-rounded and trained in all aspects of law enforcement. Now, because of the new county sheriff we're definitely looking forward to training together with the deputies and working more together.

Community Helpers

I don't know how we functioned before our chief got the volunteer program going. Slowly it developed into the program we have now and I'm proud to say that my Dad is the coordinator. They raise money for uniforms, they have in-house training. They do training with us sometimes. There's a hard core that actively participates weekly. Some of them work in the front office, some do parking enforcement, others do vacation checks. We call on them if we have an accident where we need traffic control. They do the signs for our special events and post them and take them down. They make life so much easier. It used to be the officers who ran around and did all that so it was a lot of extra work, a lot of overtime.

We have a cadet program for kids 14 to 21. They go through a little academy, ride with officers, sit in corrections and communication and up front. It's a great program for kids who think law enforcement is where they want to go. It gives them a taste.

Family Issues

If my kids think I'm being overprotective, they say, I hate it that you're a cop, Mom, because I would get to do this if you weren't a cop. Everyone sees Port Townsend as this little innocent, sweet town, which for the most part it is, but not entirely. So I am constantly preaching to the younger two. They'd be the first ones to tell you, Yeah, she preaches. And my grandchildren will get it too some day. At times when I'm talking to my daughters, it sneaks in that they still worry. They were most concerned when I first started, especially when I went into nights. They've learned to manage their fears, but in the beginning they had trouble sleeping, bad dreams where I got hurt. I had kids sneaking into bed with me.

From a Very Traditional Hispanic Family

Sergeant Belinda Ferguson was born in 1961. She is married to a police officer and they have three children, 10, 12, and 14. In 1997 she was hired by the King County, WA, Sheriff's Office where she is currently their recruiter. Belinda is Hispanic and Native American and hails from Harbor City, California.

Long Before I Got into Law Enforcement

College would have placed a huge burden on my low-income family. After a year of business, communication, and leadership courses, I decided to go into law enforcement. My older brother worked for Rockwell International and as soon as my Dad heard that I wanted to be a cop, he said, You can't be a police officer, not in Los Angeles. Once they understood that I was very serious, my brother spoke to his boss who was looking for an assistant. I wasn't qualified for the job, I took a typing test eight times and then they changed the classification so I didn't have to pass the typing test.

I was 20 years old and they offered me $35,000 a year in 1981. I stayed with them in marketing for 14 years. I learned a lot and ended up a supervisor. Marketing and communications skills have blended in perfectly with my current career.

I come from a very traditional Hispanic family. I have three siblings and we're close-knit. My father and mother both were very strict and had very traditional ideas. I went against all of that. I was always a rebel. My father thought I'd got the idea of being a cop from TV and because it was so far-fetched I was going to do it. He thought it was too dangerous, and in his father's eyes I was too small, delicate, fragile, even though I was quite a tomboy. Mom expected me to marry and have children, which is what Hispanic daughters are supposed to do.

My mother attended my graduation from the academy, my father did not. It scared him. I understood and accepted his feelings because as a parent I'd have mixed feelings if my daughter said, Mommy, I want to be a cop. I also told him I'm an adult and this is a decision that I've made and I don't need your approval anymore. I'd like to have it but I don't need it. He said, You're going to do what you have to do. When I visited my parents my talk about work was very limited. My husband could talk until he was blue in the face about being a cop and that was fine.

Changing Careers

I wanted to make a difference, and be a contributing member of society. The idea of working behind a desk was extremely boring to me and I don't do very well with supervision. Being able to sit in my own police car, being independent appealed to me. Being a female in a career dominated by males definitely was a factor. Could I accomplish this? The more resistance I received, the more I wanted to do it and that's just part of my personality.

I had my third child. I had a live-in nanny. I was working long, long hours, 14-hour days. My children recognized their nanny more than they did their mother. I was getting burnt out on the corporate ladder and my husband, who was blue-collar, had the opportunity to relocate to Seattle. I asked myself, Am I ready for this change? We didn't know anybody in Seattle. All our family is in California. Then we experienced the Northridge earthquake. That was the final straw. I said to my husband, Do I need a rock to hit me on the head? I am ready to make a change for us and our family to get a better quality of life. Other factors were the long commute to my job and the fact that when my child turned five he would be bused to another area.

Within six months we packed up and moved our family here. I decided I was going to take a year off and be a stay-at-home Mom. That was a disaster. My children at the time were four, three, and a year. My husband would come home from work at four and I would still be in my pajamas, a glass of wine in my hand, watching Barney. My children started bringing me the classifieds. That was my first clue. Mommy, do you need a job? Even though I love my children dearly, they are my life, I am much more of a quality parent when I am working.

The one question I had was, If I'm not able to make the switch from being a cop to being a Mom, and be the kind of Mom that I respect, I will be the first to say this isn't for me. The first year was difficult because you're in training and on probation and everything's about that job. But once that's been successful, you can prioritize correctly. Now, as soon as I leave, I'm Mom. This is simply my career. And my family will always be first. The first thing I do when that garage door closes is take off my gun and secure it in the vehicle. Now I am Mom. And when you walk in the door there are these three kids. Clamoring, Mom, I need a new backpack. Mom, when's dinner? It's not difficult to make the transition.

My police experiences have made me appreciate my family rather than it jade me and change the way I treat them. I see how much I have versus people who don't have stable homes, people who don't have food on the table. It's enhanced my family life, which goes against all of the statistics. I have so many friends involved in law enforcement who have gone through a divorce. However, I call my husband a cop 24/7 because he's always thinking that way and it drives me crazy sometimes. He thought I wasn't interested in what he did because I didn't ask him what was going on with him. It's just that at home I became Mom. But I make it a point now to say, How was your day?

I Was Fast-Tracked

There was a part-time opportunity at the Renton, WA, PD for a support personnel position. It was graveyard so I'd be home during the day. It was a position where you worked at the front counter and in the jail. There was an oral board interview and I was very fortunate because 200 people applied for it. It was a huge pay cut from what I used to make but it was a four-day week and I could come home and sleep a couple of hours and then be able to see my children. At the same time my husband decided to quit his job and go back to school and pursue his lifelong dream of law enforcement, something he had always been interested in.

We had support from our families financially and he went back to school and began testing for agencies. The more I worked at Renton the more I thought, I want to pursue this dream, but I'm 35 years old. Can I still do this? I'll never know unless I try. My husband had applied for the King County Sheriff's Office, I decided to apply as well. We went through orientation together. I was fast-tracked, meaning I tested and was hired within two months. My husband had been testing for a long time and after my very first test, I'm offered employment. I remember coming home and he said, There's a message for you from King County. From the look on his face I said, This is going to strain our marriage. I won't do this. He said, You absolutely will do this and you'll be wonderful. I accepted it and he was offered employment by Renton, which I left a month later.

If I hadn't had the stability of a live-in nanny, I don't know that I could have committed myself and been successful. She still occasionally comes over and stays with my children. I hired a Hispanic not just because that was my upbringing in terms of values, but it was an opportunity for my children to learn Spanish. But instead my children taught the nannies English.

I now work Tuesday through Friday, 9 a.m. to 7 p.m. My husband's schedule allows me to be home with my children and get them off for school and he picks them up. Our children are our top priority. It's been great for our marriage. We miss each other. We go on dates. The kids say, Mommy, after 16 years, you guys still love each other? Yeah, we do. I'm fortunate to have a very strong relationship with my husband and my family.

My Job, Recruiting

I'm an example of the opportunities with this agency. I'm very straightforward and honest about the fact that I do not have a college degree but a humble upbringing and life experience count for a lot more. I worked patrol for three years and then I went into a detective unit, burglary and larceny. It offered me a very stable and flexible work schedule. I got specialty training in sexual assault and domestic violence. I went to crime scene school. I got involved in a variety of things early on in my career.

People come up to me and say, You don't look like a cop, you don't sound like a cop. I take that as a compliment because it says to me there are no stereotypical cops anymore. The fact that I can break that old mold appeals to me. I'm able to connect with young and old people. I can empathize because of personal experiences and even dealing with a difficult crime scene, I'm able to touch people, even the bad guys.

In January 2000 I was approached about the recruiter position. I thought, I can do that, I can do that very well. But I also thought, I haven't paid my dues because I have only been with the department three and a half years. I went through the process, I interviewed, and was selected.

As a recruiter I get to travel and I do a lot of public speaking. That is very rewarding but the bottom line is I still want to be out there responding to calls. We wear many hats. We recruit, process, and hire because the hiring process is very extensive. I have minimal supervision, which I like, and when you don't have a budget for recruiting you have to be very creative. I have a personal interest in who we recruit and who we hire because these new people are going to be working next to my coworkers and friends.

Promotion

My children think I'm already at the very top because I work the Mariner games. I have been approached about another position, instructor at the academy, teaching criminal procedures. I need to have credibility with the people I'm supervising. To me that means going back to the street and refamiliarizing myself with the basics. How much credibility would I have being off the street for three years, promote, become a supervisor, and make decisions for people when I haven't done it in three years? So, do I go back to patrol to prepare myself to promote or do I cover the basics in a different arena, at the academy?

I got to be a member of the honor guard last year. It's a specialty unit where we do memorial services, funerals. I'm going to Washington, D.C., in May and we're going to the law enforcement monument and participate in the services. There are ten of us, two females. They said I would really mesh in. Most of the people on the honor guard are SWAT, ex-military. You have to march in formation and I am so not that. Am I going to be able to do this? My first assignment was memorial services for a deputy who I worked next to for two years. I got through that entire memorial service and I never cried. I felt honored to be part of the service.

The Testing Process

I give a workshop where I instruct new candidates on how to take our test and what to expect. It includes a three-hour written test which has 54 scenario-based questions shown on a video. You have ten seconds to make a multiple choice of four answers. In ten seconds you have to evaluate what you saw and determine what is the best step for the officers to take. For example, a woman is at home with her children. This woman just got a warrant for a traffic infraction and two officers decide to go to her house and possibly arrest her on this warrant. The woman is inside the house. Another woman is standing outside the house with a baby in her arms and child. The child says, Are you a real officer? Is that a real gun? They answer yes and ask for Mary S. The child says, That's my mother. The mother comes to the door and it freezes and says, What would you do? One might be, I tell her I have a warrant for her arrest. Two, I tell her I have a warrant for her arrest, arrest her, and remove her from the house. Three, I ask the woman if I can speak to her privately and let her make arrangements. Four, I ask the other woman to take the children inside so I can talk to her. We're looking for common sense for which you wouldn't need law enforcement training.

I see my job as not just to recruit but to make candidates successful in the process. I give an orientation for the physical fitness test. I walk them through it, I demonstrate it. In the workshop I go over every single step in the process. In the workshop we do a mock oral board. Other steps include a very intensive background investigation, polygraph, psychological interview, written psychological test, medical exam, another command staff interview, and that's all prior to consideration for hiring. I try to familiarize them with each of those steps.

In the orientation I use many examples of myself, things that I did that were absolutely stupid and how I learned from those examples. One of the dumb things I did when I first hired on had to do with roll call. It was my first week and I thought roll call was once a month. So I walked in on Monday, brand new, the only female recruit. The whole squad was looking at me. I'm thinking, What's the big deal? My FTO says, Where were you for roll call? Roll call's once a month. No, roll call is once a week on Monday. I had never been so humbled in my life. And she wanted to see me. I walked in her office and what could you possibly say? I looked at her and said, It'll never happen again. She said, I know that it won't.

I tell this story to illustrate how someone my size can handle a unique situation because of my training. I was dispatched to a family disturbance call but my backup unit was a good 25 miles away. So that person was heading toward my call but I thought, it's just a family disturbance. There was no indication from dispatch that weapons were involved. When I get to the front door I see two people on the floor and a man very upset, speaking very loudly, agitatedly, and he has a sword in his hand. I thought, Hmm, this isn't any old family disturbance. I got on the radio and indicated that I needed help. I'm told that my nearest backup is from the precinct, which, lights, sirens, full speed ahead, is a good 20 minutes away.

I've got my gun drawn, I'm ready, and I directed him to drop the sword and put his hands up and he just looked at me. I was aware of the danger but I was not afraid. At that moment I knew that I was cut out to do this and I could handle myself and was very confident that if I had to make the choice, I was going home tonight and maybe he wasn't. I looked at him and said, That's a great sword. Where did you get that? It distracted him and he said he was a Vietnam vet and we started talking about the sword, its mother-of-pearl handle. In a matter of minutes I was able to get him to put the sword down and handcuff him. I talked my way out of it without having to use my weapon or pepper spray. Then lights, sirens, the whole world arrived.

My Teaching Assignment

I have a specialized certification and I teach a varied curriculum of law enforcement to high school students at a special occupational center. I was invited there as a guest speaker and the students liked my presentation so they asked if I could do it on a continual basis. It is a specialty program for students interested in a career in law enforcement. The instructors are commissioned officers or detectives. I have done this for two years and next year I will have a paid position. They have funding for three paid officer positions. I never thought I could be a teacher. But you start to connect and find yourself as a mentor to these students.

We go out to the schools, introduce ourselves, and let the students know that this is available to them off-campus. There is an average of twenty students in the class. They receive high school credit and they can take it for a year or a half year. What I do as a recruiter for the King County Sheriff's Office is put them through a mock testing process. I have them apply and we go through a background investigation, polygraph, physical fitness test. The course is two hours a day, Monday through Friday. Bus transportation is provided but some drive themselves. It's a very diverse group from different communities. My future educational plans are for a teaching certification so that I can instruct within the school district that I am currently volunteering for.

The Advantages of the Older Applicant

L. Faith Ratchford wrote an article for the summer 2003 issue of *Women Police* that describes a program to train older applicants. "Hiring the 'Total Package'" is how she refers to it. The Ontario Provincial Police are not only interested in mature candidates, but positively enthusiastic. Older recruits very likely have college degrees, work experiences in a range of fields, volunteer work, and varied talents based on years of experiences. By living and surviving the "school of hard knocks" they have developed good decision-making skills. She urges more police services to champion older applicants. After reading these portraits, I couldn't agree more. How about you?

10

Independent Personalities

It's never too late to be a pioneer. "Promotion a milestone for trooper and Patrol" was the headline for a *Seattle Times* article of September 18, 2003. When she scored 92.633 percent on the sergeants' exam, she was the first African American woman to place first among the 200 troopers who took the test.

At the age of 35, Monica Hunter enrolled in the Washington State Patrol Training Academy, 10 years older than most of her classmates. Like so many women you meet in this book, she brought lots of life experience to the job. She had studied communications in college, she was a licensed cosmetologist who owned her own beauty salon. She was a flight attendant with United for seven years and delivered traffic updates on TV. She is a single mother with a ten-year-old son. She has had lots of support for her career change from her mom, siblings, and a group of girlfriends from junior high, as well as many, many people in the agency who have mentored her.

The racial composition of the women in this book: Fae Brooks (Chapter 13) and Renee Winston (Chapter 15) are African American; Sarah Cortez and Belinda Ferguson, whom you have already met, are Hispanic; Annette Louie (this chapter) and an unnamed officer are Asian; the rest are Caucasian.

The Question of Personality

The answer to the question of whether one's personality is a good fit with police work is the focus here. We've already seen how patient a woman can be with someone threatening suicide. We've also seen how resourceful and creative she can be when facing muscle-bound 200-pound guys. We've learned how even a 22-year-old can have "officer presence," taking control when she enters the room. This chapter will fill out that personality profile with independence topping the list.

There are 1,002 male troopers and 82 female troopers in Washington State. Here's another sergeant who like Monica Hunter also has had groundbreaking experiences. Karen DeWitt was born in 1960. She is married to a retired state patrol lieutenant. When we met in the autumn of 2001 she had two sons, ages 20 and 16, and a step-daughter age 17. She has a bachelor's degree in management. She left office management and joined at the age of 29, having been recruited by state troopers on her volleyball team. When I asked her what she was proudest of, she got tears in her eyes and said it was doing CPR on a kid who only lived for three days. But his parents wrote a letter saying that they had donated his organs and she was able to see who, by name, and where, the organs went. It also made a difference to his family that she had been there to keep their son alive so they could spend those three days with him.

I Make My Own Decisions

I have a very soft voice. My first sergeant was brand new. I'm thinking, Oh, great, he's got a brand new recruit and I'm female. Everybody was petrified of him. Because I'm quiet and reserved, he assumed I was meek and mild and worried that I was going to get hurt, until he saw me restraining somebody. He realized then that I wasn't willing to put up with too much, and that if the button got pushed, I was right in there. He called me into the office and said, I'll never worry about you again.

I joined because I wanted to be a sergeant or above. I like the freedom to do my job. You know what you have to do and you do it. You don't have somebody looking over your shoulder constantly. If I have a question, I've always been comfortable with finding the answer. If I can't fire it to my immediate lieutenant because I can't find him, there's always somebody else out there I can get the answer from.

My lieutenant gives us freedom and obviously trusts his sergeants to make their own decisions. Since I've been a sergeant I've always had a captain or a lieutenant who has been very positive. I've been willing to take more on and they've always been willing to let me do that. Just let me work through it and let me manage things and I get my projects done ahead of time. It's helped me prepare to be lieutenant because I've been given the opportunity to do lieutenant-level material. I have to pat my captains and lieutenants on the back for that.

I Was Definitely Prepared

Fortunately I was athletic, a runner, volleyball player. I was doing a hundred sit-ups and push-ups two months before I entered the academy. I'd been running distance for a long time. The first day at the academy we had to do so many push-ups and sit-ups in a minute. There were 40 in the class, three women, and I was number four in push-ups. I did 61 push-ups in a minute. The instructor came by and asked the male cadet I was partnered with, How did she do? He said 61. He asked him three times, until a sergeant said, I was standing here. It was 61, so he backed off. I was definitely prepared.

I had it fairly tough. I had just gone through a divorce and I had two children who my parents took care of because the first six weeks we were the state patrol's property. We didn't go home. I'd been through a real bad divorce and while I was in there my ex decided he was going to try to get custody of the boys just to make my life miserable. So I was dealing with some extra things that I shouldn't have had to deal with.

Ways to Keep Learning

We're given sabbaticals for educational purposes for up to a year. We're very fortunate in the state patrol because the administration works very well with us when we're trying to get our education. We have a new chief from Louisiana who has a Ph.D. and encourages us to get more education, the higher the better. If you have a four-year degree, go after your master's. I'll start work on my master's in public administration next autumn and they've made arrangements for me to make sure I can adjust my shift. Troopers are usually willing to adjust their shift so you can go to a class.

I went to Evergreen State College to pick up my four-year degree and I was in uniform. Walking across campus I got a few stares and when I got to the administration desk to pick up my diploma, this kid walked past with green hair and his clothes hanging half off. He turns around and says, What happened? Did you get lost? I said, No, I'm here to pick up my degree and he starts shaking my hand and saying, Congratulations. He was totally stunned that a state trooper would graduate from college.

I've attended a couple of IAWP conferences. In Anchorage I thought the classes were great. I thoroughly enjoyed Toronto. A lot of men attended. I was very pleased to see that. They need to know what we're doing in law enforcement. I made a life-long friend from South Carolina highway patrol through the

IAWP. I met her in Anchorage. We communicate all the time. I've been to visit her. We met up in Toronto again with our husbands.

You meet a lot of different women at these conferences that you can draw things out of, and you share with them, so there's a lot of mentoring going on. You hear their experiences, the hoops they've had to jump through. Like I said, I've been very fortunate, everybody's been very encouraging throughout my career. That's nice to share with people who have had a difficult time coming through. If a woman is having a difficult time, talking with somebody who has gone through the process helps her understand what's going on and how to deal with it, or at least the right people to go to to solve the problem.

We had a women mentoring program within the patrol but we took a lot of flak from some of the men. It isolated us so we decided to make it a whole mentoring program, not just for women. What we were doing was focusing on new women coming in. They were assigned a female mentor who had been in the patrol awhile and took them through the steps and who was willing, basically, to take calls at any hour and check on them, How're you doing? Is there anything I can help you with? A lot of new officers didn't want anything to do with it because they were fearful that the men will look down on them and they wanted to be one of the guys.

If I Make Lieutenant

We're all encouraged to take exams. The vast majority of women coming in now have four-year degrees, and more and more take promotional exams. I think there's a correlation between higher education and taking the exam. A degree says that you're more motivated for whatever you're trying to achieve. I wouldn't want to be a police chief. I wouldn't want that responsibility. I made sergeant on the first exam. If I make lieutenant in the next couple of years, I think I could attain the rank of captain by the time I retire.

I'm on the lieutenant's list currently. You first submit a resume. Then you have a command recommendation. After that you come in for an oral board where they give you a topic and you have an hour to prepare for it. You sit in front of a panel of three, two of them normally are from outside our agency, the other person is our number three in command. You make your presentation and they ask questions. They also throw you three different scenarios that you have to respond to on the spot. You come back a week and a half later and take a written test that covers three texts that we have to read, our rank manual, unusual occurrence manual, administrative manual. We're tested on them, about a hundred questions. After that you do an in-basket. You get a pile of documents and they tell you, You're the new lieutenant and your captain just came to you and said that they need you to go out of town for a week by five o'clock today. So you need to go through that in-basket and write on everything who's going to be doing what while you're gone. You have to decide what's top priority down to what can wait. The last is a writing skills exercise where they give you a complaint letter from a citizen, and you have to respond, and another exercise from within the patrol, and you have to respond to that.

I was eligible to take the lieutenant's test by three days. You have to have three years as a sergeant. But then I had an opportunity to go to Washington, D.C., for a year to teach our patrol's aggressive driving program and once that came up, getting promoted went out the backdoor. I have another 13 years to become a lieutenant and I wasn't going to miss a once-in-a-lifetime opportunity. I shelved it but I went through the process because I thought it would be good knowledge. I think I placed 32 out of 35. The material's just coming out for the next exam that will start in March 2002. I'll finish going through the lieutenant's process and start my master's in public administration in September 2002.

We Use Our Brains

There are a thousand plus commissioned personnel and only 12 female sergeants and when you go to an outlying, remote area, you're dealing with these rugged men who've grown up in remote areas and have never even experienced a female trooper. So here comes this female and you always wonder how you're going to be accepted. One of the guys in my academy class is in my detachment. I'm supervising him now. But I went down there and they were having some problems with my being assigned there, and they've totally done a flip-flop. I don't know why, other than I know I set a good example. Because I like to get out there and work with them and I give them pats on the back when they have it coming. As a female, we shouldn't have to go the extra mile, but you always feel that you have to.

This speaks to a safety issue, but probably the most important quality is that most of us realize we're not big and strong like a lot of the men, obviously we have a different muscle mass and different structure. Women bring to the job being able to immediately think about what's going on and know how to talk our way out of a situation. Most women in the patrol can do that successfully. I have avoided conflict because I was able to think my way out of it and use the correct tone of voice. If you come across somebody violent who decides he doesn't want to go with you, you can't act like you're 6'4" and you're going to bully this guy. You have to use a softer tone and reason with the individual. It's gotten me out of some bad situations and I've seen it with other women. We've been able to use our brains and that's the most important quality a woman can have if you're out there working the roads.

We have a different mentality than men. A lot of men can continue with the job off duty and most have their buddies in law enforcement, so they'll go out shooting, hunting. Most women aren't into this when they're off duty. When I get home I am able to totally cut the job off. Once I'm out of the car, I'm a mother. I could be called out, and I have been called out, but I have a very supportive family and there was always somebody right there who was able to come over and watch the boys. When a lot of the guys get home from the graveyard shift, they can't sleep so they sit up watching TV. But within five minutes I'd be out of my uniform and in bed, out like a light.

If a woman is a ten-percenter—we supervisors spend most of our time with ten-percenters—she gets pulled in by the men who are negative, disruptive, misbehaving. That she happens to be a female, so be it. But if women are with men who are ninety-percenters, just wanting to do their job, women don't have that need to be one of the guys. You're just one of the troopers. The ninety-percenters, who are trying to follow the straight and narrow, don't like men or women misbehaving. They'll say, Gosh, she's got a filthy mouth. Or, I don't want anything to do with him.

I would guess the proportion of gay women in the patrol is at least a fourth. They have been very well accepted not only by the men but by the women. It's kept fairly quiet about the men in the patrol. Most people probably don't even know who's gay. The mentality is, if you're doing your job, we really don't care. It's probably a bigger issue with the straight men, maybe they've never been around gay men. I'm athletic, I've been around lots of gay women and I don't even blink.

Captain Annette Louie

Annette was born in 1957. She is married to a detective, has a daughter age 6, and a BA in business management. She went to the academy in 1980 at the age of 22. Her current role in the King County, WA, Sheriff's Office is commander of the Internal Investigations Unit, which handles complaints about commissioned and non-commissioned personnel from volunteers and interns on up.

The Chinese Family and Law Enforcement

I have worked since I was seven years old because my family owns a variety of businesses. Our father wanted us all to get accounting degrees and work in the family restaurants. I had no interest in restaurants or accounting. I had a boyfriend who worked in adult and juvenile detention who had acquaintances in the police department who said, You should test for this agency, it's a good job, good income, good benefits. I wanted to pay for my college education out of my own pocket and needed the income. My boyfriend's friend kept saying, I need you to come out here as a decoy prostitute. Back then Asian women were "in" on the streets.

I only had a high school education and I wanted to be on my own, making my own decisions. It was, Dad, you have your life but you're not controlling mine. I have always been the black sheep in the family. I'm the middle child. I had two above me and two below me who had their college education and everything paid for. But I was not going to be beholden to anyone, including my father. I don't know where that came from because everyone else stuck with the family. I moved out when I was 19. I come from a Chinese family and you don't do anything to embarrass them. I didn't think I was embarrassing anybody.

Needless to say, my parents were not pleased with my choice. Why didn't I go into accounting and became a CPA, a quiet little job a bookworm would do quite well in. That was not me. I'm a very outgoing, social person whereas my family is very introverted. My mother and father came from China and my mother is very old country, very quiet. Curiously, I'm the one who has been in a career the longest, 22 years. Everybody else has had changes in their jobs. Their companies would sell out or merge and they'd lose their job and have to find another. It happened again and again. My brothers and sisters are a great resource for me when I have a need to vent. Friends are great but they weren't raised with you, they don't know you inside and out.

Thoughts about Promotion

When I got promoted to a captain I worked three years in precinct field operations and administration. Last year I came to internal investigations as a captain. I've already been offered another promotion, a major's position, and turned it down. I would have had to go back to a precinct as a commander. But it would have meant that my husband would have to be transferred out of his current position. You want a happy home life, you don't do that. He's in a career path that he's enjoying, he is in a location he enjoys.

I'm not a fast-tracker. When people fast-track too fast into a promotional position when they have never learned their first position, then how do they mentor and guide people coming up? They don't, because they have never learned the answers themselves. I prefer to put my time in and learn the job inside out, so when somebody comes up behind me, I can train them. In a couple of years, if life has settled down at home, perhaps a major's position wouldn't be too bad.

Internal Investigations

We take complaints and decide if there is a misconduct component involved, and, if so, then we investigate it. Volunteers and interns, too, can do things that violate our policies and procedures. If it is so egregious, they're no longer volunteers. If a person is using their position in the department to influence, intimidate, obtain something of value for their own personal gain, they're not representing the department. If what they are doing is misconduct, they're no longer going to be here. We don't sell widgets out there. We provide a service to the community, which is law enforcement, and the community has to have trust in us that we're doing the right thing.

If you were a juvenile, 10-15, and you did something really stupid back then and now you're 35, we'd look into it because you still might have some criminal tendencies. Although most of the time with juveniles, the records are sealed. We all take a polygraph test and they ask, Did you ever commit a crime? Didn't we all do something as a kid that we knew was wrong? We knew the difference between right and wrong but we still did it. And if you got caught and got in trouble, you should have learned from it. Well, there are people out there who will never learn from their mistakes and that's why we have repeat offenders.

We don't want people who haven't done anything in their lives. We want some life experience. Some individuals try to get hired on who have a very clean record, have never had any problems, but they've lived at home forever, never been out on their own. They've gone to school but how will they deal with citizens who have all these dysfunctional things going on in their lives? Sometimes having led a very sheltered life knocks someone out, not understanding people who have problems.

Ethnicity an Issue?

I was the first Asian female cop hired in the department so that was a unique situation. I've never had any serious problems with the public. When I first got hired, the public would see this little person driving around and the department would get calls about some kid stealing the car. I was short and I looked pretty young. Every once in awhile I was called a derogatory name. My attitude was, That's your mindset, and I'll still treat you with respect and look objectively at whatever laws are affected, and whether or not you get arrested will be based on those laws, it won't be based on the color of your skin or anything else. But if you're operating at the level of calling people names, you obviously have no other skills.

The department has quite a few Asian males from a variety of backgrounds and there are a few other Asian females, but they're not full-blooded. When I first tested, I had my choice of either Seattle or King County. I didn't want Seattle because I knew where they'd stick me, in Chinatown, the international district, and I wasn't in the mood to be arresting relatives. I didn't want to be pigeonholed in one area. Almost all Seattle's Asian officers worked in the international district.

I think of myself as educating people culturally who have never dealt with a lot of Asians. Why do the Chinese do certain things? Why do we act a certain way? In some cultures you shouldn't look someone right in the face because it is demeaning. In other cultures touching is not all right. You don't touch me, you don't look me straight in the face, because if I'm looking down there's a reason, it's a sign of respect. But some people might interpret not looking you in the eye as untruthful. In Vietnam if you ordered an individual to get down on their hands and knees, a kneeling position, that means you are going to come up behind me and shoot me in the head. It is a suicidal position.

Different cultures come here with a lot of baggage from their countries. It's important that new recruits get this cultural education from people from these other countries as a part of their training. Not only for information but to teach them to respect other cultures. Our community service officers come from a variety of backgrounds, Cambodian, Vietnamese, Russian.

If you want an example of an issue from my own experience, I had problems with the firearm that I was given at the academy because the firearm had problems. The armorer we had kept telling me that I needed to strengthen my hand. He blamed it on me for being female and weak. Well, there was nothing wrong with my hand. When all the other instructors and other students who were expert shooters couldn't pull the trigger back, because it jammed, it was not a matter of the gun being too big or my hand strength being too weak. I decided not to use the department-issued gun. I bought my own.

Also on my own, I needed to work on my strength training, so I got into karate. I wanted to deal better defensively than with what the department had taught me. I did it so that when I got into situations where there was going to be a hands-on, the guys would know that if I was their backup, I'd never give up.

I had only been in the department a short while when I got into a fight with a guy with a gun that made me think, Is this the right job for me? The information that this guy probably had a weapon did not get out on the radio so I was the only officer responding to this call. I talked to him and maneuvered him into my patrol car, but I had this gut feeling. I got on the radio and said, I need backup, now. A sergeant came and I told him, I think this guy has a gun. When we get him out, we're going to have to deal with that.

We got him out and he wouldn't comply with us. He pulled out his gun and pointed it at me and we knocked him down. It was a fight of my life. We got him handcuffed and we finally got backup. We didn't have a personal assistance team back then, so I was on my own to deal with this emotionally. I kept thinking, I could have died tonight. Is this job right for me? I had to work it out for myself.

Solutions to Family Problems

A lot of females who have families start seeking positions in which they have a Monday through Friday schedule, weekends off. Daycare facilities mostly run Monday through Friday. So if officers are interested in having a family, the department is not going to stop them from applying for these jobs.

I carpool with one of our professional staff who lives close by and we chat about what's happening at work and other things that veer us off of work, such as plans for the weekend, what happened at the last Weight Watcher's meeting. From there I go to my daughter's daycare where sometimes it is chaos. The first thing I ask her is, How was your day? What happened in school? What did you learn today? What do you think we should do when we get home? What do you want for dinner? And when we get home there are certain things that we need to do, like deal with the school paperwork in her backpack. Now my focus is on what her needs are and work is no longer on my mind.

As far as housework goes, I can't stand to let things sit. If there is a certain project in the house I want done and my husband has said, I'll do that, and he doesn't, I'll do it myself. Because of my independence, I don't wait for him to do something. If I want to be happy in life, I am not going to be dependent on other people to make me happy. So my daughter has learned that if I want something done, it's going to get done. I also want my daughter to know that she doesn't have to be dependent on a male to do things for her.

Being in a nontraditional position helps me know that I'm competent. I have the respect of my coworkers. The troops out there know that I'm fair. If something were to happen to my husband, I wouldn't buckle. When I've had hardships in my life, I just worked harder. There are some women so dependent on men, that when that relationship fails, they totally fall apart. Not only has a long-term nontraditional career been good for me, but it's also proven that if I need to, I can take care of myself and my family.

From Cop to Professor

In June 2002 I interviewed Retired Captain Linda Forst in her office at Shoreline Community College in North Seattle where she is a Professor of Criminal Justice with a horrendously heavy teaching load. She was born in 1955 and is widowed with two daughters. She retired from Boca Raton, FL, PD in 1996 and moved to Seattle with her retired police captain husband, who two months after their arrival died of a heart attack playing golf.

For a sophomore writing assignment Brynn, Linda's older daughter, wrote about her Dad. When she shared the manuscript with her mother, they were finally able to talk to one another about their grief. They talked about how there wasn't anything to help teenagers whose parents are suddenly taken from them. Brynn said, "Maybe I could write something that would help other teenagers." So she did and Linda edited. They were almost finished when 9/11 happened. The younger daughter said, "Oh, all those kids whose parents aren't going to come home tonight."

Shoreline CC printed the booklet, *Heart to Heart: For teens who have lost a parent, From one who has been through it*, by Brynn Duke. Linda absorbed the cost as her contribution to the victims of 9/11. The booklet has been sent to hospices that sponsor grieving groups for teenagers and children. Through word of mouth the booklet has reached school counselors not only in Washington State, but also Florida and Texas.

When we met, Linda had 46 publications on her resume. Her bachelor's, master's, and Ph.D. are from Florida Atlantic University, Boca Raton, where she has also taught. Additionally, she has taught at Palm Beach Community College, Boca Raton, and Northwestern University, Evanston, Illinois.

Road Patrol Fits My Personality

I started off pre-med and didn't do as well as I had hoped which was disillusioning because I'd always been a very good student. I tried a bunch of different courses, one of which was Introduction to Criminal Justice. The instructor had been a police officer in California and Miami and I loved the course. On the internship I rode patrols, that's what I fell in love with, being out there in the middle of everything, Jack-of-all-trades. Road patrol meshed with my personality because I'm very outgoing and assertive.

My Dad raised us, four girls and a boy, to believe that you had to be able to support yourself. He had health problems so my mother often did support us. My Dad owned a restaurant, but told us to get civil service jobs where we'd have sick days, vacations, things he didn't have. He was very pro-police officers and the men in our town never paid for food. He wanted them hanging around in the restaurant. There were 17 officers in this small town, an hour outside New York. We had a volunteer fire department and when the fire whistle blew, Dad knew the codes and knew where the fire was, so he would go out and direct traffic in the middle of the town square. He was very excited when I joined, but unfortunately he died three years after I got on when I had just gotten into the detective bureau.

My Mom was a teacher who always told me to get a teaching degree to fall back on, which is what I'm doing now. She was nervous, she wasn't keen on it, but she felt the most important thing was that I liked what I did. I didn't think I'd stick with it more than a few years. I tested in 1976 and Boca Raton called me in 1977. My family moved to Florida when I was a senior in high school and I went to the state university in town.

At the time I went to the academy, New York PD had laid off 3,000 cops and they were all in Florida taking tests to get on. There were 300 applicants for every two positions. The city decided to use physical fitness first as a way to cut down the number of people taking the test and it virtually cut the list in half. I prepared for months in the Florida heat. I was a swimmer, and we had to swim. I ran a couple of miles a day, did push-ups and chin-ups. I was living at home so I had a chin-up bar installed in my bedroom door. I did well in the running and swimming but I just squeaked by in chin-ups.

One Person at a Time

I wanted a job where I could support myself and be independent, my own person. When oral boards ask people why they want to be police officers, they say they want to help people and make the world a better place. That sounds trite but it's very true. That's what you want to do, but after a time you're frustrated because you think you can't make those changes. But you can, one person at a time, one incident at a time. My husband and I talked about this a lot. We felt that if we could make the world just a little bit better than before we started, it was worth it. That's what keeps you going.

Unfortunately sometimes, the higher up you go in rank, the less it seems you get to do. You no longer get the, Thank you, Officer, I really appreciate your help. Instead you get officers who don't like you when you discipline them. But you can still make changes because you make policy decisions that benefit other officers or the public. I was very involved in domestic violence, sexual battery, and stalking legislation. I worked with the state representative to change a couple of those laws. And within the police, I worked on policies as to how we handle sexual harassment.

Back in the 1970s, if you didn't pay for a rape exam, they would bill your insurance company. Well, people didn't want their insurance company to know. We got the law changed so that the state covered it instead. We didn't have a stalking law, as most places didn't. I arrested a guy for stalking but I had to arrest him on another charge. He was a bad guy and was stalking this poor woman, making her life miserable. It was a classic case. The judge, very reluctantly, said I have to let him go because this statute just doesn't apply. There was a lot of publicity about the case because the victim was very open and helpful. So Florida developed a stalking law. I was very vocal and I feel I contributed to something that has made women's lives easier.

Most directly I was involved in changing the environment within the police department on the sexual harassment issue. Looking back, I tell my classes, I went through so much stuff that was sexual harassment but I didn't know it. To me it was, if you want to do a man's job, then you put up with it. As I moved up the ranks I got educated on those topics and looking back at it, I didn't have to take any of that stuff. We had four shifts. Of course, I had to go to a shift that didn't have a woman because, God forbid, you wouldn't want two women working the same shift. They picked my training officer on the basis of one criterion, that he was married. They didn't want to put me with a single guy riding around in a car for eight hours. He didn't have any training as an FTO, but because he was married that's who I got.

I spent a year of my shift handling the serious traffic accidents when there was a homicide. This particular evening the fatality guy for my shift and I got a call that somebody had encountered an accident and said it looked bad. Listening to the radio you could tell it was bad, send medics, send this, send that. When we got there, he said, Don't go over to that car. I said, I have to. He said, No, you can't. I said, It's my job. He said, It's a father and a daughter. The daughter's dead on top of him and he's groaning and you don't want to go there. I said, I appreciate your concern, but I have to measure and do all the things I'm supposed to do.

When I started as a road patrol officer our shifts rotated together, so I stayed with the same group of people basically for five years and we knew each other really well. In my third year we got a new sergeant. We got a call about a hostage situation at an apartment complex, a guy was threatening to throw a baby off a balcony if the girlfriend didn't come back to him. I got there, another officer and the sergeant got there right after me. I started taking control. I talked to this big guy in his early twenties and the girlfriend's crying and pleading. I spent 15 minutes calming him down and discussing what's going to happen if he does this or that. Eventually he gave the girlfriend the baby. My sergeant stood back and just watched. For days he went on about what a great job I had done. He was totally shocked that I had handled this potentially critical situation. The guy who backed me up said, What did he expect? We all knew you could do that.

On the Job as Captain

When I left Uniform Operations as captain, I looked over my shift lineups. On our evening shift we had three squads and each squad had six or seven people and four out of the six would be females. People bid for shifts and got them. We didn't say, Whoops, wait a minute. Too many women on that shift. Or too many Blacks in that squad. We now have females training females, females training males, and female sergeants. Not only was it hard to recruit females sometimes, but it was hard to get them to take the promotional exams.

Because of the seniority system, when you get promoted, you go to the bottom of the barrel for picking shifts. When I'd encourage women to take the sergeant's test, they'd say they didn't want to give up weekends off or the pick of the shifts. The only other objection I got from males and females was, Why should I?

Who wants the hassle? I just want to worry about myself. I don't want to worry about what other people are doing.

A student the other day said, I'd really like to go into law enforcement but I also want to get married and have a family and I don't think you can do both. I said, You can work it out. Take it like school, one quarter at a time. The one word of advice I have is to wait a little bit to have children because childcare is difficult, and the more seniority you have, they'll know you're a good worker and they'll bend.

Uniform Operations was my biggest job as captain. It was basically all the people on the street—road patrol, traffic, marine unit, bicycles, motorcycles, canine unit, special operations. I had a hundred people working for me of which 15% were females, most of them working in road patrol.

I Swore I Would Never Marry a Cop

I met him first when I did an internship in college, then later when I joined the Boca Raton Department he became a kind of mentor. Before I went to the academy I was working midnight shift, dispatching, and he would bring me coffee and we would talk. He was one of the few people who I felt was supportive and encouraging. We were just friends for a couple of years because I swore I would never marry a cop, but we did get married.

We were both officers, then he got promoted to sergeant, then I got promoted to sergeant. Then he got promoted to lieutenant, then I got promoted to lieutenant. Then I got promoted to captain. It was all testing up to the captain's process of appointment. Personally, I felt the chief should have asked my husband because he was the better candidate, but for whatever reason he felt I was. I said to my husband, This is what happened. What do you think? He said, Well, what do you think? You're the one who got offered the job. Do you want it? I said, I don't know.

We'd had problems in the past because a lot of men are threatened by women's promotions, so they would say nasty things to him, not when I was around, but anonymous notes, or make comments about his masculinity in this anonymous little publication that went around once a year. I said, You know how people are. He said, Linda, if they say something, that's their problem, not mine. I can handle it. If you want the position, take it. I took it and he ultimately got promoted again.

Making the Switch from Work to Home

My husband said to me, many times, You're not on the street at midnight. Relax. I worked midnights for five years until we had the kid. At midnight you had to take control. Midnight was more violent and disruptive situations than nicey-nice stuff. I was used to taking control and speaking in certain way and sometimes I would use that same tone with my kids. When I came home I ran to de-stress. But sometimes I would forget and when I wanted something done, I wanted it done now. He had no trouble making the switch. I'm a Type A person, he was a laid-back Type B. He was known as a listener in the department. People would go to him to talk. They would talk and he would listen. He mentored a lot of people.

The Constant Need to Prove Myself

We always had chiefs that came from within the department, but one time they went outside the department and a guy came in from Chicago where he'd just taken the sergeant's test. He'd been in the department a year when I took the ser-geant's test and came out number one, far above two, three, and four. No one else passed. He had acquired cronies by then and they were the ones who did not pass. He didn't like any of the four of us, so he had his cronies say the test wasn't fair and sue, saying they wanted the test redone. The union came to the defense of the four of us and hired a lawyer and ultimately we got promoted. But during my probationary time he made my life hell. I had the backing of all the people in between, the captain and lieutenant. He still did have those cronies who were patrol officers and they'd go straight to him instead of using the chain of com-mand and say whatever about me.

I always felt the need to prove myself. I knew as a patrol officer I had proved myself. But when I became a sergeant, I had to prove myself all over again, that I could be in charge and run the show. My husband and others would say, We know you can do the job, you don't need to prove yourself. But it's always there. I have to be the first one into the fight. I have to be the first one to pull up at the scene of the bloody mess.

I miss everything. I miss being out and about and involved finding out what's going on. Retirement is very hard. It's an adjustment and people don't realize it. I tell my students, you need to plan for retirement. We thought we'd planned. We planned finances and second careers. But psychologically it's hard. I went from being a police captain, where I would be just driving down the street, and wonder what's going on and pull over. What's going on? We got a situation, blah, blah. There was not a thing happening in that city or county that I did not know about.

Mentoring Experiences

I had no female mentors. I had a few people to talk to, my husband being the big one. I could totally trust him. They say you shouldn't bring your job home and we tried not to, but we often did, more so as we got promoted, and were dealing with personnel issues where you make a lot of hard decisions. The thing that he constantly reinforced was, You have to look yourself in the mirror every day. As long as you can look yourself in the mirror and believe you did the right thing, then that's what you should go with. When I was interning I did a little research study on, "Should Women Be Police Officers?" I gave out my survey to all 90 patrol officers in the department and they all filled it out. I tucked it away and didn't do anything with it. When we were packing stuff up to move out here, I found it. It's been 20 years that it's been sitting away in a file. It was disheartening. There were seven or eight who thought women could be police officers but only two or three that thought they could do patrol. Because I recognized handwriting, I knew my husband was one of them.

I mentored several women and several minority males because they faced a lot of the same obstacles and sometimes had a hard time fitting in. Both my husband and I encouraged one woman with a lot of potential. Although she was being trained by another officer, I made myself available and said, If you ever want to talk, come see me. We worked different shifts but we met routinely and I got her to join IAWP. My husband mentored her as well and she went on to become a lieutenant and then captain.

Teaching Criminal Justice

I started doing in-service training in sex crimes for the troops. I went to a special sex crimes school at the University of Louisville. Then the chief asked me to do in-service training in other areas like accident investigation. I just did this part-time because I liked what I was doing on the road or in the detective bureau and I didn't want to deviate from that. But at some point, I went back and got my master's degree, which lent itself to doing more teaching. I figured it was good experience to have if I wanted to do it when I retired. My husband was very supportive of my going to school, especially when I was going for my doctorate and we were in the process of adopting our second child. I could never have done it without him.

My teaching is an opportunity to influence future police officers because I came from a progressive department and a lot of people I've met out here are also progressive. But there are departments and people with antiquated views. If I can help educate them in a light matter, I like to do that. I teach Introduction, Investigations I, Investigations II, Juvenile, Criminology, Policing. I got into law enforcement because I happened to take an intro course. I'm committed to teaching the intro course because you get a wide variety of people, half are majors, half are not, they're trying it out. I've had a number of them say, I'm going to change my major to criminal justice. I like this.

I did recruiting and hiring for awhile, and I never understood why more women weren't going into law enforcement. I didn't know how to break that barrier. But now in my teaching, I can bring up the issues of women and minorities in police work more than might be addressed by another instructor. That also goes for getting discussions going on sex crimes and acquaintance rape. I give students a viewpoint that they might not otherwise get.

How the Men Have Changed

When I first started, most men would say they really didn't think women should be in police work but I was okay. Or, Cathy's on my shift, and she's okay. However, when I got promoted, it's one thing to work with a woman side by side, and another thing to do what she tells you to do. Over the years, it got easier, especially with new officers. We were hiring a lot of minorities because we had a very diverse population. A lot of men today have worked for women already, so they aren't averse to working for a female sergeant or lieutenant. My biggest challenge was when I got promoted to road patrol captain. I was promoted over a bunch of lieutenants with 20 years on, who went about sabotaging a lot of my efforts.

A lot of minority males, Asians and Hispanics, are not real big. I encouraged them at briefings to talk their way out of situations, that it's the safest thing to do. Nobody wants to get hurt and we don't want to hurt other people. They were very agreeable to taking the easier road out, physically, by trying to talk their way out of, or into, situations. Over time I also noticed big differences in other supervisors' handling of their personnel. More and more guys have childcare duties while their wives work. So the department as a whole became much more open to making little adjustments. If you can make a person's shift start a half hour later and now he's not late anymore, you still get the same amount of work out of him, even if he has to brief himself.

Resisting Marginalization

Independent personalities do not like to be oversupervised, overprotected, or channeled into "women's work." So they deal with it. Maybe not right away, especially when they're young, but eventually the offenders have to be challenged.

Retired Kent, WA, Officer Trisha King-Stargel: "I felt very good just getting through the academy and moving on. I wanted to get out of the classroom and into the street. I spent about four months on the training watch and then got put in at the receiving desk, an inside job taking in all the prisoners, getting them booked, managing that whole function. I had been there about four months and didn't see any light at the end of the tunnel. So I made up a list of all the female officers in the department and opposite their names what their assignments were. There was only one female officer working the streets. I posted that up on the bulletin board and my sergeant asked me, Are you trying to tell me something? I said, Sir, if I had wanted a desk job, I would have kept my last one. I want to be out on the street. He said, I thought you were happy working here. I said, I am happy working, but I'm not happy working here. It just so happened that there was an officer working patrol who wanted to go back to school. And he wanted to work in the booking area because when there were slow times, he could do homework. So they traded us out. But had I not complained, I may not have been considered for that.

My captain at that time, my first night on the job, called me into his office and he said I just want you to understand that I don't believe women should be in policing. And I will do everything I can to keep you in this assignment so that you're not out on the streets doing dangerous stuff. I thanked him for his opinion and had very few conversations with him after that even though his office is right off the booking area. He had to approve of my shift change and he did because I was outspoken about women's issues and rights and I knew what my rights were and I was willing to go to bat for them—I was a shop steward at that time—I don't think he wanted to take on the union. He figured I'd get hurt and come crawling back.

I continued to work for him out on the street, and my next big move was to the motorcycles. We had three-wheeled Harleys that patrol officers used rather than blue and white cars and I wanted to use those. Every time my name came up, he'd just shake his head, God, she wants to do this now. There was a lieutenant who worked in a different area and he used to come in a lot at night and sit and talk with the captain. He treated me with such incredible respect that when he came in, I would always make a point of getting him a cup of coffee. One night he was sitting in the captain's office and I gave him his cup of coffee and the captain said, You never get me coffee, and I said, Maybe you should talk with him about how to respect women that work for you. And I thought, I'm going to get so fired for this. When I left the police department there, that lieutenant wrote me a letter of recommendation and said if I needed any help at all getting jobs to let him now. He followed my career and was very supportive.

I had to ask the guys on my first cruises to quit interfering whenever I came up against somebody who raised their voice or started posturing and it looked like this was going to become a physical confrontation. My male partners would literally, physically, step in between us. And I told them, You've got to quit doing that. Most weren't even aware they were doing it. It was a reflex action for them. I said, I may need to get my clock wiped a couple of times before I figure out how to do it, but I need to figure this out for myself. They were very good at taking a step back and doing what I asked them to do. The other women, we were all so new in it together, I didn't get mentored by them except for the mother of eight boys, all in the police department. Her husband was also a cop. She filed the first lawsuit and eventually got promoted to sergeant detective."

More American Characteristics

Robin Haarr in a 1997 *Justice Quarterly* paper warns women police to resist "marginalization." Like Trisha's experience, marginalization means being placed on a light-duty shift, spending your time taking reports of stolen cars, answering alarm calls, and taking missing persons reports. It means handling dead-on-arrival calls, writing speeding tickets, and being placed in a one-person patrol car when two-person cars are the rule. Marginalization is accepting dead-end jobs such as radio dispatcher and desk attendant. Robin says when men attempt to direct you off the streets, stand up for yourself, speak your mind, and ignore sexist comments and behaviors.

Frances Heidensohn, a British social policy professor, says in *Women in Control?* (1992) that the most striking difference between British and U.S. police women in the '80s was that the Americans were establishing a distinctive female cop culture with the hallmark of networking and getting together to swap war stories. There was a great deal of laughter and mutual support when the women got together at conferences, meetings, and courses. Everyone returned home ready to fight the good fight once again.

Another key difference between U.S. and U.K. women police was American optimism that things were gradually getting better. She noted that the concept of pioneering was a very American thing and that her American interviewees saw themselves as pioneers. So, too, did the women now in their forties and fifties whom I interviewed. It is obvious from their stories that they endured hostility and harassment from the academy forward and persevered to prove they could make it. And getting promoted and moving up the ranks was a part of making it.

I'll end with Trisha's advice on getting through the academy. First and foremost she said: "You have to make up your mind that you're going to survive: You have to know you can play any game that the academy wants you to play for four months, six months, whatever it is. When I started in law enforcement I was 25 years old, a little older than some of my classmates. I already had some life under my belt. I knew I could play any game they wanted me to play because the end result was I was going to get a badge. So I could, Yes sir, with the best of them. I could stand tall at inspections. I could take the absolute most pointed criticism, some of it unnecessary, without shedding a tear.

Many academies are stress academies. The slightest thing you do wrong, they're on you. They want everybody to look, act, and talk the same. They want conformity and if you don't say it or do it the 'right' way, it's like, Down and give me 20 (push-ups). Yet we want people to come out of that experience being independent thinkers, especially when you're dealing with ethical issues and corruption."

Trisha made an arrest before she was out of the academy: "We had taken a test and we were given a longer than usual lunchtime. Because our academy was close to a mall, a bunch of us went there to eat. As I was walking into the mall, I saw these two guys running through the parking lot and one was yelling, Help, help, stop him, stop him, he just robbed us. The guy was running along some parked cars and he turned to come in between the cars trying to evade the other guy, and I was standing right there. I was in an academy uniform, a white dress shirt and navy blue pants, very military. I had my police department hat on because we weren't allowed to be outside without a cover on. I put my arms out and shouted, Stop, police. And he did. The guy behind him was a security officer and grabbed the guy, cuffed him up, and we got written up in the paper."

The chief way in which training could be improved according to my interviewees was having instructors who understood gender differences and worked with them. Number two was more practice at ground fighting, grappling, boxing.

Number three was informing women that they need to get in shape before the academy. Number four was mentors assigned to everyone for the whole time. Number five was constant review of the testing process so that it wasn't discriminatory. Lastly, they said, Get rid of age restrictions.

What personality traits can readers identify from these accounts to add to patience, resourcefulness, creativity, and the ability to take control of "situations"? And the big question, do you possess these characteristics?

11

Command Thoughts about Recruitment

One of my first interviews in the autumn of 2001 was with the University of Washington's Chief Vicky Peltzer. She was born in 1955 in Landstuhl, Germany. She is divorced and has a 23-year-old son. She'd been on the job two years, having retired from Albuquerque, NM, PD for which she worked 20 years. Her BA is in criminology, her MA in public administration, and a law degree is a future possibility. She has 54 commissioned officers (including seven women) under her command and an equal number of noncommissioned staff. Like other chiefs who have not been on the job very long, she had no time for anything but work, which goes against one of her firmest beliefs, that is, living a balanced life. I like to think that one of her biggest hurdles is behind her within a university community, comments like, Oh, You're so tiny, oh, you're so cute, I can't believe you're a police officer.

How to Get Promoted

I never expected to get the chief's job. Years ago I was very happy being a patrol officer. I had no desire whatever to be promoted, but eventually I needed more challenges. I got my master's degree and when I got promoted, I thought, Gosh, I think I can go to the next level, and went to the next level. The rank of captain was by appointment, not by a selection process, so that was a barrier and I didn't get promoted for whatever reason. I started accepting the fact that I might retire as a lieutenant, but I also started applying for other positions.

This job opportunity came up and I thought, What the heck. It looked interesting. I was prepared and here I am. My 20-year retirement gives me a different perspective; it's something I can fall back on. I always loved Seattle so we moved here even before I applied for the job. Still, my background is in city work and a university is a much different setting. The benefits are good and they're treating me very well. The administration is supportive but with budget cuts I had to lay off three people and that's the most difficult decision I've ever made.

There were times during my career, when I asked for a special assignment, that I was told specifically I would not get the job because I was female. For example, I applied for a criminalistics commander position. I studied real hard for it. I really wanted the position. I was competing against all males. After the interview I went back and talked with the captain and said, What could I do better, do different to help my career? The captain said, I'll be honest with you, it came down to the fact that you two finalists were both equally qualified but we thought because you were female, you wouldn't have as much prestige as a male. I was very disturbed by that, but I said, Okay, so what do I need to do now to overcome this barrier?

What I decided I needed to do was get better at interviewing. I started attending assessment centers so I could see better how they graded. I became an assessor, the subject matter expert for our own department, and used that to my advantage. When I interviewed for this job, it benefited me to use my losing not as a negative to fight back, but as a positive, What do I need to do?

Women need to understand that our management style is different from men's. Coming into this organization that was run top level by men for a long period of time, I recognized they had a real adjustment to make. When women order somebody to do something, it comes across much differently. We need to do a better job of teaching women how to use their management style in an effective way. This can be done through individual mentoring or in group sessions. From our own experiences we can say what worked and what didn't work for us.

To get women to take promotional exams we need to tell them how to prepare, then make sure that they are prepared, and have taken steps to get a broad view of the department where they work. I always preach that when you have an opportunity, you gotta take it. You can't wait for things to be handed to you on a silver platter. You have to get the training you need to work in different job assignments, get to know people, understand policies and procedures. You have to take the initiative.

What I get most from the National Association of Women Law Enforcement Executives is inspiration. When I came back from the NAWLEE conference in Orlando, I was all fired up. They have positive speakers and support groups for networking. When I applied for this job, because of my network I called two chiefs at other universities and said, This is my first time applying for a university position. What can you tell me? They were absolutely wonderful. If I hadn't had that network, I wouldn't have been able to talk to anybody. They gave me insights that helped me get the job.

What I Like Best

I like making decisions and problem solving, always looking at what's best for the entire department. What better place to be than a chief's job to problem-solve. My job is to convince people that what they've been doing all these years is okay, but there are more efficient ways to do it. With budget cuts I have to be very effective with what I've got and also come up with creative ways of finding funds.

They've been doing everything by pen and paper in dispatch. Computer programmers out there have developed very effective systems, record management systems, to log and tie in together everything. Once we get that in, it'll save so much time, we'll be able to do crime analysis, have accurate information about how long it takes us to get to calls. We'll be able to tell the university what we actually do for them. We've also been changing the budget process; again, it was by pen and paper.

It used to be that top-level only made decisions. We're pushing decision making further and further down, allowing officers to do POP, getting them involved in problem-oriented policing projects. They love it. There were officers in the dorms but there's much more to community policing, such as involving the community to help solve problems. We're empowering committees within buildings to solve some key issues.

Take the problem of skateboarding. There is even a web site that says this is the place to come skateboard. Recreational skateboarding is dangerous not only to the skateboarders but to people walking through Red Square. We have had beautiful art pieces there that were ruined. We involved Facilities and had benches installed that are inconvenient for skateboarders. We involved University Relations and the Student Association in putting up signs that recreational skateboarding is prohibited.

I'm a big proponent of long-term recruitment, getting officers out talking with kids. Explorer posts are good. Through the high schools you can get students involved so they can see what the job is and if they're comfortable with the environment. I've had them change the recruitment brochure to show pictures of women and racial minority officers.

Our department has seven students who meet on a regular basis. They have uniforms, they practice crime scenes, they go to a week-long exercise in the summer where they do accident investigations, and they're graded. We send them out in uniform and have them attend crime prevention groups when they're set up on campus, so they're visible and another recruitment tool. We also speak to Society and Justice classes and tell them about the career opportunities, including the Explorers.

My Mentoring

Where I used to work as soon as women told the department they were pregnant, they were put in office jobs. We fixed it so that it was their choice and their doctor's choice whether and when they should come off the street. We also changed maternity leave, so that they didn't have to burn up all their vacation and sick leave and then go on maternity leave without pay, at the end of which they were broke. We worked it out so they could take some days of leave without pay throughout that period and keep their vacation and sick leave so that it didn't have such a disastrous financial impact. That program benefited the men, too. By having men sitting on committees and listening, they get a better understanding of and buy into women's issues and we get their side, too, their perceptions.

When I hire a new female officer, I sit down with her and say, What you do at the very beginning of your career affects the rest of your career. I made the mistake when I came on, thinking I had to be one of the guys, talk like them, act like them, use foul language, go to the parties. Luckily I realized pretty early on that I could be me and still be a good officer. I didn't have to give up my femininity. I encourage new females to think of what they will do, faced with certain situations. The message is, Think before you act. I've had women come up to me later on in their careers and say, Thank you for giving me that talk. I now realize what you meant. I didn't at the beginning but I did later on.

I'd tell them how when I had a male partner, and he would take over, after the call I would say, You probably didn't realize what you were doing, but this was my call and I would appreciate it if you would let me handle it. You stepped in front of me. He would go, Gosh, I didn't realize I did that. Or where a citizen was addressing me but would look at him and not me. I would say afterward, You probably didn't pick up on it but did you notice how he gravitated towards you? The way for you to deal with this in the future is to say, You need to talk to this officer. I'm only here to assist. When I started doing that, it worked. If someone said, Ahh, you're too sensitive. I'd challenge him and say, Okay, you watch the next time and see if I'm right. I'd make it a joking thing, and, sure enough, it would happen and they would say, Oh, I see what you're talking about.

In spite of what Vicky said about having no time for anything except work, she hosted the seventh annual NAWLEE conference in Seattle in August 2002. Says their brochure: "NAWLEE has been involved in numerous selection processes throughout the United States as assessors, mentors, resources and decision makers. More women hold positions of executives in law enforcement than when NAWLEE began."

Chief Kristen Anderson

When I interviewed Kristen in autumn 2001, we sat in a back room of her new house in the woods of the Olympic Peninsula. Kristen was born in 1968 in Oakland, California. She's married to Brian, a county deputy sheriff, who chopped firewood while we talked. She is Chief of Port Townsend, WA, PD, where the population is 8,500 without the tourists. But usually there are tourists, the lifeblood of this restored Victorian town. She joined this PD in 1997 as an officer after four years with suburban Lynnwood, WA, PD. She was promoted to sergeant in 1998, and in 1999 shared the acting chief position with another sergeant until her promotion in August 1999.

Making My World Bigger

It made me angry that there were so many parts of the world and so many things off-limits to me as a small female, limitations imposed on me through no fault of my own. I wanted to make my world a little bit bigger. Every time you conquer a fear, your world gets bigger. I wanted to be able to face those challenges head on, and it's done that, and much more, for me to be in this career.

I graduated from the University of Washington in 1991 with a degree in English with a writing emphasis. I started working in health clubs when I was 16 and started teaching aerobics when I was 17. I aerobiced my way through college, teaching eight to 12 classes a week. Then I was the aerobics coordinator at a health club and started my own personal training business for people in their homes. How I got into law enforcement was kind of an accident. My fiancé at the time was a firefighter so I was familiar with the EMS system. It intrigued me but I didn't want to go into the fire service or medical. One of my aerobics students was a female officer who was a recruiter and she encouraged me, so I rode along with some female officers from different departments and got a lot of my questions answered. I had thought it was unrealistic for women as small as myself to get in over their heads to try to prove something. But the training, the tools, and the preparation are very adequate and women definitely have their place.

My Mom wasn't crazy about it. She wished I wouldn't subject myself to the perils of law enforcement. She still worries, that's what you do when you're a mom. But she's very proud of me. She would never tell me not to do something that I wanted to do. My Dad has always been supportive of anything I decided to do. My brother thought it was nuts, but he's nuts, too, a buck-the-system kind of a guy. It's ironic that I chose this line of work, but he's been very supportive of his little sister becoming a cop.

I started testing as soon as I graduated and got picked up by Lynnwood in 1993. I love to write and I had hoped to pursue a career in writing, but journalism wasn't my thing. I also thought about teaching but I hate sitting still. My orientation is much more active and physical. Police work drew me because it's a wild mix of both. No day is ever the same, however, it has also become quite academic. I write more now than I ever did in college.

Defensive Tactics Was My Thing

The academy is tough, physically. Women need to work harder to keep up. A lot of guys take their brawn for granted and don't keep themselves up, so women have a great advantage if they continue to work at it. I see a lot of females, at a very young age, who are terribly out of shape, overweight, and who don't have healthy lifestyles. Even in elementary schools, more and more kids have sedentary lifestyles. You definitely have a leg up if you're in shape. Then when you get into the career, exercise is a great stress release. You'll keep your longevity personally and career-wise.

I did very well in defensive tactics. Also, at that time, they had the Thousand Minutes and Hundred Mile Club. If you were a runner, you would log your miles and if you did other things aerobically, you logged your minutes over three months. I did both. I dispute different physical standards for males and females to enter into police work. It sends the wrong message. When you get in your patrol car, and you're out there, you're not going to get sent to different calls because you're female. The demands on you are not going to be any different. Lesser standards for women suggest to males in the class that you are weaker because not as much is expected of you.

In my academy class we had more women than any class to date, ten women out of the 29 who graduated. My roommate and I were the only two who could make the obstacles courses, get over the wall consistently. We ran together every morning and lifted weights in the evening. It disappointed me that the other women made it through without ever having to meet that standard. If you're out there and your partner jumps over that six-foot fence to get the bad guy and you can't get over it to help, that's a very bad thing. When I got to Lynnwood PD, the chief asked me to apply for a defensive tactics instructor position. I was the first and only female ever in that position in that department. I went through the level 1 and 2 defensive instructor classes and level 2 in ground fighting and weapons. When I came out of that class, I was so covered in bruises that my husband didn't want to go anywhere with me in public because he thought he'd be accused of having inflicted them. There was a lot of hair pulling, getting thrown to the ground, arm twisting, wrist twisting, the chances for injury are fairly high. Nobody really relishes pain, even me, but it was very confidence building.

If You Go to Them

The first 18 months of being chief it was nonstop. I didn't do anything else. The department is too small for me to be able to staff things out, so I wind up doing a lot of things myself. I don't have an assistant. I keep my own schedule, for better or worse. I wear a uniform to work every day. It's a small building, so I interact with the staff and patrol officers every day. The community of Port Townsend was pretty clear with their complaints in past chiefs. They wanted somebody who would be a community member, involved, visible, so my role is being the face of the police department, the personality that people associate with the PD. Even if the community doesn't get to know all of the officers, if they feel like they know me, they will transfer that feeling to everyone in the department. The future of the department depends on how I present myself in public. And it's a small town, so there's nowhere to hide.

Ownership in the process is important. What do you want? I'm not going to tell you to work four 10s. I'm going to ask you, instead, If you could come up with the ideal schedule, what would it be? We now have a mixture of four 10s and five 8s. They can choose, they can swap, they know when the rotations are. If you go to them, rather than telling them, This is what you're going to do, it works.

Women have a tremendous amount to offer in public service. They tend to be detail-oriented, compassionate, and talk their way through things, by necessity largely. My husband is a police officer, 6'3", 230 pounds. He doesn't have to take the time to talk things through. If he decides to take somebody on, and they decide to take him on, it probably won't go well for the other person. But when you're my size, you're forced to use your verbal and communication skills. Law enforcement in this country, as it has evolved over the last 30 years, has moved more toward accountability and away from "the end justifies the means" methods, which the public used to support—"I don't care what happens to the bad guy after you've get a hold of him, just make him go away." People are much more scrutinous of law enforcement, as they should be. Women bring balance to law enforcement, which is critical.

Recruiting Girls

There is still a lot of mystery about what police do. We need female police role models in the educational system starting at an early age. When I go to schools now, it is not such a shock to those kids. They don't have a problem accepting me. I hope that little girls meeting me tells them that girls can do anything. Teenagers are my favorite age group. They are idealistic, motivated, cause-driven, and believe that when they graduate from high school, they can change the world. Adults tend to lose that and that's too bad.

I like working with teenage girls. The high school has a mentorship program. They ask various businesses in the community, if there are students interested in what they do, would you let them be interns? We have done this for years, and curiously enough since I've been there, it's always been girls. The young gal that we had last year took on the cadet program that I had always wanted. But I needed somebody with motivation to take the ball and run with it. She did a lot of research and we wound up putting together a joint cadet program with the sheriff's department. Both agencies felt the kids would get broader experience by working with rural county deputies and the city police. It's also been a bridge between the sheriff's department and the police department. She was so enthusiastic she'd come in and we'd spend a lot of time talking. We have eight cadets, and half are girls she recruited from school. She's has now gone off to study criminal justice in North Dakota.

I'm not sure there is one central place to recruit the group I'd like to—women who don't have a college degree, nor the most privileged upbringing, and are on the fringe financially, struggling to make it. But they're motivated and their intentions are to make their community a better place. They just haven't been given the opportunity. I'm not sure how to reach them. Our economy is depressed, and most of the jobs that young adults wind up with are food service, tourism, and retail.

One Size Doesn't Fit All

My biggest frustration as a line officer was feeling that departments had a cookie cutter approach to rating and training officers. They had an ideal of what an officer should look and perform like and everybody had to do it that way. It's a field so broad, that to force everybody to do the same things, things they aren't necessarily comfortable doing, they don't like doing, means they don't do them very well. In the meantime the department is missing out on their special talents. More women would stay in the police if they were allowed to move in the directions that motivate them the most, and where they could excel and succeed. The women who do stick around in law enforcement are women who successfully found that place.

Law enforcement, like every other business and profession, needs to look for new ways of doing things. The world is changing and we have to change with it. My feeling is not to try to make every person fit some ideal, but to figure out what makes that person go, why did they join up, what do they really like to do, and then support them and give them extra training in those directions. And not say, "You need to write 25 tickets a month and if you don't write 25 tickets a month, then you're going to be sanctioned for it." That person may be an excellent investigator, and spend lots of extra time on investigations, but isn't into making traffic stops. There's always punishment associated with not performing to a standard. But there aren't the rewards to make up for it on the other end.

What The Job Does to You

Creativity in scheduling and letting officers have ownership in the process are important. Whenever you work 24/7, somebody's going to have work nights and shift work is a fact of life. Shift work is a huge issue in terms of morale and keeping good people. Your schedule impacts when you eat and sleep, when you see your loved ones, when you get to play. Scheduling is not addressed as an important issue as often as it could be. Some agencies have done very creative things in scheduling, but a lot look at alternatives and say, No, that'll cost us more in overtime, it's not efficient, doesn't serve the department's needs. In a small department like ours, coverage is always an issue, but a few years ago, the officers had been saying, we'd really like to work four 10s. It had been denied and denied and denied. They had a bizarre rotation system through a five 8s schedule that didn't maximize coverage anyway. So when the last permanent chief left, we came up with our own schedule, which was a product of what the officers had wanted.

Even though there was an extended period between chiefs, the officers' morale stayed up and people stuck around who probably would have left otherwise.

Departments also need to do a better job of telling recruits what the job does to you and how to deal with that. Now, in the year 2001, given what we know about the effects of stressful work, a lot of agencies don't make allowances for counseling and time off. Being involved in a shooting can have severe long term effects because of the way an officer is treated afterward—no leave, no counseling.

We recently had an officer whose wife was very sick. This was a second career for him. There were a few weeks where it looked like she might be terminal. They were waiting for tests to come back. She was in a lot of pain and he said, If she's dying, I'm quitting and we're going to travel until she can't anymore. I don't want to spend her last days working. What we were prepared to do was ask him instead to consider a leave of absence, knowing that if she passed on, in a year's time or so, he's going to need to do something again, and to leave that option open. As it turned out, she's okay, the cysts were benign and he came back to work. This kind of decision builds loyalty and we didn't want to lose a good person.

Mentors Are Important, Too

Chief Anne Kirkpatrick of Federal Way is one of my mentors. She was my tac officer in the academy years ago. She has a very good reputation among her staff. The officers love her. She works a patrol shift at least a few hours once a week. She's down there in the trenches with them. It's difficult to come into an organization, regardless of your gender, and bring about the kind of respect they have for her. That agency had some big problems when she came in so she's doing very well down there. She has a law degree and is a practicing attorney. She taught criminal law at the academy when I was there and is a very good instructor, great sense of humor. She's hilarious. She's had a long career in different parts of the country, through different ranks, has worked at the academy, has been the chief in different organizations, and she has a very interesting perspective.

If you go into an organization and you're different in any way, the more time and energy you spend making it the issue, the more of a problem it's going to be for you and everyone else. When I was hired at Lynnwood, I was the only female on patrol for my first year there, and those guys hadn't worked with a woman for well over a year. I didn't want me being the girl the issue and I didn't want to make locker room humor the issue—"Don't talk like that in front of me." I decided that I'm just the gray person. I'm here to absorb the culture and learn and become part of it.

Overcoming Overprotection

Definitely, when I started out, whenever I would go to a call, for example, a burglary alarm, I'd get there, door's kicked in, so I'd set up a perimeter, and call for the dog. Somebody gets to go in with the dog and search if it's a large commercial building. And where I didn't want to be was at the southeast corner of the perimeter sitting there for the next 45 minutes doing nothing but shivering in the middle of the night. I wanted to go in with the dog. It was my call. It kept happening. I'd get sent to the southeast corner because the guys were going to go in and do the man thing. Or going to domestics, a two-officer response. I found myself always being the secondary person. The officers would push past me—they were going to take care of things. Brian was an officer there at the time, we worked the same shift, and he and I had become friends. I told him one day, I'm really sick of this happening. And he said, Well, that's your problem. If it requires physically grabbing them and moving them out of the way so that you get to take the lead, then that's what you're going to have to do, because they're going to keep doing that as long as you let them. He was right. I had to grab guys and get them out of my way, or demand, This is my call. I'm going in with the dog. You go here, you go there. The same thing happened when I came to Port Townsend. Even though I had more experience than many of the guys, initially there was that overprotective thing. But it goes away if you make it go away.

As far as channeling goes, I always got sent to interview rape and child abuse victims. The men would go talk to the suspect. With female suspects and prisoners I always got called to do searches when the guys had been doing them for years before I got there. They just didn't want to. They would always find an excuse to get me to do something that was kind of a girl thing. However, with the rape victims and kids, I really like doing interviews.

Supervision Can Be Very Lonely

When this police department sought a new chief in '98, they had over 80 applicants, weeded it down to four, and did an assessment center on those four. They made a job offer that the guy turned down. They decided there was no number two and quit. They did it again the next year. Same thing happened. There was not one single woman who applied either time. The interim chief told me that chiefs hire and promote in their own image. If you are a middle-aged white male who has been in law enforcement for twenty-plus years, you're looking for a white male who reminds you of yourself when you were that age. And if most police administrators are middle-aged to older white males, they don't see themselves in the women who are coming up through the ranks.

The standards and qualifications made for the position created a résumé that most women don't have yet, because women haven't been in law enforcement long enough to get that kind of experience. I didn't fit the qualifications either time so I never applied. It was not where I was headed or where I wanted to go. It was more a series of bizarre circumstances that led me to get the job because I did not meet those criteria.

A lot of women don't want to get promoted because they know what they're going to face when they get there. If you have to supervise a bunch of alpha males, they are going to try to pull that rug out from under you at every turn because they can't stand the thought of a woman telling them what to do. Supervision can be very lonely. I felt a sense of alienation when I became a sergeant even though I was still out on patrol and part of the team. But when you move beyond that, you don't have that one-of-the-guys feeling and that is one of the reasons why people stay in law enforcement and why people who leave law enforcement come back. It's being a part of something. It's unlike any other culture, any other organization anywhere.

I don't feel lonely now. Certainly initially it was harder. Now the only time I feel lonely is when I have to make really tough personnel decisions. I've had to encourage some people to leave. And you can't be a friend. You have to be professional and supportive, and when it's time to go, it's time to cut it off. The rumor mill in law enforcement is pretty powerful; everybody likes to talk. So when those particularly difficult decisions need to be made, they're made alone, but certainly with input from my command staff. My command staff is very supportive and I rely on them heavily. I am very fortunate in that respect. I don't see that everywhere. I see organizations where the people at the top have people just below them doing what they can to undermine.

I don't think I could have survived the last two years without Brian. He has no issues about who he is, or his place in the world. He's incredibly supportive and he's a great cook.

I don't think that the way to get ahead is to disparage anyone else. Two of the biggest problems in police administration are the issues of power and control, and who gets the credit if things go right, who gets the blame if things go wrong. You need to be willing to relinquish power and control, and say, this is a team effort, it is not about me or you, it's about us. It doesn't matter who gets the credit. If someone else wants the credit, that's okay. The point is the job gets done and it gets done right. I don't like to see finger-pointing or hear blame assignments.

My Proudest Moment on the Job—So Far

This has been a particularly busy summer for our department. August was really, really difficult. We were short-staffed with two supervisors on vacation for two weeks. During that time some major things happened, one right after the other. One of my sergeants, a woman, organized what wound up being a multi-agency search warrant where we recovered six bombs, a bunch of narcotics, made two arrests, took a 10-month old child who was meth-addicted. We used animal control, the sheriff's department, Washington State Patrol, their bomb squad, their bomb dog, child protective services, our citizen volunteers—our citizen volunteer force outnumbers our paid staff, by the way. They did perimeter and traffic control. There was a huge, huge effort put into this mission that she coordinated. Brian is the firearms and tactics instructor for the county. We have a joint training program with them, so he worked with his counterpart from our department to do the entry and search. We don't have a SWAT team out here. They spent several hours that morning getting everybody trained up for this specific mission. They had a raid plan. The fire department was standing by. Hundreds of pieces of evidence were gathered.

Then that weekend we had a fair. We were supposed to staff a booth at the fair. The ferry system imploded and we had to staff three people a day three days in a row, eight hours a day, to control the traffic at the ferry dock. When the weekend was over, we had a homicide, a live-in caretaker for a gal with MS took her out into the woods, shot her, was supposed to shoot himself but he couldn't get the nerve up. In desperation he brought her to the police department, so this woman who is shot in the head in strapped into the passenger seat, and he drives up and says, Help me. I just killed my girlfriend. The same evening we had a suicide.

The thing that I was so proud of was how everybody came together, the officers were beyond reproach with their work ethic, their willingness to work together, the face that they presented to the other agencies on the search warrant made the whole organization look good. Everyone was a part of the effort and in a time of crisis to see everybody pull together like that and do things right, that is my proudest moment.

Improving Recruitment

It is way too early to see the success of agency efforts to adopt the National Center for Women & Policing's *Self-Assessment Guide* for recruiting women, however, one vital factor should be exploited, and that is each officer's family and friendship network. Within this network every officer can influence the career choices of significant others. From the chief on down to patrol, on and off the job, everyone needs to pester, prod, and persuade women whom they judge have "the right stuff" to take that test. Studies of recruitment by the New York State Patrol found contact with a trooper was the single most important influence on people and recommended that chiefs and other police executives find ways to get all sworn officers involved in recruiting (Campbell and Christman, 2000).

"Accept the Challenge" is Washington's King County Sheriff's Office recruitment brochure. It shows women on patrol and doing detective work indoors and outdoors. It features a photo of eight deputies of whom three are women, a blonde, a brunette, and an African American. Every department I visited had stacks of little "Accept the Challenge" cards on the counter. "Continuous Testing. Apply Any Time." Some researchers have opined that once the proportion of qualified females is large enough, there is no longer a need for aggressive recruitment. The King County Sheriff's Office begs to differ.

In tallying ideas of how to improve recruitment, word of mouth won hands down. "We should all play the role," is how one woman put it. Number two was high school and earlier recruitment: career days, cadet programs, interns, summer teen academies, Explorer posts. Number three was ride-along programs. Number four was community college criminal justice programs and athletic departments.

Other ideas were more women recruiters, state fair booths, improved police web sites, military recruitment, citizens police academies, health and fitness clubs, and targeting other departments' officers to get lateral transfers.

The Albuquerque Police Department will be hosting a Women in Policing Career Fair August 3, 1996, at the Albuquerque Police Academy. You are cordially invited to join us for a few hours to learn about a woman's role in law enforcement as one of Albuquerque's "finest."

If you are interested in a challenging career where you make your own decisions, help the community solve problems, and help those in need, come to our career fair. The career fair will include Chief Polisar, a panel of policewomen discussing issues involving women in police work, salaries and benefits, how to apply, and what the application process means.

So read a letter signed by Lieutenant Vicky M. Peltzer.

Retired Kent, WA Officer Trisha King-Stargel agreed with Vicky about the many, many jobs one can do as a police officer: "It has an incredible breadth of different niches that you can fill, and you can do them all over the course of your career. If you never want to get promoted, if being a supervisor or manager isn't your style, you can be a trainer, work with volunteers, be a school liaison officer, be an investigator. Some people like investigative work but don't like the basic stuff of patrol. You can work where you want to live. If you want to work in a rural area, you can. If you want to work in a high population area, you can. When I came to work for this city it had 52 police officers and I was coming from an agency of over 1,800 officers. This department was specifically what I was looking for.

One strategy is showing success for women and minorities. You have to start at the high school level, letting people know that they can be successful as a police officer, and that it isn't like what the drama shows on TV make it, like NYPD. Even COPS shows all of the hot action stuff but doesn't show what the job is like on a moment-to-moment basis. We need to teach students that their gifts, talents, and skills can be used to better their community. It's not like you're going to go out and save the world but you can enter it saying, If I can make a difference in one person's life in the 25 years that I do this job, it's going to have been worth it.

The other piece is letting women know what the breadth of work is. Yes, you have to participate in the patrol division before you go anywhere else, but that is the foundational work. Yes, sometimes it's scary, and, yes, in some cases you're dealing with people you'd cross the street to avoid. But you can override that instinctual stuff and find interesting and varied ways of dealing with situations other than brute force. Because women's first instinct isn't to beat somebody over the head but rather to negotiate, we have made a huge change in how policing is done now. The agency I went to work for in 1977 would be totally extinct had it not been for the influx of women. We bring something so incredibly necessary to where the work has evolved to today. Both men and women are necessary to get the job done.

As far as how to recruit, everybody's going to get the nudge from a different place. I remember lying in bed all day on a Sunday reading this book, a true story, about the experiences of a woman who went to work as a police officer for the NYPD transit authority. After that book, I was positive I wanted to be a police officer. So in addition to schools being a good place, it has to be in truthful, genuine writing. And we've got to be smarter in marketing. You have to take your brightest and best women and put them out on the forefront. I used to do a pre-test orientation for people who had applied to take a test—how to take it, what to expect, and answer questions. One of the things that I preached to them was, You've got to want this and you've got to want it for all the right reasons. It's not something you're doing because somebody else wants you to. So all of the ways that we can possibly attract and recruit women should be used."

Sequim, WA, PD Sergeant Sheri Crain emphasizes policing's service orientation: "That if you want to give back to your community, this is a great way to do it. I talk about the whole criminal justice system because people get a little fixated on police officers, whereas there's detention officers, corrections and probation officers, a wide range of jobs that need good people. I tell high school students, Go to college, get a job, use those three years productively because the more experience you have under your belt, the more likely you are to get hired. Don't dwell on, Oh, I have to wait three years. Use those years doing things that are going to get you your goal."

An academy lieutenant wants educating children to the realities of law enforcement to start early so little girls grow up thinking of it as a possibility: "In high school young women need to get to know and talk with female officers. It's like anything else, if you plant the seed there's a possibility that it'll grow. I've only been involved giving talks in my kids' schools. My oldest son when he was little I had him in town one time and we saw some firemen on a fire truck and stopped to chat with them. And one asked him, So are you going to be a police officer like your mom when you grow up? And my son said, No, that's for girls. I want to be where the guys are. I want to be a fireman."

In all my interviews, only Major Robin Fenton and Deputy Debbie Kronk were recruited at a community college via a criminal justice class. No one said job fairs, career days, or open houses had drawn them in. What just about everyone said was that they had been encouraged to take the test by family members and friends in law enforcement. An army reserve colleague of Sergeant Dianna Klineburger told her the Port of Seattle was hiring. The state troopers in Karen DeWitt's volleyball team urged her to apply. A female patrol officer in Kristen Anderson's aerobics class pushed her to do ride-alongs. Fathers and uncles, brothers and sisters, male and female friends who were police officers or wanted to become police officers recruited these women.

This chapter has been more than lessons on how to recruit. It also has good advice on how to get through training, how to supervise and mentor, how to get promoted. But perhaps most important, it reminds women officers to regularly review their relatives, neighbors, members of groups they belong to, to see if there is someone they should be encouraging to enter law enforcement.

12

A Suburban Commander and a Small Town Chief

What's it like for a woman to be a chief of police? How are their personalities, motives, values different from rank and file officers and male chiefs of police? What sort of management style do they use? What do they want to accomplish? What are their major job satisfactions? Here we'll add to what you already know, however, most of the women I talked to do not aspire to be a chief or a sheriff. Both are political positions and they don't want to get involved in politics. So this is a worrisome sex difference in that more men, already a far greater proportion of police officers, are willing to get political.

An academy lieutenant put it this way: "I don't know a whole lot of women who want to be chiefs of police. I know a lot more men who want to be chiefs of police. Now why would that be? I never wanted to be, not because I didn't think I could do it, but because I don't want to mess with the politics. It's been driven into the men of my generation, you've got to move up or you're nothing. If you don't advance, that's a bad thing. You don't see that so much in women. Five years ago I might have wanted to be a chief but you have to sacrifice a lot to be the head of anything and my priorities are changing. I'm focusing more on home and life away from work as I get closer to retirement."

Retired Kent, WA, Officer Trisha King-Stargel opined that men approach competition differently than women: "There is so much emphasis on competition, as opposed to, Do you want to become a supervisor because you have the ability to supervise the work of other people so that the job gets done more efficiently and effectively? We need to teach women how to deal with that competitive edge. It would be wonderful if you could change the process, but they're not going to, because they've done tests and assessments for eons and they don't know what else to do. And in defense of the administrations, you've got the issue of civil service and unions. You've got to have some kind of criteria, you can't give merit-based promotions because then you get into favoritism and that doesn't work well with people who have gender issues. One of our officers who got promoted took the test and came out number one on the list. We were talking about the oral interview, which is very rigorous, and she said she was lying in bed the night before and thinking back to when she was little and how every time she'd had an opportunity, she'd always taken charge of something. And when they asked her the question we know they're going to ask, Why do you think you'd be a good sergeant? she said, Because I've been preparing for this all my life. I've done this and this and this, and I've always been in charge of these things and I've always progressed. This fits me. She's been a wonderful sergeant and a lieutenant's exam is coming up soon and she'll take it and do very well."

In looking over what the women had to say about promotion, they were adamant that the same testing process straight across the board be given everyone. The best person for the job should get that job. Several recommended in-service training on promotion, teaching women the process and how to go through it successfully. Several mentioned that people close to age 50 should be encouraged to retire. But there's still the issue of how can we get our young women to promote? Why don't they have the incentive?

Commander Gail Marsh

Born in 1953, Gail Marsh is divorced with two sons, 27 and 16. She has a BA in liberal studies and an MA in organizational development, both achieved while working full-time. She described her role in the suburban Redmond, Washington, PD as oversight of the criminal investigation division, all the community outreach programs—volunteers, crime prevention, family violence unit—and the department's national accreditation effort. Women constitute 22% of Gail's commissioned officers. When she joined Redmond in 1980 she was the first woman they had ever hired. Gail's e-mail signature is "Happiness is a journey, not a destination. So—work like you don't need the money, Love like you've never been hurt, And dance like no one's watching."

How I Fell into Police Work

I was working my way through college apprehending shoplifters at a big department store. To tell the truth, I never thought about being a police officer. I took the test on a dare to get one of my girlfriends off my back. The next thing I knew I was passing all these things and got hired. She really, really wanted to be a police officer and kept saying, You need to do this. Finally, I said, Where's the next test? She said it was here. I didn't even know where this place was. It was a little tiny town back then, 23,000 people. When I'd passed the written test and they told me what the physical was, I didn't think I could pass the physical, going up and over a six-foot wall. My brother-in-law was sure I couldn't do it so I bet him a steak and lobster dinner. The morning I woke up to take it, it was snowing. The only thing that got me over that fence was that lobster sitting up there.

My mother assumed I would be running around with some guy in a car or be a detective working behind the scenes. When I explained that I was a patrol officer working by myself, she was apprehensive. I ended up graduating number one in my class and my Dad got up and started whistling. I was so embarrassed. He was very proud and ended up having a second career, after the military, as a supervisor in probation and parole. The military upbringing I had and the work ethic of our family are reasons why I've ended up where I have. Plus the fact that I went to Catholic schools and wore a uniform all my life meant I didn't know how to dress myself, so here was a job where they'd give me a uniform.

All Seven of Us Graduated

Running, exercising, sit-ups, and push-ups were already part of my life. Back then, we had a series of challenges including the six-foot wall and the chain-link fence. I was the shortest female and the first time we were tested I was the only one who did them all. Then a woman who is now my best friend got over the wall and another gal did, so there were the three of us for the next three months helping the other women get through. Sitting in class the first couple of days the captain said, There are seven women here, but not all of you will graduate. The odds are that several of you will fail because of the physical. But we all practiced on weekends and some women bruised themselves up so bad hitting the wall. They hung in there and all seven of us graduated. I was pretty proud that I was elected our class vice-president, proud of the fact that people decided I was a leader, back in 1980.

They Did Everything I Said

I spent four and a half years on patrol and in the process I proposed a new detective position that dealt with juvenile issues and crime. I got it passed through the city council, so in 1984 I became the first juvenile detective. We had a mandatory rotation and I went back to patrol as an FTO. After that I went into crime prevention and public information, was promoted to sergeant in 1990, to lieutenant in 1994, and to commander in 1997.

When I began on patrol, they deliberately assigned me to a slow district. Then if there was a fight in progress there, they'd call me off and tell the big boys to go. I remember going to a fight in progress in a tavern where I was the first officer on the scene. I was waiting for my backup and a man came out with a bloody nose and said, Come in, come in. We need your help right away. I went in, people had pool cues and were yelling and screaming, I said, All right, you guys, knock it off. Calm down. Put those down. And they did. They did everything I said. They were very nice to me and then officers came running in looking for a big fight. They didn't get one because it was all calmed down. After that, they called me off all the time because obviously they wanted a big fight. I finally went to my sergeant and said, You need to let me handle my calls in my district on my own.

My Passion Is Involvement with the Community

I don't know that my being channeled is anybody's fault but my own. It is not a coincidence that when women began to enter policing that laws around child abuse, domestic violence, women and family issues started to change. The more the administration could do to bring me into these areas, they did. My feeling was, if we're dealing with a rape victim, she needs someone there who wants to be there. I took on a lot of those roles right away, like teaching about date rape. I'll never forget watching this tape a male information officer was showing high school students and he said, Rape is just having sex when you don't want to have it. I was horrified.

I developed a rape prevention program, which we now call personal safety for women. I watch over it like a hawk. I try to get more females teaching it because when women teach it, women will disclose. They'll say, You know what? That happened to me. In your audience you will have a lot of victims. I've taught across the state on domestic violence issues.

Law enforcement is similar to social work in that you're solving problems and helping people find resources and doing something for the good of the community. My passion is that, being involved with the community. I'm ingrained in it on a lot of different issues for several reasons. If you do your job well, you can affect change, maybe more than within the bureaucracy of DSHS doing social work. I've been able to implement lots of programs that I don't know if I would have been able to do in other departments where the organizational culture is totally set on doing things a certain way.

One thing I did early on was work on a maternity policy that recognized that pregnancy is not a permanent handicap. These women will come back. I did it because I was interested in having a family myself, but as a commissioned officer there's the expectation that you can do the basic job you were hired to do. Wear a uniform, get in a patrol car, answer calls for service. If the men think women are being given preferential treatment because they have special needs around families, the guys say, Well, I have a family and I have those needs, too.

I've been very involved with the FBI Law Enforcement Executive Academy that I went to. I'm on the state chapter board. We're the only chapter that has women in three out of the five board positions. The next president will be a woman. I'm the second vice-president. Our secretary-treasurer is a woman from the gambling commission. The FBI national academy trains law enforcement executives throughout the world. When I went through there were 20 women out of 260 law enforcement managers and 20 students from other countries. I took three master's-level classes there in organizational issues through the University of Virginia. It was the impetus for my master's degree.

Making the Switch from Commander to Mom

Making the switch is hard. If I had gone to a teenage suicide, for example, I would deal with the scene and then I'd typically come home and wake up my kids and hug them and say, Do you know that I love you? Do you know you always have options and choices? They would go, We know, Mom.

I'm not as good at separating work and home as I'd like to be because I live in the community, work in the community, volunteer in the community. Everybody knows me. They call me all the time. I'm their personal cop. They'll say, My son played baseball with your son in 1992. I want some advice on this or that. I get those all the time.

I did an okay job as a mother but I told my boys, unfortunately I'm the mother that I am because I'm a police officer and I have more information than you want me to have. I know about kids and drugs, kids and partying, kids and guns. Just recently, my 16-year-old son snuck out of the house. He was only gone 15 minutes but when he came home I was so angry I threw him up against the trunk of my car and patted him down. He didn't have any drugs on him but I found a pack of cigarettes. I said to myself, Relax. We came in and I took a deep breath and I said, I love you but I know what's going on at night. And you cannot leave this house without my permission.

Years ago, a young man who grew up with my son was selling drugs. I cut him a deal once, because his mom begged me to reduce the sentence. But then he went back to doing it and the next time I was really cold and said no. One day he walked in here with a rose and said he was in a 12-step program and he wanted to apologize to everybody. He said, I remember you with tears in your eyes saying to me, You are going to be held accountable for this.

Recruit Women from All Walks of Life

Accreditation is a voluntary set of standards that are nationally recognized in policing services. It's like medical accreditation or academic accreditation. It will hopefully be the standard we want to achieve in all law enforcement services. We were the first police department to become nationally accredited in the state in 1986 and we maintain it every three years. One of the components of national accreditation is to try to reflect the community so we try hard to recruit women and ethnic officers. It's hard because we are primarily a Caucasian community. We just lost a fantastic African American female officer because she wants to raise a family in an environment that is closer to what her family looks like.

One thing I started, which is exciting that can help us recruit, is a volunteer program. I got official funding for it two years ago, but before that I hired a woman I met at the leadership institute who is very good at program management. Now she's been hired permanently. A civilian in her 50's. I gave her the vision that I wanted our volunteers to help out throughout the whole department and that we valued diversity. She has managed to recruit three Latino women, two of them are from Bogota, one was a lawyer, one now works helping people, Microsoft recruits from other countries find housing. We have Muslims from the Middle East, a number of Asians.

For recruiting we also use our citizens' academy and our Explorer program. In 1994 I started a community policing advisory board that meets every month and we talk about the problems we're working on and they give us input. They're not political. Some have become full-time volunteers. They do some of the most menial jobs, data entry or shredding. We use them all over. We have an officer in charge of the Explorer program because these are young people who are exploring this career in law enforcement.

Public speaking is another way to recruit. I just spoke at a community college to 300 young, 18-year-old women where they were recruiting women in the trades and nontraditional jobs. People look at me and think, If she can do it, I can do it. If she can do this in her forties, I can. Women typically don't fit a mold in policing, which means we can recruit women from different walks of life and ages.

The Importance of Mentoring

Recruitment also depends on the fact that the women in this department support and mentor each other. You can look at a nearby agency with the same demographics, and they still only have two or three women. You have to have an organizational culture that appreciates women's contributions to law enforcement. We have that here. As far as women being successful with patrol, with detectives, as first-line respondents, the word gets out. If you're a woman and you're looking for where you're going to go work, you would rather work at an agency where women already are being successful. We talk about the agencies where women fail all the time and why would you go up against that when you can go to work for an organization like ours?

Some mentoring situations are more casual, some more formal. We were at a homicide scene the other night. One of our new recruits was doing her first ride-along and happened to be out with an officer who was on the perimeter of the homicide scene. I went to see how she was doing and asked her if I could give her a ride back to the station. She'd been sitting in a patrol car at the crime scene for hours. I told her who I was and that I would help her in any way I could to get ready for the academy. It was three o'clock in the morning but we sat in the parking lot and talked. I told her we don't have homicides very often here and she said, Oh, yeah, the other officers told me that.

I have the responsibility as the highest ranking woman in this department to make sure that I reach out to the younger women, to let them know that, first of all, I'm here to help you to succeed, and, second, one day I may work for you and I want to make sure you get the best preparation you can. I remember when I first started. I didn't know anything about makes and models of cars. My supervisor would say, Go over there and pull out that '73 Impala. And I'd say, Can you give me a color? I'd never shot a gun before. I didn't know anything about calibers of guns, makes, models. What's an automatic? What's a semi-automatic? What's the typical use of a handgun? They gave me all these boy clothes and said see if they fit. I didn't know how to put a vest on. I didn't know how to put a gunbelt on and there was no one to help me.

Now, as soon as we see a female officer getting her stuff, we say, Let me show you how this goes on and how you can go to the bathroom the fastest. I didn't realize how arduous a task it was to go to the bathroom. Those kinds of things are mentoring, too.

A woman called me from another agency for help. She had a female officer there with the same seniority I had, so I said, I don't mind sitting down with you and explaining all this basic stuff, but why don't you talk to this other woman? She said, She told me that if she had to learn it the hard way, I had to learn it the hard way. That's crazy. I wouldn't do that to anybody, male or female. There's a saying, "One ah shit wipes out all of the atta boys (girls) you have."

Women Changing Work

Eight years ago we hired a lot of female officers. The older men said, Every time I turn around, they're hiring another woman officer. I said, Now you know what I went through for 15 years. Every time I turned around, they were hiring another male officer. The newer, younger officers nowadays, in their twenties, grew up with their mothers working, some in nontraditional jobs. They just accept women in the workplace. They have women in their academy class. They're likely to be mentored by women field training officers.

After I started the women's personal safety class, some of the men wanted to teach it. Now I'm getting kudos on some of these men. They are very compassionate. I told them that you will never know what it is like to be a lone woman walking down a street at night. You don't have that innate fear. Most men feel they can handle themselves. So do not tell women that you know how they feel. Relate it to someone you're close with. Say, my wife feels that way, or my Mom feels that way, or my sister.

A Proud Moment

I went to a call when I was a patrol officer, a young girl had called 911 and said her dad was hitting her. It was 11 o'clock on a school night. The dad called back and said she was overreacting. It was just parental discipline and nobody needed to come. I was working with a male officer and he called himself off. But I said on the radio that I'd check on it.

I went to this upscale house and this man answered the door and I smelled alcohol. I said, I'm sure everything is fine but I'd just like to see her. We went back and forth, but finally he opened the door. There was broken glass everywhere, the house was torn up. Here's this little girl bleeding from her nose, her ears, her face was all swollen. I called for backup, had him arrested, called an aid car. She was a step-daughter, living with her mom who had two babies with this man. The mom was being abused and didn't know how to take care of the kid. The mom had tried to leave that night and couldn't.

The mom said, I can't protect her from him, so we went to court. I found out where her dad was and placed her with her dad. The mom never, ever contacted her. We went to court three months later and her mom walked right by her when she called out, Mommy. Her mother stuck with her husband. He lied about the whole thing, said I made up the statement. I was devastated; I was a new officer. All I was trying to do was help her. They sued us for five million dollars. They kept taking everybody else off the claim but left me. Eventually they didn't sue me because they had missed the filing deadline.

She was eight years old at the time. Twelve years later I got called down to records. There was this beautiful woman there with this tiny girl. She had come to thank me. She said, You don't remember me but I was that little girl. She was so successful and so pretty and being a great mom. She said the best thing was she grew up with her dad who gave her a loving environment. People like her come into your life and sometimes twelve years later you find out you did the right thing.

Soldotna, AK's Chief

Chief Shirley Gifford was born in 1951. Both she and her husband are retired captains from the Anchorage Police Department. He is currently a cold case homicide investigator for the Alaskan State Troopers while she is Chief of the City of Soldotna PD on the Kenai Peninsula. Shirley has a daughter, 19, a sophomore in college. Her plans for retirement are training and education and she already has taught criminal investigation as an adjunct college professor. Shirley was given a "Breaking the Glass Ceiling" award from the National Center for Women & Policing in April 2003.

It Was the Perfect Fit for Me

I decided to go into law enforcement my senior year of college and then took nothing but criminal justice courses to get my BS. It was the perfect fit for me. Before that I had taken psychology, child growth and development, teaching K-3. My final year I picked up a book of my boyfriend who was taking criminal justice classes and it just clicked. I finally knew what I wanted to do.

I had worked out when I was going to college. I was a runner and I liked running, so physically I was prepared for the academy. I did sit-ups and push-ups. But it was so strenuous, my muscles hurt so bad every day. We had this ex-Marine Corps drill sergeant for PT. I had never been through anything so brutal in my life. If I hadn't been working out, I don't think I would have succeeded. He always called me the meter maid as a demeaning kind of thing and he tried really hard to make me cry and break down and leave the profession. But in my mind I felt, he's trying to make me strong. We had to hold our arms out for ages and if you do this for very long, it hurts. It was our last day and he got right in my face and I didn't know what he was going to say, but he said, You're going to make it. What an impression that made in my mind. I can remember it today as vividly as if it were happening. I was in too much pain to say anything so I just smiled.

I went to the FBI National Academy in 1991. Everybody goes into it thinking I'm not prepared. They talked about doing the Marine Corps obstacle course or the Yellow Brick Road. You get so set up mentally, you think, Oh, my God, I can't do that. But you work out and you get ready and then you find out when you get to the academy that they don't start you out running ten miles, you start out running a mile. You work up from there, every day building on your physical condition.

APD Was a Very Satisfying Career

I started out as a deputy sheriff in a township in Michigan and was there for a year. Then I had an opportunity to come to Alaska with a different boyfriend and eventually we got married. After I left Michigan I wasn't sure I wanted to stay in the police because things happened in the department that I didn't care for. That department didn't feel right to me and my intuition was right-on because after I left indictments came down against members within the department for receiving stolen property. I was told to go pick up my bottle of booze at the towing company where we had a contract. I didn't want to do it and I was ordered to by the chief.

But I came to Alaska and found out that the pay scale of the Anchorage Police Department was three times what I made in Michigan. I couldn't believe that police officers made that much money. I thought, Maybe I'll give it a second try. And the Anchorage Police Department's philosophy was, You didn't take free coffee. You didn't go into a theater to watch a movie in uniform. You didn't take free pizza. That fit for me and I thought, This is where I belong. Because accepting freebies makes you feel like you owe people and you should never be in that position as a law enforcement officer.

I spent 20 years with the APD and it was a very satisfying career. I rose through the ranks. I started out as a patrol officer and then got bumped into a traffic officer position after one and a half years. They needed somebody and they did reverse seniority. If people don't put in for a position, then the person with the lowest seniority after 18 months on patrol gets bumped in. I went kicking and screaming but I wound up with very good training, good experiences, and did traffic accident fatality investigation on midnight shift. It helped me throughout my career both in investigations and in dealing with people who have had some of the worst trauma dealt to them.

Then I did hit-and-run investigation for a year and from there I went over to the burglary unit and got promoted to detective, then corporal and sergeant within the burglary unit in the detective division. I spent six years in burglary and then got promoted to lieutenant in charge of training where I spent one year. Then I was transferred back to property crimes so I was again in charge of burglary, in addition to the theft unit warrants section, fraud unit, and auto theft. Did that for two and a half years and then got transferred over to person crimes where I was lieutenant in charge of homicide, robbery, assault, sexual assault, crimes against children. I spent a couple of years there and then got promoted to captain in charge of technical services where I was in charge of human resources, budget, computer section, property and evidence, records section, and dispatch. I did that for a year and then got transferred to captain in charge of patrol, a couple hundred people. Spent two and a half years there and then transferred to being captain in charge of detectives for a couple of years. I retired in 1997, put in for this position and came to Soldotna in June.

I had a chief who had the foresight when I was in training to take me out of training and get me back into property crime investigation. I loved property crime investigations so when the person crimes position came open, I wasn't particularly thrilled about going over there. I didn't care about dead bodies too much. I was perfectly happy where I was in property crimes and he said, No, you're going to person crimes. It was the opposite of traditional channeling. He forced me into new areas. And another chief allowing me to go back to patrol as captain; I was very appreciative of that.

I taught in the academy in Anchorage and watched women decide early on that policing was not their thing. There were also women who were not willing to put up with the stuff you have to put up with in the academy. Academy staff could do a better job of encouraging and hanging on to recruits instead of giving them such a difficult time. On the other hand recruits need to be told not to be so sensitive. They need to understand that this is just the academy, it's just the training program. Say to yourself, I've got 20, 25, 30 years ahead of me and I'm not going to let this bozo get to me.

Over the years I have observed women supporting women grow very strong. In the '70s and '80s women vied for few available positions or promotions and there seemed to be more competition. Now, to a larger degree, mentoring and outwardly helping one another have come of age. When I was a captain in Anchorage I had women come seeking advice about promotion but then ask that I not tell anyone. They didn't want anyone to think they didn't do it on their own, or that they received special favor. The men who came to me for advice prior to a promotion never asked for the secrecy but boldly came into my office.

Managing Motherhood

My husband and I divorced when my daughter was two so I was a single mom for 16 years. I became pregnant when I was in the burglary unit so working light duty in burglary was not a big deal. I didn't have to worry about how my uniform fit because I was in plainclothes. The difficult part came when we did divorce and I was moving up the ladder, more responsibility, more phone calls in the night. It really hit me when I was in charge of the person crimes section where we were getting 30 homicides a year and my requirement was to go out to the scene and work the case with the sergeant and the rest of the detectives. It wasn't like I could load my daughter up and take her to a babysitter. So I paid quite a bit, $10 an hour, to have my daycare person come out at night. When I got the call, my first call was to her and then it was to the rest of the team. She has become a very good friend and she helped me raise my daughter.

I compensated to my daughter by taking vacation time at Christmas and her spring break, and a large amount of time in the summer when she was off school. Through the years I gave her quality time. But there were many times when I had to call someone out at night or I had to work evenings. Her dad was there in town and we had shared custody, so I tried to do my administrative work on the nights that he had her. He was a sergeant with the Anchorage Department and I absolutely believe that my job was the cause of our divorce. My job took its toll. I had a young child. I had a husband. I had a career and it was in a place where I was moving up. It was overwhelming and it got to the point where I couldn't do it all.

My Roles as Chief

I'm in charge of public safety for the city of Soldotna. Internally, my role is to ensure that the officers in the department have a budget that they can work under, and the training and resources to do their jobs. I make sure they have the tools, the vehicles, radar guns, etc. Externally, my role within the community is to be there for different groups where they can see me, touch me, talk to me, let me know what their needs are. I am connected with the community in a variety of different ways. I work on committees, boards, and councils, not only within the City of Soldotna but for the State of Alaska. I'm vice-president of the Alaska Association of Chiefs of Police. I've had membership work, for example, I served five years as a member of the Violence Against Women Action and Implementation Planning Committee. Part of that was making sure that other departments throughout the state had equipment for interview rooms and training in domestic violence. I see my role as very broad-based.

Our main issues are domestic violence, juvenile-related crimes, criminal mischief like vandalism and abusive skateboarding. We have drunk driving, alcohol-related issues. I have to laugh because at high school graduation night my husband was still with the Anchorage Police Department up at one of the high schools and he has this bullet fly by his head because they were shooting outside the graduation. And what I dealt with down here was one of the kids after receiving his diploma did a little dance on the stage. And he's the big rebel. It's a very close-knit community. Everybody knows everybody and that helps to keep criminal activity in check.

I was raised in Eaton Rapids, Michigan, which is a similar-sized town to Soldotna and I was very comfortable being raised in a small town. I knew what I was getting into here. We didn't care for the deputy sheriffs where I grew up. We thought they were mean and not very nice. My interest in law enforcement may have begun subconsciously in my teens. I thought, it's not necessary to talk to us like that and be mean if we smashed a pumpkin in the road. You can get people to do things without ordering or commanding them. You say, Hey, kids, look at the mess you made. I can either call your parents or you can clean the mess up, it's your choice. Then they clean the mess up and think, Hey, this is a cool cop.

What I enjoy is the support I get for the job. The city has a good manager who is very supportive of me. The city council's attitude is, If Shirley wants that, give it to her. Not all chiefs enjoy that and have to fight for what they need. The mayor is marvelously supportive of me and so are the members of the department, and the community at large. I'll go have lunch over at the senior center or at the high school and everywhere I go I get thanks for being here. I've been able to call the shots and be in charge and have things done the way I feel they need to be done.

Troubles Recruiting

Departments across the nation today are having a hard time attracting people into law enforcement. I'm in the baby boomer era and there were a lot of people wanting a fixed pool of jobs when I was hired on by the Anchorage Department. When I was hired on I was one of four out of 500 applicants. Anchorage was getting thousands of applicants for a 25-person academy. Now, they struggle. They're going out trying to recruit from other departments.

With the age of technology a lot of students are going into computer-based jobs, programming, because the money is good. They're going into these wide-open technical fields where the pay is good and they're not putting themselves in harm's way. Because we never know what's going to happen. I don't know what kind of call I'll get this afternoon where everybody might have to be called out, if we're going to get involved in, say, a drug bust. We just never know and that's very unsettling to the Me Generation. And now we're getting into the X Generation and their focus is different. In the baby boomer era, it was I want to help people, I want to get out there and be of service to people. For the Me Generation, it is I want a good career, a safe career, lots of money, I want to retire early, I want to have fun. It's very frustrating. At least my female patrol officer, I'm in the process of promoting her, has wanted to excel and get to the next level.

I'm now starting recruitment at the high school level. We do job shadows. We invite the students to come in and work with us for a day. They spend some time with the detective sergeant, then spend a little time with the administrative sergeant, seeing what he does taking care of property and evidence, resources, preparing material for the district attorney's office on cases. Then they spend time with the patrol sergeant, or in a patrol car riding around, and then they spend time with me to see what the police chief does. In the six years I've done job shadows, the girls clearly outnumber the boys. We do half a dozen job shadows in a year. We also go in for career days where we talk about our work. We teach in the classrooms. I've taught search and seizure in the history classes. The detective sergeant teaches about drugs. We go into all the schools. Another way we connect with the community is the DARE program. I've got one half-time detective and half-time school liaison who is my DARE officer. The kids really love this officer.

I've also had intern programs where I pay college students to work here through the summer. I don't use reserves but I have a community patrol I run through the summer time. I have 20 members. They are a fantastic group. In the winter they serve as my citizen advisory group. In the winter it gets very slow and I don't want them to get bored. The officers get bored and I don't want my volunteers to get disaffected. So once a month in the winter we talk about cases and philosophy, their view as citizens as to how the police department is doing. If they give any criticism, they always buffer it with, Now, I'm not saying anything against the officer. I've been on other citizens advisory groups where the members see themselves as watchdogs but that's not the mentality here. Here their role is to participate and help and it makes this a better police department.

The community patrol started two years before I got here. It was under the city manager over at city hall. Then two years ago we took it under the police department at the request of the community patrol because they wanted to be connected and closer to what the law enforcement officers were doing. I would encourage other departments to have this. It's working out better where we're working hand in hand. They meet with the officers before they go on shift and the officers tell them where the problem areas are.

Overprotection and Underprotection

Overprotection was horrible in Michigan, horrible. I would get to a bar fight or a domestic dispute and I would literally get pushed back. I was their little clerk-typist. They already had it ingrained that they were going to protect me and when I got out on the road, I wasn't allowed to talk or take charge. I was so frustrated. I thought, Let me talk. I know how to talk to people. I also know how to fight. Let me get into the mix. After the fact I would say, Don't push me back like that. Let me back you up. If I'd stayed there any length of time, they may have come around.

This did not happen in Anchorage. When I hit the street, the FTOs' approach was they wanted to see me in fights, they wanted to make sure I could handle myself because there was no other way to evaluate me as a solo officer. I was so mad at my first FTO one night. We worked partners back in Michigan and if we had a passive resistant guy the two of us would get that person into the car. So I'm trying to get this drunk into the car and my FTO is just standing there, watching me. I could not believe it. You're here and you should be helping me. I was so mad at him I took it out on this drunk and picked him up and threw him in the car. I got into my share of fights and loved it because they not only allowed me to fight, they expected it. That's another reason why Anchorage was a good fit for me.

Camaraderie

The camaraderie within the police profession is very strong. The sense of belonging keeps you going, and makes you want to be there. We know what each of us is going through and we depend upon each other for backup. Sometimes we get wrapped up in some black humor that people outside the profession think is wrong. However, we all know it's a survival mechanism. If you don't make light of some of the things you see and have to deal with, you probably are not going to survive the career. That doesn't mean that we don't respect people and their dignity, or that we don't have empathy or compassion, it just means that we choose some things to laugh about that others outside the profession may think sick. Lots of funny things do happen and being able to laugh with your fellow officers strengthens the bond. We can go anywhere in the world, identify ourselves to a police officer and gain a new brother or sister. That's a pretty great feeling.

Major Coping Strategy

Not surprisingly, camaraderie with coworkers has been identified empirically as a major coping strategy in the police for handling stress (Robin Haarr and Merry Morash, 1999). This comradeship consisted of getting help and understanding from the women one worked with, from male coworkers as well, and from mentors. It meant getting together with other officers to joke and blow off steam. Small wonder that women's conferences and meetings are so important to women commanders and chiefs because they can meet up with other commanders and chiefs to get that help and understanding.

This chapter reminds readers that there is as much variety in chiefs' jobs as there is in detectives' jobs or sergeants' jobs. Women officers ruminating about whether to seek promotion should be inspired by Gail and Shirley and the programs they have established to better serve their communities.

13

Command Thoughts about Family Life

Port of Seattle Lieutenant Myra Harmon opined: "Here it is, the twenty-first century, and affordable, safe, and available childcare for working mothers of all occupations remains an unfulfilled goal for American women. For most full-time women police, private childcare is too expensive. Only in socialist states like Cuba and western European countries such as Sweden, Denmark, Belgium, France, and Italy is public daycare easy to find. So women cops use parents, grandparents, sisters and brothers, neighbors and friends to be there for their kids when duty calls."

I'd like to tackle the crucial issue of childcare here. One way women manage childcare is having an understanding, flexible boss. Another is having an understanding, flexible spouse or partner. Even better is if both are understanding and flexible. Here is more information on how women officers solve the childcare problem.

Sequim, WA, PD Sergeant Sheri Crain said: "Both times I was pregnant I was blessed with really good managers and as soon as I was uncomfortable in my uniform, I was put on light duty. I did investigations with the first baby and with the second I worked on a lot of different projects, like rewriting policies. It was a great learning experience; I did things I wouldn't have been exposed to otherwise. Some of the broader-minded guys will say I set precedent because our department now has light duty for those hernias and heart attacks, shoulder and knee operations."

Trisha King-Stargel, retired officer from Kent, WA, PD, talked about the men who alternate childcare with their wives, including Trisha's husband: "If one of the girls was sick, and I stayed home, the next time it was his turn. Our department is very flexible and lets officers bid on shifts. Dual officer families will bid for two different shifts so that one can take the children to school and the other pick them up. Many police and firefighters could use childcare at night, because even if the kids are sleeping, during your shift you could pop in and let them feel that parental presence."

When Major Carol Cummings and I sat down at my patio table in July 2002 she had recently moved from a major investigations section to overseeing security for King County, Washington's bus system (Metro Transit). Carol was born in 1958 and has a BA with a history major, English minor. She is married to a geologist turned nurse who works part-time and is largely responsible for the care of their three children ranging in age from 5 to 15. Carol is very proud that in her previous assignment she was instrumental in getting the Revised Code of Washington State (RCW) changed to lower the bar for child neglect. Her goal now is to have a major impact on Metro.

To My Utter Surprise, They Hired Me

I worked as a nurse's aide in a nursing home while going to college and moved to a hospital emergency room as a clerical specialist in 1980 when I graduated. I liked the environment but I didn't want to do medical school. After a rigorous academic life, I was tired. I earned a little money and traveled around Europe for six months. Then I went to my college job placement office and had a couple of unsuccessful interviews for corporate jobs. At college we wore jeans, some wore shoes. I blush to remember that I wore a dress to the interviews that my mother made. I had long hair and wore no makeup. One guy was pretty blunt and said, I suggest that you find somebody to teach you how to dress professionally.

As a joke, a friend gave me a brochure saying the county was hiring deputies. I thought, Well, they pay you to go to the academy and you can work out there and get in shape. I didn't have a place to live, so as a lark I filled out an application. I had an interview and I'm thinking, This is too weird. Like the corporate jobs, again I'd be coming from a very different world. There was one person from my college, a Hispanic male, who was working in the sheriff's office. I called him up and he explained what the job was and the freedom really appealed.

I applied and to my utter surprise they hired me. I was asked if I would shoot a guy in a situation they lined up. I said, Of course I wouldn't shoot him, he's not threatening my life or anybody else's life. He's threatening his own life, but that's not an appropriate use of force. I wasn't going to give them the answers I thought they wanted and that is probably what got me the job.

I Was Relaxed

I started out in Multnomah County in Portland, so I went to the state academy in Oregon in 1981. This sheriff's office was a very innovative agency, one of two in the nation that required a four-year degree. They were hiring attorneys and people with advanced degrees. There were four women in a class of 35, the largest group of women they'd ever had. I graduated number one and my roommate graduated number two. We felt a lot of resentment from the men, yet once we'd all gone through that camaraderie together, we felt positive about it.

You have to be able to pass a physical fitness standard to be hired. When I hired on, they gave men and women different tests. They wanted me to take a lower step test than the men. I said, What are you talking about? I'm taller than at least half of the men. I won't do it, it's insulting. But they made me do the women's test and then I did the men's too. The department had you do a mile and a half in a certain time, a stretch test, a certain number of sit-ups and push-ups, because they didn't want to send somebody to the academy and pay all that money only to have the person fail. You had to be able to do it at the front end.

I ran and swam in college as a stress reliever and I had just backpacked around Europe so I was very strong. Another advantage was I was very tall. There was no question in anyone's mind that I could take care of myself. We went through a mini-academy at the sheriff's office for a month and then they put us out on the street. They had not trained their trainers so when I got in the car in the driver's seat mine simply said, That's the radio. This is how you answer it. It's all yours. And on my first night there was a stabbing.

Then we went to the real academy for three months. It wasn't my heart's desire to be a cop so I was relaxed as far as the outcome. There was this general sense that women were not physically capable of passing, so that got my competitive spirit up. My roommate and I clearly wanted to be great, we didn't want to be any less than at the top. When they'd say, Run one mile, we'd go out and run five. When they'd say, Do ten sit-ups, we'd go back to our room and do a hundred. And after college, how could studying for tests at the academy be difficult?

Not Sure How Long I Would Stay on the Job

When I began my attitude was, I'll do this for a year and a half, get off probation, and I will have proven women can do it. Then I'll quit and go to law school and become a prosecutor. But after 18 months, it was a lot of fun being able to go behind the yellow line. It was the antithesis of college full of ivory tower intellectuals. I was seeing a completely different world. I got it in my mind that I'd do it for three years. At three years I will have really proven it.

But in 1983 this RIF came down and they laid all of us off with four years or less. I came up here and lateraled over. I didn't have to go through the Washington State Academy. I showed up, took a test, and went to work under a field training officer. However, at three years I had just gotten married so I thought, Five years, then I'll quit. But at five years I had a baby and my husband had thrown his back out in a major way, in fact he had surgery the day I went into labor, so that obviously was not the time to quit.

I went back after five weeks and decided to stick it out for another year or two. A year later I got pregnant again and didn't want to get off the street so I didn't tell anybody. Back then, they didn't know what to do with pregnant women. I decided to take the sergeant's exam. I went up to the oral board, eight months pregnant, which was highly embarrassing, because I tried to keep my personal life completely away from work.

Having a Family

Making the switch from home to work was, and is, very difficult. When my husband was going to nursing school, we worked odd shifts to keep the children out of daycare as much as possible. I'd hand my husband a baby and take off for work where somebody would say, What's that on your back? Baby vomit. Using a breast pump when you are a police officer is not easy. However, I had a very good boss who let me come in early in the morning and take no lunch break so that I could go home early in the afternoon. But there was very little time for sleep.

I remember the day I went out to a call, a burglary in progress with a potential armed suspect. I was driving to it, lights and sirens, and the adrenaline was pumping. You need that because it gives you that ability to see things quickly and you use that. I thought, This adrenaline is not good for the baby. I deliberately took deep breaths and calmed myself down and I showed up at the scene totally relaxed, which is not what you need in that situation. I realized my lack of disclosure had gone on long enough and went to my sergeant and said, I'm going to need to go light duty. He said, Why? I said, Look at me. He said, Oh shit.

How Women Were First Treated

When I joined King County, I was trained, I had confidence, I had done it. But they had not had lateral officers before. They were used to rookies. I went to a domestic and my FTO took over my call and talked to this man, who was mad and drunk. So I stepped in front of my FTO and told this guy, I am the one making the decision whether you're going to jail tonight or not. So if you've got any issues, you tell me. My FTO commented later, I can't believe you did that, but you were right. I was being slightly protective.

They never put women on the same squad. You had an A side and a B side to the precinct and they'd always put one woman on the A side and the other on the B side. If there were ever two women on the same shift, they wouldn't let the two of you work in the same area. The first time a woman and I had an adjoining district, a shock rippled through the guys and they referred to us as the Broad Squad.

My old boss recalled when the first woman was put in uniform. She had hired on as a matron and she wore skirts. Now they'd put her in a uniform and given her a car. My boss's sergeant called him and his buddy in and said, It's not going to last, it's just another of those stupid programs. But for now we've got to deal with it. She's going to be in your area. And the two men went, Ahh, man. You're on that side of her and you're on the other side of her and if she gets a call, I don't care what you're doing, one of you break free and go with her. Eventually this will end and we'll get back to normal. For the next nine months, any time this woman went on a call, one of them would go with her. But my boss admitted that she did a good job and developed a grudging respect for her.

I have some statistics with me for women. When I hired on in 1983 we had 28 females out of 486 commissioned personnel in the county. Now in 2002, we have 674 commissioned personnel and 119 are female, which is 18%.

Learning the Ropes

My father was in the military so we moved a lot. I went to three junior highs and four high schools. I never expected to fit in and that has helped me a lot. It never bothered me that I was not part of the inner circle. I never necessarily wanted it because I'm a very private person. That's why it was no problem being the only female and on my own. No one ever told me how to do anything. When I went into a new situation the men would watch me to see if I was going to fail. Then my need to be competitive would kick in and I wouldn't fail.

I was a new sergeant and I'd been hazed before but this was different. Being a private person as a patrol officer, I could blend in. But now I'm a sergeant? With all guys? I was supposed to be running the squad. There was no training. There was no anything. I didn't know how to enter a roster into the computer. I didn't know how to approve a report. One sergeant was so phenomenally hostile, he wouldn't look at me, he wouldn't talk to me, he was so hostile when I came into the office, he'd walk out. I remember I grabbed a senior patrol officer, who I will be forever grateful for, to show me how to enter the roster, show me what the paperwork was. I asked for help, which I almost never do, and he gave it in a professional, respectful way.

The next part of the week I had another partner who was considered hell on earth. You still hear stories about this guy, devious, mean, vindictive. I'd already had a couple of to-do's with him. He asked me once, Are you going to file a sexual harassment grievance against me? I said, No. You're an asshole to everybody, not just women. So I didn't know what to expect from him.

I went to the roll call and all these guys came in and I sat down on the side of the table and we had our little chat and I came back out and he said, You are the sergeant. You do not sit on the side of the table. You sit in the front and you call them to order. You run it because you're the one that they're going to look to for advice. I thought, Shit. He's right. It was that male role. Where you sit, how you look, and how you conduct yourself generates respect or not. It was the first time anybody had given me feedback and I appreciated it because it was good advice and he did that in a number of ways for the next six months. I've always liked him since.

What Is Metro Transit?

Metro is like scuba diving. All of a sudden you are swimming in this world you never knew existed. Buses. Time tables. Bus routes. Crimes on buses. Metro was having a lot of difficult personnel issues and they are one of the things I handle well. If there was ever going to be a challenge in my new role as major, this is it.

The bus system's policing force used to be off-duty people with county sheriff's sergeants overseeing them. Then they started a few officers full-time until a tragic incident occurred with a bus going off a bridge. There was a huge outcry and an obvious need for people to be more secure in the transit system. We now have 20 full-time and 250 part-time off-duty officers. There is a limit to how many hours they can work a month. You don't want somebody working a 40-hour-job and 40 hours of off-duty. We handle in a secondary fashion the crimes that occur on the transit system. If there is a shooting on a bus in a certain part of town, that police department would be the primary responders.

Two ongoing problems are fare evasion and sleepers. Fare evaders jump off the bus without paying and what's the driver going to do? Drivers are reluctant to do anything about it and driving the bus is their primary responsibility. If you look at fare evaders statistically, they frequently are the ones who vandalize buses. Sleepers are a real problem, particularly on specific lines, because we've got so many homeless people now.

I Want to Say I Made an Impact

The job gives me the ability to make an impact in my community in a way I think is important. An excellent example is the revision of Revised Code of Washington. The bar was very high for law enforcement to investigate cases of child neglect. You had to show substantial risk of bodily harm before there was any charge, so infants that were left alone for hours, toddlers eating out of dumpsters for days on end, children whose teeth were rotting out, 10-year-olds left alone to take care of toddlers, babies without diapers changed for days—no charge, nothing. You had no probable cause that a crime had occurred. For a variety of reasons CPS was not capable of following up. If they could show a pattern maybe they could go in. Most of the cases involved drug abuse, alcoholism, mental health issues. People usually don't want to neglect their kids. But offering a carrot like CPS did, like parenting classes, wasn't enough. We needed a stick to say a charge will be filed against you.

I'd like to have an impact at Metro as well. But you don't just rush in and start making changes willy-nilly. There are little things that can be done immediately like updating the computer system and doing an analysis in regard to the security with the correct emphasis on terrorism. With this job I need to take a global perspective. In contrast, on patrol the focus is getting the bad guy, finding the burglar, catching the kid who is speeding up and down. The focus is on the individual. But now the focus has to be broader.

My dream is pre-training. If we're targeting certain groups of people in recruitment, then we need to give them the skills to compete at an even level. Rather than pursue selective treatment, we should aim for an even playing field. Let them know how to take tests, let them know how to dress. Offer remedial classes to everybody in how to take tests, how to improve physical fitness, how to do push-ups and sit-ups. If women routinely can't do part of the physical test because they don't have the necessary upper body strength, then three months before the test, open up training, make the opportunity available to everybody, men, women, minorities, but when you have that test, let it be equal.

My current assignment is one I truly wanted and I have a wonderful mentor who has been crucial in my career. I had spent too many years in uniform and never learned any fashion sense. My mentor said, You need help. We met for about an hour and a half talking about likely interview questions. Then we went to Nordstrom's and she brought out various things and I tried them on. She worked with a clerk and they put together three different outfits. We went to a hair stylist the day of the interview. She told him what she thought, and he did my hair. I drew the line on makeup. I'll never do makeup. She got me earrings. She's got me wearing earrings again. She lent me her purse and a pair of shoes because we wear the same shoe size, and she showed me how to put a scarf on because I'd never worn a scarf. It was absolutely wonderful.

Chief of Shoreline, WA, PD, Denise Pentony

Denise places top priority on accommodating women who want to combine the job with childrearing. When we met in the spring of 2002, she had been Chief for two years. Born in 1958, Denise stressed the importance of education if a woman wants a crack at promotion to her level. She has a BA in law enforcement administration, a MA in public administration, and a State certificate in executive leadership. She has attended the FBI National Academy and was a research fellow for the Police Executive Research Forum in Washington, D.C., for six months. She teaches criminal justice classes for the Sea-Tac campus of Central Washington University and is interested in earning a Leadership Certificate at Washington State University. The percentage of women in her department of 45 is 31%, which means the job of police officer under her supervision is no longer nontraditional for women.

Denise grew up shooting with her dad and sisters. They even had a range in the bottom of their house. Her dad was a Portland police officer and her sister had a 25-year career in the police. Denise didn't join until she was 27, but she started thinking about it when her dad's partner would come over and let her sit on his motorcycle.

Proving Myself

When I decided to quit dabbling in reserves, I had two mentors, my sister and her best girlfriend, both Alaska State troopers. They coached me through the oral board, the background investigation, polygraph, they were there rooting for me at the physical. Every woman should have that kind of support. These women knew what was going to come up and helped me psychologically. Our department hires through the County Sheriff's Office. If we could assign a mentor to everyone, she could be out there riding with the person, making sure they did their sit-ups, push-ups, all the stuff you've got to do to get you the job.

When I first started, I felt I had to be tough, chase down the bad guys, get my butt kicked a few times, back up the men, bail them out. A suspect got away from me once and another officer was really mad at me for not being tactically smart about having more people there to help me. I was so mad that I was stupid, I tracked the guy down again and arrested him just to show that I could do it by myself. I had this group of friends on motorcycles and they were like my big brothers, checking up on me, backing me up on calls. I worked graveyard shift on one of the worst areas of the highway and tried to make as many warrant arrests as I could, another way of proving myself.

Yes, I've been channeled. I didn't have the opportunity to go into special operations. After two years on, my goal was to ride motorcycles. It was all males in special operations and I couldn't break the barrier. I had taken the initiative and learned how to ride on my friends' motorcycles. Also I'm an expert shot, yet I couldn't get on the SWAT team to be a sniper. So, because of my earlier background in banking, software, and computers, I started working in white collar crime, the fraud unit. Ironically, when I was a major, I managed the special operations section, 90 people. I was their commander for a year so I finally got there. One of the last things I did going out of there was bring the first female motorcycle officer in.

Family Issues

Many women leave because they feel a greater need to be at home with their children. There's nothing we can do for them other than make sure they have a good experience while they're here. For those that want to make this a career, we need to have a mentoring program, a reward system that always recognizes good performance, and opportunities to be challenged and to take on new leadership roles.

I have a woman here who's been with us 15 years and she has a small child who's five and she wants to spend a year at home before the child goes to school. She's just taken a leave of absence. She was a master police officer, a corporal, but she is such a great person, we've left the door open. We would always hire her back. It would help so much if we had alternative work schedules, like job-sharing, that would attract more family-oriented women. We don't have that currently, but it's not out of the question.

As far as marriage goes, if you are married before you come to the job, you've a 99% chance of losing your marriage. Because you change, your eyes are opened. You accept these new responsibilities and become much more competent and capable. You're able to do everything yourself. You pull down an excellent wage. You don't take shit off people anymore. You see the kind of games people play. You go to so many domestic violence calls and see so many families that have trouble that you look at your own relationship and say, I'm not going to be a victim anymore. My perception is that husbands feel threatened—she's no longer this nice, little wife I once had. Very few men are attracted to women who are very successful and competitive and have positions such as mine. If they are attracted to you, it's not for a long-term relationship but to see if you can be conquered. A man has to be very secure in himself to have a woman in a nontraditional role as a partner.

On-the-Job Mentoring

We have a mentoring program here for new supervisors and it's a most rewarding experience. I've been a mentor for a female who was just promoted to sergeant. Her first year was very difficult because it was a controversial promotion and she'd gone to a work area where people resisted her. We met once a week and talked about her experiences. She'd vent and then check with me about things she was thinking of doing. She complained, Nobody's inviting me for coffee and no one wants to go to dinner with me and I feel so isolated. I said, Then you need to show up on a call and say, Can I buy you coffee? I'd like to get to know you. She started reaching out to her staff that way and by the time she left the precinct after her probationary year, they did not want her to go and she did not want to go. She was able to turn her whole self around with that group and they're tough. Cops will eat their young, that's how tough they are on one another.

She also had the reputation of always taking the underdog's side. I was honest with her about what I'd heard and she said, Here's why I championed the underdog's cause. I understood what she was saying but at some point she had to make the transition and pick up the company line if she wanted to be successful. Again she changed. But if somebody hadn't been there to help her, she would have ended up a management issue, because she'd always be bucking the system.

I had a problem with not having a lot of people skills. I was pretty much by the book, top-down, rule-oriented, until I learned that I had to change how I approached people and talked about the rules. My mentor took me through that. She was always so calm and cool and thoughtful. I was action, go, go, go, mow right over people. She showed me that things work much easier if you have that human component.

I Would Not Be Shy

Being a chief is more than I ever dreamed of. Going up even higher would mean becoming chief of a larger agency. I like the quality of life I have now, the level of stress, the amount of money I make, the security. But if opportunities presented themselves to me, I would not be shy about looking into them. A year ago I applied for the Washington Patrol Chief's job. I was in the top three. The governor went outside, instead, and selected somebody not on our list. What I learned from that experience was invaluable. I would share it with whoever wants to know how you get a high-level job.

If you really want to be promoted, you've got to be committed, prepared academically, and know what the issues are. You've got to prepare yourself for the oral board, the test questions you might be presented with. I would advise a woman to go to anyone she respects who has been promoted over the years, male or female, to ask what to do to prepare. You should have a bachelor's degree. You should have researched current issues by reading publications. You have to develop yourself personally, develop a reputation of excellence, high integrity, and proven leadership.

Conferences Are For Fun and Learning

I've been a member of the International Association of Women Police for 15 years. I'm very active in the International Association of Chiefs of Police and the National Sheriff's Association. I also joined the National Center for Women & Policing in 1996 and have been to three conferences, Washington, D.C., Palm Desert, and Los Angeles. We talk about our issues and different strategies for handling them. I've learned from women who have been through hell and back how they survived. It helps knowing you have people who care about you and will be there for you. Because when you get to this level, you don't have many people on the landscape to talk to.

When I was at the NCWP conference in Anaheim, I met an assistant chief with the New York State Patrol. She told me a story of how she worked to get a program in. She used a fishing analogy. How brilliant because for men it's all sports and fishing. She was thinking in full circle: I want to get a fish and how am I going to get that fish? She had a perfectly laid-out plan. She decided who was the target, what bait would attract that person to make the decision she wanted, and what were the obstacles. She gathered together all the things she needed to be successful—net, rod, boat. Then when the hook was set, she reeled it in and she got what she wanted. This is just one little nugget that I've gotten from other women.

At conference I seek out the fun group, women who are outgoing and have a lot in common with me, and we talk, have a ball, recreate, drink, whatever. There's another group at conferences that commiserates about all the woes and troubles of being a victim but I have no time for the negative.

What I Have Been Looking For

Community service was my main motive, but also the opportunity to have a very exciting career. Being in a nontraditional field appealed to me. I'm very competitive. What I like best about my job as chief is the freedom to create the job. I love working for the community, I love feeling a sense of achievement that I made it this far in my career when I never ever dreamed I would. Every day it's a blessing to come to work. I'm filled with pride that I have great people who work for me. The officers on the street are connecting with the community every day and I try to give them the tools they need, the training, the time they need to go out and do community policing, and support them when things go south on them. My style is simply to be available to them, to listen to them. Our four core values are leadership, integrity, teamwork, and service, and if you're not stroking with that boat, you're not here. We have a very good accountability system, meaning, what are you doing every day to contribute to the goals and values of this department? If you're not, your supervisor should be talking to you. The people here like each other, they work well together, and that makes a big difference. I can't take total credit for the environment here because these are good people.

Empathy is a good thing, compassion is a good thing. For the moment you're there for a crisis in someone's life, and you're helping them, you should be emotionally involved. But taking it home or making it personal is the wrong thing to do. Here's an example of the kind of community service I'm proud of.

A 74-year-old woman came out from Minnesota on a Greyhound bus to visit her daughter. She arrived at the downtown bus station, which is the dregs very late, on graveyard shift. She fell when she got off the bus and was injured. The daughter wasn't there to meet her. The bus people did nothing for her, left her sitting on a bench with $50 in her pocket. She kept calling her daughter and the daughter didn't answer. The next day she decided to spend her $50 and take a taxicab out here. She wasn't sure exactly where her daughter lived and the taxi driver wasn't very friendly, drove her around for awhile and couldn't find the address she had, and finally left her at a McDonald's. The officers got a call from McDonald's that there was this distraught woman who's been injured and dumped off by a cab. They didn't know if she was a victim of crime. An officer listened to her story and tried to find the daughter but couldn't. So he brought her to the precinct and got her lunch, coffee, turned the TV on for her and tried to identify her family. He found the house but nobody was there. It was getting into five hours of sitting here in the precinct, so I said, Find her a hotel room. The officer got her a hotel room, paid for it himself, bought her dinner because the cab driver had taken all her money. He left notes on the daughter's answering machine as to where the mother was. They do things like that all the time. They're unbelievable. I've never heard from the woman or from the daughter. But it doesn't matter, because in their minds they'll remember policing here as a very positive experience.

People should go to a department only if they value what it stands for. Every woman should make sure the department is the kind she wants to work for. Do they have good people? What's the leadership like? The vision? Would I fit in? If you'd fit, great, you'll be successful. But don't ever go to work for an organization where you're going to be unhappy.

When She Met Her Boyfriend's Parole Officer

Seattle Assistant Chief Cynthia Caldwell was born in 1954, and she is divorced with one son, age 19. She earned a BA in sociology in 1976 and her first brief jobs before joining the Seattle PD that same year were as probation and parole officer and women's prison officer. To quote from the Central Kitsap, WA Almanac, "Her introduction to law enforcement came in a surprising way—her boyfriend was arrested for burglary. When she met her boyfriend's parole officer, she knew she'd found her career field." The article noted that Cindy was, at 5'9" and 145 pounds, very athletic.

I Liked the Idea of Police Work

I was 18 when I decided to become a police officer. It was a job that paid well and had a good pension, unlike traditional women's jobs—secretary, teacher, low-level bank employee, nurse—jobs where women did all the work and made less money. My personality meshes with policing because I'm people-oriented, gregarious, and domineering. I don't take any guff but I'll be really nice when I engage people. In addition to my boyfriend's parole officer, there was a female Bremerton police detective who was a tall, blonde, stunning woman who knew my parents and I'd see her on the street looking elegant and regal and think, Wow, I like the idea of that.

I played a lot of intramural sports in college, softball, volleyball, badminton, and I ran. I took a lot of PE classes, I loved PE. I was in pretty good shape for the academy. I practiced my push-ups at home. That's all I needed to do because I aced the physical all the way through. I was fifth in my class in my total score for shooting, academics, physical. And the four people ahead of me had all taken the academy before so I felt I was number one.

How Things Have Changed

I was one of 16 women who joined the police together. We were about the same age, got married about the same time, had our babies about the same time. And we were all married to police officers. The guys would work one shift and we would work the other, so the men really got involved raising their children. But talk about hard on relationships. You're totally tired because there's nobody there to spell you when you're home for your eight-hour sleep but that's how we had to do it. Today some younger women leave, others take leaves of absence. They wish they could have part-time work and so do the young guys who are pretty good about cleaning the house, cooking, taking care of babies. Because their mothers worked, they learned it from them, and their wives work, their daughters work. This is not a new phenomenon like it was when my mother first started working.

There were no rigid roles anymore, but that's not just in the police department, that's out in the real world. When I was a precinct captain there were men who took a two-month leave of absence when their wife had a baby. Another thing, community policing used to be a women's role, but today, nationwide, both men and women do it. Guys who yell at people and throw them around end up in internal investigations. The stuff I saw when I began, it's no longer allowed. You have to behave, you can't be obnoxious.

My best friend is a sergeant and we have been friends for 26 years. Our husbands were both cops, our kids are the same age, we live in the same neighborhood, we couldn't have had more in common. She's due to retire any day. We shared everything because we experienced the same non-acceptance at the beginning, the same trouble of balancing home life and work life, the same trouble of having a baby and having to come right back to work, shift hours different from your husband. Basically we listened to one another's stresses and trials and successes and supported one another emotionally. She does horses, I do horses. We have a lot in common.

Men today don't tell as many dirty jokes or make sexist comments as they did when we first came on. They don't automatically exclude a woman from being considered for a certain position because she's a woman. You see men now wanting to help people and do problem-solving, men who are excellent community police officers and sex crime investigators.

When women were brand new, every time we went to a call the guys would critique the call and tell all four precincts, Did you hear what Sherry did this morning? Did you hear what Debbie did yesterday? On one occasion a woman was violently raped and she was sobbing and my girlfriend went over to put her arm around her to comfort her and this big macho guy who was with her came back to the precinct and said, Damn it, if that's what this police department is coming to, I don't want any part of it. How dare she act like a mother and touch that woman! That's not the case anymore. The men may not physically touch a victim but they're very sympathetic, very much so.

It used to be that you went to a call, yelled at people, threw them in jail, and left. You didn't worry about the system or people's real needs. We didn't have a list of service agencies you could refer people to. We went to roll call and everybody is 6'4". We called the men "trees," because they were hired for their bulk, not their communication skills. When we go to roll call now, there's every size of man out there because they're hired for their communication skills and education. They don't feel that it is beneath them or degrades their manhood to help people.

We Thought We'd Be Paving the Way

The sixteen who began together wanted to take promotions, we wanted to get the best jobs, we wanted to rise up, we took on all kinds of new things. We were cutting ground everywhere we went. We'd be the first woman in a unit, which was difficult, but we were willing to put ourselves out. Today there aren't many women taking the promotional tests. Our current captain and lieutenant rosters have no women on them, which means there's going to be a big gap of no promotions to the command staff ranks. There is a handful of women on the sergeant's list which just came out.

But when I and another female assistant chief leave, there will be only one female captain and two lieutenants. Women are going to be sorely underrepresented in the ranks. We have asked young women, Why aren't you doing this? They say, we want to have a home life. We want more balance and we don't need the money and we're not competitive. We don't have to be the top dog, we make enough money. Leave us alone. We don't want your problems.

We thought we'd be paving the way for other women. Maybe it's a generational thing. Remember the '80s? We were competitive. We were brought up with that go, go, go, and the generation behind me just doesn't care. They're into minimizing their lives where you don't have to have a fancy car, fancy furniture, fancy clothes. They're content and maybe it's more healthy. When you do patrol you don't have anything waiting for you the next day. You go home, it's done. Each day is a new, fresh start.

Another assistant chief did a survey, and extended leaves, career breaks, part-time, flexi-time, job sharing are what women want. Unfortunately the Law Enforcement Officers and Firefighters state pension system I was in for the first group of women did not allow job sharing. As of 1977, when LEOF 2 started, apparently part-time work is allowed and we could have job-shared. Instead we became workaholics and did not have balanced lives.

The Importance of Variety

I've had 13 jobs in 26 years. One day I was in the patrol car. One day I was doing community work. I can't imagine sitting at Boeing at the same desk working on the same widget for 30 years. I'd shoot myself. You can work with dogs, you can work with horses, drive patrol cars or ride the motorcycles. It's unbelievable. I've got the investigations bureau now and I'm really debating, Do I want to go into personnel next, with training, because that would groom me for a job in the outside world in training or human resources? Or do I want to be the very first female precinct operations chief?

I was an officer, sergeant, lieutenant, and captain on patrol longer than any other woman, ever. I could step into one of the operations bureau chiefs and handle two precincts I've worked in. I could wear my uniform and ride around with officers but I wouldn't handle calls or make arrests unless it's an accident. I like the idea of being visible for the younger women. My selfish part wants to groom myself for my next job and my unselfish part wants to help women by taking a visible position that says, We can do this.

When I retire I want to work in the private sector, security or white-collar crime or investigations for an insurance company. It would be nice to be head of security for a big corporation. I don't want to be a police chief. Maybe at a campus level but not at a municipal or sheriff's level. I don't have that thick skin to handle the politics and I'm too outspoken.

How We Got to Know One Another Back in 1997

Chief Fabienne Brooks of King County, WA, Sheriff's Office, and I go back a few years. Cliff and I had seated ourselves in the aisle and middle seats off to the left of that football field called a 747 to fly back from Heathrow to Sea-Tac. A petite, café con leche lady approached, smiling, and pointed to the window seat, which was hers. Cliff helped her off with her somber winter coat and put it and her hat up in the overhead compartment. She quickly donned earphones, sank her head into a pillow, and closed her eyes.

But you know how it is. Airplanes are as bad as hospitals, every 20 minutes waking you up with water, juice, dinner menu, another pillow, blankets, customs forms, *The Times*, duty free. With meals there's all that passing of trays, glasses, and cups back and forth. Then if it isn't the call of the captain, it's the call of nature. So as time passed we got acquainted. She was returning from a six-month sabbatical devoted to the ins and outs of equal opportunities in British law enforcement. We were returning from our 6-month annual sojourn in London, where we wrote statistical texts and books based on interviews with interesting people. I said I'd be happy to read and comment on the draft of her report, if she'd like, and she did. So that's how we came to know one another back in 1997.

Fae was born in Harlem, New York City, in 1951. She is married to a retired firefighter captain who spent 32 years with the Seattle Fire Department. They have four children, all in their thirties. A graduate of the FBI Academy, Fae has a first-level middle management and executive certification in law enforcement with the state. Her goal is to finish her BA in business management before she retires, with an eye toward law enforcement education as her next career.

I've Always Liked Change

My first job was legal secretary for the Public Defenders Office but law enforcement—FBI, criminology, something along those lines—was what I had always wanted to do. I've always liked change, new and different assignments. I started as a regular secretary and ended up as the executive secretary to the head of the agency. Throughout that time I was also the investigator office manager. I had a lot of contact with the Sheriff's Office. You can tell from people's voices, whether they're happy to talk to you or not and these deputies were always happy to talk to me. I thought they'd be a pretty nice group to join. That's why it was the only place I tested in and the only place I've worked.

As far back as I can remember, I was probably nine, I would visit my great-grandmother in Washington, D.C. One of her sons, my grandmother's brother, was a police officer. He would come home in his uniform and I can remember being in awe of how handsome he looked. My Dad was in the Navy, so being in uniform wasn't a foreign concept for me.

My grandmother and mother came out to watch me graduate from the academy, and Grandmother came out when I was appointed to major and Mom saw me appointed to chief. They're very proud but my Mom, because of the environment we're living in now, is nervous. She understands that my role is different than front line, but she still worries.

It Was Like Going to College

When I was going through the recruiting process, one of the tests was the Harvard step test. They check your heart rate before, during, and after. The Sheriff's Office offered training to prepare people for that test so I did that because I had no idea what I was getting into. I also had a friend who helped me run.

One day at the academy all 26 of us were in a circle and we'd just finished doing push-ups and this guy comes over and picks me up—he's one of my colleagues now, he's a deputy—by my hand and my leg and starts twirling around and I'm yelling, Put me down, put me down. He didn't put me down when I said to, he put me down when he got ready. And when he did, I hit him in the throat and knocked him on the ground and said, Don't ever do that to me again. He looked at me and said, All right. After that I had men helping and motivating me because they saw that I wasn't afraid to stand up for myself.

Overall, I was number two in the academy and I would have been number one but I didn't know how to shoot a gun. I had never held a gun, never fired a gun. Six months later I found out why I was having so much trouble. One of the guys who took me under his wing said, You know, that grip looks too big for your hand. Let's go get you another one. He got me another one and I did better. It was a .357 magnum with a stock grip. That's huge for a small hand. I was able to do it with a different grip. Shooting has never been my strong point. I have to carry a gun, but if I didn't have to, I wouldn't.

Two years of college helped me develop the study habits I needed for the academy and once I got in, my husband, who I was dating then, had been through firefighting academy. He helped me through that process. It was like going to college. I had to come home and type up my notes every night and he would have a hot bath ready for me because I'd be sore. Sometimes he cooked dinner for me. He knew what the pressure was like. The day I graduated from the academy was when he asked me to marry him.

I also had the experience of growing up as a Navy brat and being the only minority in the school on the base. Groton, Connecticut, Adak, Alaska, Sasebo, Japan. I'm used to being the "only." I'm used to being able to come out of a shell and talk to people. Being the only woman in my academy class was no big deal after being the only Black in high school for so many years.

Sex Crimes and the Job

I joined in 1978 and after a year and eight months the Sheriff's Office was expanding their sex crimes unit, which was three males. The sex crime counselors had asked to have women and a bigger unit. Most officers expect to wait five years to become a detective.

I was in that unit for two years when I got involved with the Green River investigation because I was able to talk to prostitutes and many of the victims were prostitutes. After a few months they disbanded the investigation and I went back to sex crimes. When the investigation got big again, I was back in it. When they cut it back again I became the department's media relations officer.

In April 1984 the Green River investigation hit another peak. We needed a media relations officer for Green River and one for the department. I was media relations officer for Green River until January 1989. Got promoted to sergeant and did a graveyard shift for a year.

Then became sergeant over the sex crimes unit and did that until 1991 when I got promoted to precinct operations lieutenant until 1993. I had developed a very good working relationship with the precinct commander, and when she got appointed to Chief of Technical Services she brought me down to be her administrative services commander. This included personnel, recruitment, training, civil process, property management.

From August of 1996 until March of 1997 I was on an Atlantic Fellowship in Public Policy, living in London and doing research on equal opportunities policy in law enforcement. After that my assignment went back and forth between precinct captain or commander and CID (Criminal Investigation Division) captain. In July 1999 I was appointed chief of the CID and I've been doing that ever since.

My span of control is diverse. I have homicide, robbery, child abuse, child neglect, domestic violence, computer forensics, criminal profiteering investigations, criminal warrants, child find, which is primarily custodial interference-type cases, special support enforcement unit apprehending people who haven't paid child support, court protection and security, criminal intelligence.

On the Home Front

My husband and kids have told me that when I came home I was always like a Mom. I wasn't a cop. I'd just leave everything from work on the ride home and pick it up on the way in. But one of the downfalls was that my husband never knew what I did. He would hear me on the phone and that's how he'd find out what was going on. I never shared stuff I was doing. Every now and then, the kids would say, Oh, oh, she's got her police voice.

Other than that, I have this thing about wanting the kitchen clean before I go to bed. But one night I went to bed early and when I got up the next morning I discovered plates all over the place and I got everybody up and into the kitchen and said, What is this? Can't you guys just clean the kitchen up after yourselves? I'm not your maid. They stood there looking at me like, Has she lost her mind?

How We Recruit, Retain, Reward

We have a slick recruitment brochure and we do a lot of target recruiting aimed at nontraditional programs that teach women to be mechanics, riveters, carpenters. Our chief recruiter also targets community colleges, parades, community fairs and festivals, gyms.

In terms of applying for positions, it's an open process. Anybody who wants to apply, can. We have women who have been canine officers, on motorcycles. We have a woman commander of our helicopter unit and we had a woman at one point who was over in our marine unit and we've had a woman in our major accident reconstruction unit. In our special assault unit, sex crimes unit, we try to make sure it's at least 50-50, and that's 14 detectives. If a woman can compete on an equal basis, if she's the number one, she gets the job. We have a woman everywhere except SWAT.

In terms of rewarding people, I like to send people little cards saying, I've nominated you for an award from the department or I've put you in for recognition. Last month the computer forensics unit I nominated for an award got it so I participated in the award dinner. It was sponsored by an association of security investigators. My unit got a certificate and a plaque.

Last year I finally, after persistent pressure, got people more involved in our division's Christmas-holiday potluck. Last year my two captains and I made baskets, which we raffled off. This year we're going to have awards for detective and employee of the year. Here everybody's so focused on their work that they don't want to take time out to celebrate. Up until now it was always just a get-together over food but nobody interacted and talked. But if you put the food in one room and dessert down the hall, it encourages people to mill around and eat and talk as opposed to taking your plate back to your desk.

She'd Shut the Door and We'd Vent

The mentor who has had the biggest impact on me was a woman. It was 12 years before I worked with her. The way we communicated, we just clicked. I could talk to her about issues, things that I had to decide as the ops lieutenant. I could pick her brain and she wouldn't look at me as though I was stupid. The fact that she was able to provide that mentorship helped me quite a bit during 1991-1994. Toward the end she was at the end of her career. She was the first woman chief that we had and she was working with two men who would make decisions on the golf course affecting her division and she wouldn't know about it until after the fact. As she was leaving, she said, Don't use me as a role model because I'm burned out. But I continued to because she was still in there, handling it. She'd shut the door and we'd vent. Then we'd open the door and she'd be okay, for awhile. She cleared the path. She made it easier for the second woman to come in and be a chief and that woman made it easier for me to come in and be the next one.

My first year as a chief, if I had continued at the same pace, I would be burned out by now. I was trying to be everything to everybody, be here from 6 a.m. until 6 p.m., and at the same time out in the field. I was coming in on weekends and I couldn't do it all. Fortunately I realized after a year it couldn't continue.

Women's Issues, Racial Issues

When I was on patrol as a deputy, people called me "colored bitch," but nobody called me the "n" word. My attitude was they can call me whatever they want. That's fine with me. Most of them were handcuffed and going to jail, and I was going home. You know that about my Mom? Sure. Whatever. People would say,

Get me a real cop here and I'd say, I'm it. I'm the only one you got. So either you tell me or you don't. I had situations like this one. I was dispatched with a couple of other officers to a bar disturbance. A big guy was in there, drunk, causing a problem. I get there first. I go in because he's not physical, he's just verbal. I go in, I talk him down, he's ready to go. We turn a corner, there's a male officer and I can immediately see him click on, he wants to fight. I told the male officer, Do me a favor. Go around the corner, keep me in your sight, don't let him see you. He did that, the guy calmed down, and went on his way.

When I was a detective in the sex crimes unit, there was an opportunity to go on an extradition to California because it was my case. But the sergeant of the extradition unit said, No, because I guess he assumed that I wouldn't be able to control the prisoner on the plane. My male partner went instead. Then there was a deputy who referred to me and another female officer as "cunts." When I heard this I approached him about it. He went to the lieutenant and whined. I was a sergeant then. The lieutenant came to me and said, I understand this happened. Are you going to be able to work with this guy? I said, Sure, if he's going to be able to work with me. I've had that happen.

We've recently been involved in a situation where a white officer killed a Black male. It was like the straw that broke the camel's back for the African American community. Consequently I spent a lot of time interacting with the African American community, in part because I am a part of it. I go to church in that community and people there have known me from before I became a cop. After I became a cop I wasn't any different. I'd hang out, party, have lunch at local restaurants. In spite of this relationship I had to tell both sides that I'm here as an impartial person, trying to do the right thing. But the white officers think I'm a spy for the Black community. I had to spend a lot of time letting people know I'm here to do my job. And my job is to talk to people on both sides, get people calmed down so that they can see the big picture.

That's been one issue I've faced, as has been my continued willingness to be a part of the Black Law Enforcement Association of Washington. Some white officers feel, Why do you need that group? Maybe we should have a white male officers group. I was president of the group. I'm still a dues-paying participant. But early on, white officers would wonder, Why do you need that kind of group? Isn't that divisive? Why do you need a woman's group? Isn't that divisive? I would tell them, No, it's not. It's a way for us to help each other get through this. Periodically I go to meetings and get re-energized and re-invigorated. They help me deal with racial issues. The same thing with the women's groups. Because of the way I grew up, I don't need that support as much as other people do, but both kinds of groups are needed.

When You Look at What Could Have Happened

From the time I was five until I left home at 17 to live with my grandmother in New York, my Dad sexually abused me. I never realized until we were going to Japan that he wasn't my natural Dad, but my adoptive Dad. I grew up thinking, that's how it was supposed to be. When I hear people talk about their childhoods, I don't have a lot of memories because I've compartmentalized my growing up. That's why this career is so unusual for me especially working with the Green River investigation. Almost to a person all of those young girls had been sexually abused in one way or another, and there, but for the grace of God, would have been me. Maybe it was because of my grandmother's influence, but I didn't use that experience as an excuse. It is a part of who I am, it made me who I am, and I believed I had to deal with it. I could be a totally different person if I didn't have a strong faith and a belief that what happens to you happens for a reason and you should use it in a positive way as opposed to a chip on your shoulder.

This chapter reiterated what we've learned earlier about meeting home and job responsibilities. Carol's husband does most of the work of taking care of their children. In contrast, Cynthia and her police officer husband shared that work. Denise goes out of her way to accommodate women who need flexible schedules and short leaves. And Fae reminds us that the way to be a good mom is to leave the job behind when open your front door.

A headline in *The Independent* of February 4, 2003, read "Met chief says police stations need crèches." Sir John Stevens, the Metropolitan Police Commissioner, said every main police station in London should have a crèche to attract more women into the police service. He said far more needed to be done to increase the "pitifully" low number of female officers—17% of the Met's 27,750 officers. He said it should be 30%. Within five months he planned to install a crèche at Hendon where recruits are trained (Bennetto, 2003).

14

The Importance of Family Support

"How did your mother and father react when you told them you were going into law enforcement," was one of my questions. Women considering law enforcement need to be prepared for parental resistance and think over ways to handle it.

One mom "wasn't crazy about it. She wished I wouldn't subject myself to the perils of law enforcement. She still worries, that's what you do when you're a mom." Another mom "was particularly shocked. Going into federal investigations doesn't sound that ominous, but doing patrol work, driving around in a patrol car alone late at night, that's much different." Another mother was very vocal about it. "What are you doing? You're a mother, you shouldn't do this." Obviously the women I talked to had dealt successfully with their mothers' anxiety, even if "success" meant simply putting it out of their minds.

Countless books have been written about "mother love and the power of fear," which is actually the title of one of these tomes. The message is that keeping children out of danger is the signature virtue of motherhood. When daughters leave street patrol for a desk job, mothers' alarm systems subside, but when daughters return to the street, the alarm systems get set on high again. One major when she started out was relieved that she was sent to her city's south end precinct because it kept her out of her mother's north end neighborhood. "Every time she heard a siren, she didn't have to think maybe it was me."

In spite of moms' worries, 57 parents of the women were supportive, equal numbers of mothers and fathers. Twelve parents were indifferent, while 29 parents reacted negatively, 16 moms and 13 dads. (Data are missing for two women.) Fortunately with the passage of time, motherly worries are joined by pride and support, and dubious fathers likewise become extremely proud and very supportive.

Born in 1959 and single, Captain Mitzi Johanknecht spent five years playing collegiate basketball with the intent of majoring in education. She is looking forward to taking criminal justice courses relevant to working at the executive level within the Washington State system. When we met she was in charge of the special investigations section of the Criminal Investigation Division for King County, WA. The CID is divided into two halves and Mitzi oversees one of those two halves. Mitzi's father got her into athletics by playing baseball in the front yard when she was four. In addition to field hockey, which she had recently taken up, she plays basketball, softball, soccer, volleyball, rugby, bowling, and golf. Mitzi is a good example of both mother and father being positive and supportive.

Mom and Dad and the Academy

There were six months between the test and a phone call saying we have a slot for you at the academy. I was working for my Dad who was managing the Space Needle so I ran the stairs there on my break. I knew I needed to work on upper body strength as well. Also, it had been awhile since I had been in the mode to read and retain at the college level. The things that are thrown at you are condensed, criminal law and criminal procedures, so I started doing general investigative reading. I was proudest of my driving skills. I was the best driver in our class. Even now when we have emergency vehicle operations I finish well. I started driving when I was 15 so I had ten years' experience by the time I got into the academy. Plus my Mom was a good driving instructor.

My parents were excited and supportive as they have been all my life, but it was telling when I moved toward more desk-oriented jobs and my Mom could now take a deep breath and not be as worried as she had been. She worried that I would get hurt, that someone would intentionally try to take my life. She'd think, I know with the training Mitzi's had that she won't do anything stupid. I know she's careful. I know she's larger than most people so she has that advantage. My parents' concern now is for my overall well-being because as I've moved up in the organization, I've had to distance myself from the people who were my peers. You have to, because now you are managing them. The other captains, there are 19 of us, who are now my peers, are spread out across the county so we don't have that much direct interaction.

My Mom understands this and checks in every weekend. How are you doing? What's been happening? She's always been a listening ear. When I played high school and college basketball we spent hours after the games, debriefing. That's the role she takes now. She listens to personnel issues I have that I can't really share with anybody else. My Dad, too, he'd been a manager for many years so I go to him for pieces of wisdom: I have this situation, what do you think?

I'm a Caretaker

Patrol is the heart of our organization, single-person cars covering hundreds of square miles. So you don't know how soon somebody's going to get there. There are now more women for the men to relate to and they've realized the gift of gab and being able to talk people out of situations is invaluable.

Law enforcement kind of chose me for a variety of reasons. Through sports I had some very good older friends who were in the field, so early on I had an understanding of it. I thought that I had the personality, temperament and inner strength required to do the job. It was intriguing, across the board, in the things you deal with on a daily basis at the patrol level.

I'm a caretaker. I worry about others and put others first frequently. Policing takes an incredible amount of patience and self-discipline. At the same time you have to be able to quickly assess and take action. I don't hold things personally and don't worry about the little things, because 99% of the time you're in an adversarial position with someone, or something horrific has happened in their life so that they need the police. You have to be able to deflect abuse that comes your way because typically it's not intended and it's not personal.

What I've experienced is that women are good at knowing their abilities and not relying on physical strength. The guys understand that now. We have, at least within our organization, men who talk and counsel and barter versus laying hands-on. The men have learned and continue to learn from women, sometimes simply from interacting with us, watching, but also from having a true bond, a relationship, with women. However, I don't know if it's just an evolution within the culture of this particular organization.

I Like to Get Out in the Field

I get out in the field now when I have command duty for captains and above where for a week we're in charge after hours and on weekends. Aside from that, whenever I have callouts for any of my units, or when my partner's gone, like he is this week, if we have a major crime situation, I go out to the scene and help facilitate whatever the needs are of the unit that is investigating. My computer and fraud group does a lot of search warrants, a lot of identity theft, and also with the drug unit, I can gear up and go out with them.

I try to be open with the people I supervise on a daily basis. I go out and experience situations with them to better understand what they are dealing with. I work hand in hand with them, for example, this morning I was down to the county courthouse. We have this high profile temporary restraining order being heard involving the Issaquah School District and the teachers who are on strike. I have a court protection sergeant there and his staff of deputies and screeners, but it's not like we're ever staffed at the level we should be. This is a fairly big media event and there were 400 people trying get into a court that holds 200. I met with him last week to make sure he had an operations plan to take care of any eventuality and that he had the personnel he needed. This morning it was just check-in. Do you need anything? What can I facilitate? And then stand in the background so he can come up and ask me any questions he has.

When the chief is gone, she appoints either me or my partner to be acting chief. This summer it happened that both she and my partner were gone when we had the death of a deputy. Then, the following weekend, three of our deputies were shot at a meth lab search warrant. Both of those times I was in charge of the division. As it worked out, I don't live too far away from where the deputy was killed, so I was at the command post in five minutes. From my level what I'm dealing with is oversight, an instant command setup to make sure we're doing all the right things we're supposed to do in the investigation, to ensure the safety of everyone else in that area until the bad guy is in custody, and then to make sure a proper investigation results in a charge and we get this successfully through the criminal justice system.

When the victim is somebody you know and have supervised, you still have to put on your professional face and kick in and be a model for everyone else who works under you. So that everybody can chug along with you and do what they have to do. You have to be there with the detective who has to deal with the body. You're balancing a bunch of different things, answering to the sheriff, answering to the chief of field operations, making sure that we have enough officers on site, that the rest of the county is still being protected and police business going on that needs to be.

I immediately assigned people to work on support services for the family and who was going to do the notification of the family. It's a mish-mash of things to be done: the criminal investigation, taking care of the family, taking care of the people that work there. I set up critical incident stress debriefs because I knew the impact this was going to have on everyone who participated. Keeping people busy, keeping track of people. When I first got there, the scene was still hot because the bad guy wasn't in custody. He had fled to his girlfriend's apartment so I had to coordinate with the patrol sergeant who was in charge of the interior and exterior perimeter. We had to establish communication with him, to get him to come out.

It's organized chaos. It's amazing. Everybody knows their job and their professionalism kicks in. The county has a personal assistance team, PATs, that is made up of officers, deputies, professional staff. And then we have mental health professionals from the county who are assigned to us and two or three of them will debrief. Those folks who were directly involved you want to take care of quickly and get to before they leave the scene. Then the next day they have another debrief, which is a time to talk about anything. Anybody and everybody can talk and there are rules around privacy. It usually starts out with a small group of those folks who were intimately involved, it may be five or ten people. Then there's also a larger debriefing for anybody who would like to come on an individual basis.

My Mentor for 17 Years

My mentor is another captain who has since retired. He's not only been my mentor for the four years I have been a captain, but before that he influenced my career a lot even though he probably doesn't recognize it. He was a patrol sergeant of mine. When I was a sergeant he was my field officer lieutenant.

He's a very fair-minded person, a quiet leader, calm, dedicated, somebody you would go into battle with and never question what he told you to do. The uniqueness about our relationship is that he and I come from really different places and when we get together, we see things differently. I sought out somebody who would give me perspectives I hadn't considered.

It's probably been a couple of months since I've seen him. The last time I had a personnel issue. I had a manager who was treating a line staff employee unfairly. The employee was like a target, a person to pick on. He and I talked a lot about the various approaches I could take. He brought in a lot of experience in his point of view based on 30-some years in law enforcement. The problem was all about personality, and in this business, personalities have to be set aside. What we came up with was to ask the manager to pre-think actions whenever possible. Is what I am about to do how I would treat another employee who wasn't a target? How would I treat that person? I hope it had an impact because otherwise this behavior will end up hurting the manager.

Chief Colleen Wilson

Monroe, WA's population is 15,000, but the Safeway draws from a population of 180,000. When I interviewed recently retired Chief Colleen Wilson in the spring of 2002, I knew that she had been the first woman police chief in Washington State. She joined the Monroe PD in 1977, was promoted to sergeant in 1986, to lieutenant in 1989 (second in command), and to chief in 1993. She would begin a new job with the state training commission in Burien the week after we met. She chaired this commission for five years at a time of transition. Again, it's a time of change and Colleen will manage police officer certification and decertification. She has trained cops, physicians, evidence technicians, the public defenders' association, the librarians' association, and lay persons in all aspects of intimate violence all over the state.

She was born in Seattle in 1950 and attended Gonzaga University, leaving two quarters short of graduation. If she goes back to college, she'd like to study organizational development. She is married to a semi-retired high school teacher of English and history. She has a son 28 and a daughter 23. She's a good example of both parents not being supportive, far from it. In 1973 Colleen was the town hall receptionist.

How I Fell into Law Enforcement

The day after Thanksgiving a woman came to the counter wearing a big heavy coat with her hands in the pockets. She leaned over and said, Hi, I just shot my husband in the head. I said, Have a seat over there and I'll get someone to help you. Fortunately she wasn't armed because it never occurred to me that I might be in danger. It only occurred to me that I didn't know what to do. I got an off-duty officer who'd been working on his truck in the city garage to come to get her. In those days they wanted a woman with a female prisoner, so I went through the works with them at the jail. Later he told me, Ohmigod, you should have gotten her hands out of her pockets. The first thing he did was take her coat off because he thought she might still be armed. After that, I went to the chief and said, If you're going to stick me up here at the front desk, I'd better have some training. That's how I ended up going to reserve school. I was supposed to just go to a few classes, but I had a 14-month-old little one and I craved adult companionship, so I told my husband, I'm going through the whole thing.

Once I got my diploma, I said I want to be a reserve officer. The officers I worked with encouraged me. They said, You're good at this. We need women.

You should try for the position they're testing for. Well, I was taking in the applications and knew there were people with college degrees and lots of experience, but I took that test to shut those men up, because I didn't think I had a chance. But when that written test was done and I had finished number five, my competitiveness got the better of me. I said to my husband, I have to try this.

I studied pre-law in college but I never planned to work. I had that Fifties Mom thing. I was going to get married and have six kids. The only reason I went to work was to pay off a bunch of medical bills. But I learned at work that I needed it and eventually I would have a career. But the choice was pure luck.

What Other People Had to Say

Dad was horrified, he was so vocal and disdainful, that my brother took him aside and said, You know you've spent her whole life telling her she could do anything she wanted to do and be anything she wanted to be. For my Dad, that meant an acceptable female profession because then it would have been cutting-edge to be even a lawyer. But being a cop and going out and wrestling people—ladies didn't do that. My brother said, You've given her this message all her life. You don't get to change now. You have to accept who she is and what she's chosen to do. It was the first time in my life that I'd done something just for me. I had done things because people told me to. You're a four-point student, you should go to college. I had done things because people told me not to. You can't do that. Watch me. But I had never said, I want to do this and I don't care what anyone else thinks. The day I graduated from Quantico at the FBI Academy—and by this time I knew I was going to be appointed the first female chief in the State—was the first time my Dad told me he was proud of me. My mother was appalled. It must be because you want to be around all those men.

Now they're totally fine with it. They were raised in that generation where what the neighbors think is important. People are more accepting now. They no longer go, She does what? They were also frightened for me. Over the years I've been able to educate them to the fact that it isn't dangerous compared to other things people do. My brother was a fisherman, a purse seiner up in Alaska every summer, and they didn't bat an eyelid at that.

My husband had a lot of objections. He thought it was dangerous, it wasn't what he had in mind, shift-work wasn't what he had planned. He said, It is not what I would choose for you or us or our children, but if it's important to you, I will try to support you in every way I can. At the time, Seattle PD was tracking their females and females who had been married prior to the academy were not married, almost 100%, by the end of the academy. The academy alone destroyed these relationships. So at times it wasn't easy, but Jerry really has lived up to his word.

Welcome to the Academy??

When I walked on to the academy grounds, I asked for directions from a Seattle officer and he said, Why? I said, I'm reporting to the recruit class. He said, You don't look like a cop. I'd been working the street for nine months, so I'd heard that before. I said, Well, I am a cop. He said, I'm your tac officer and it's my job to make sure you don't stay a cop. I said, Okay, thanks very much for sharing.

I could run but I had never done anything else physical. I'd had back surgery so I had to work at upper body strength and I especially struggled with push-ups. I had trouble with the wall the first week and no instructor came forward and said, Here's how you do it and taught me a technique. But a classmate said, Use my knee for a boost, because you've got to hit the wall above here. He explained the technique and I never missed the wall again. Dozens of men facilitated my success in that way. When it came time for the push-ups test at the end of the academy, understand no one ever told me there was anything wrong with my form, I could do the push-ups but guess who was going to count them? I did the number required but he decided I was short two because they were not militarily correct, the angle of my arms didn't meet 90 degrees. However, I had been hired before the mandatory training law so Monroe could keep me even though I was refused a diploma based on those two push-ups. Eventually the physical test was changed to the Cooper's standards and the folks at the state training commission sent me an accreditation certificate because my performance would have fallen within those standards.

Early on the Road

Graveyard worked well for me personally when the kids were little. We adopted our daughter when she was three days old. I took three months leave without pay and then worked graveyard or swing while she was growing up. I could have used my vacation and comp time, but I couldn't use my sick leave.

We were still a small community, one officer working at night, and we were very dependent on each other. My FTO was determined to put people out there who would take care of their fellow officers. I worked graveyard for years, the only woman in Snohomish County on the road all alone. This FTO was a salty old Southerner. He let me know it was okay to be afraid. Little lady, he said, There's only two kinds of people out there, what ain't scared and they's liars and fools. Everybody's scared out there, no matter whether they tell you so or not. He took it as a personal source of pride that I succeed and not wash out.

The guy hired right behind me was a defensive tactics instructor. He and I worked overlap for many years as partners in drugs, and he had not received traditional DT instruction. He was one of the first students of the movement that says, One size does not fit all. I told him, In DT they taught me this hold but it never works because I'm always smaller than the person I'm trying to control. He said, Quit practicing it. If it doesn't work for you, don't do it. When they gave me the standard baton, I had bruises all over because it was too long for my arm. They took it out to the shop and cut two inches off of it. Years later the company made batons for smaller people, but back then it was, if the equipment doesn't fit her, we'll fix the equipment, but we don't tell her she can't do it.

When I started, what I heard was, We are a very, very conservative community. But by handling everyone fairly, the community gradually began to identity itself as "We're the place where there's a woman chief." A lot of people I didn't even know were proud of it. I still have to know how to talk the good ol' boy stuff. When I go to the east side of the mountains, I train very differently than training here, especially when I'm introducing the idea of supporting officers' families.

Some of My Dealings with Men

I passed up the sergeant's exam the first time. I had found myself repeatedly being an acting supervisor and the chief had given me the budget as an extra assignment. He said, You've got to put in for sergeant. I said, I'm not interested. He said, You're already doing it. And if you don't put in, you're going to have to work for that guy over there. I said, I can't work for him. He said, Then take the goddamn test. I did and I finished way ahead of that guy.

I wasn't sure I wanted to be chief. I enjoyed being the second in command, but the chief's job did intrigue me. I was in Quantico when our chief turned in his intention to retire. The city said, Okay, we'll do a nationwide search. While I was away the officers who had been working for me to a person showed up at the civil service commission meeting and said, We'd like you to do an internal test because we think we have a candidate here. There were 80 people in the council chambers telling the city council, we'd like you to do an internal test. With that public pressure they changed their minds and even the current mayor who fired me in March was one of those people who said, We should give her a chance. They did an internal test and I became chief in April 1993 and that was the first time a woman had been a chief in Washington.

As far as overprotection is concerned, when I see male officers act like White Knights, I've told them, I know you're trying to help that female officer, but you're really hurting her. You can't do that. I went to this Rural Executive Management Program in Arkansas and this bigoted, sexist sheriff was there from Louisiana. One evening we were sitting across the table at dinner and I'd had a glass of wine and I got up my courage because at Quantico the guys would say, We want to know what you think, Colleen, we want to know how we can help our female officers. They had nobody like me to turn to and say, How should I deal with them? I coached them to let women use what they have. If they want to bat their eyelashes at some guy to control him, shut up and let them do that. Women should be taught to use all the skills they have at their disposal.

I was going to try to strike my blow with this sheriff from Louisiana. I said, I heard you say you don't let your female officers work nights. I said, Do you realize how unfair that is? You're depriving them of the really important skills and abilities they need to be considered qualified by their peers. He said, Well, I let her work nights one time but I ended up with a suspect with a broken jaw out of that deal. I said, Ohmigod, she broke a suspect's jaw? And he said, Hell, no, them other officers broke that suspect's jaw because he wouldn't call her Ma'am. I said, I surrender. You obviously work in a different world.

The Family-Friendly Department

What ended up "working" in our college recruiting was the department's reputation for being family-friendly. I always told my staff that you can't do this job and survive psychologically unless you have support. That support must come from some form of family unit, parents, partner, spouse. You have to have that or you won't make it. It's true. People don't stay single through this job. It's tough on relationships but the relationships are the real foundation. I call my husband my rock.

We were one of the first agencies in the area to modify a space in which to do child interviews. Back in the '70s I had to use the chief's office to do interviews on the floor because his was the only room with a carpet. We wallpapered a corner, bought children's books, crayons, put in a gumball machine, and we not only use it for interviews but it's a comfortable place where officers can bring their kids, say if they were making shift exchanges and needed 15 minutes here.

Officers who come in on their day off for a meeting, for example, don't have to do daycare. The kids would sit and color.

When I became chief in '93, we started a tradition of hanging family flags. First we did it with the group that we had and then we were going to do a lot of hiring and I wanted to keep the team together and emphasize that families were important. Every family made a flag that was the symbol of their family. We had prizes for the one that involved kids the most, the one with the most ethnic statements in it, the best over all. The flags are four by four and they hang way up in the work area, which has tall ceilings. Then whenever a new officer came, we would have a potluck and hang his or her family flag and they would talk about it. Their kids could come by with their friends and say, That's our family flag.

We also developed a new officer packet for families. It has the "I Love A Cop" book by a psychologist in it, the trigger lock for the spouse or partner if there are children, color books, and books appropriate to the ages of the children, if they have children. It contains our family questionnaire in the event of death or injury. The partner gets a copy and the officer gets a copy so they have to get together to fill that out.

That we support families has become a value that's clearly understood. If you talk to anybody who grew up under me in law enforcement, it's about giving people support, say if they need time off. It goes back to that salty old guy who hired me. He was supportive of families, in his own way. He would always say, If you don't have things straight with Pappy, then your mind isn't on your work. You can't do this job unless you keep things straight at home. I struggled with my marriage and I know what it's like to juggle the kids. Women shouldn't forget those years of juggling as they move up through the ranks.

We should try to accommodate a woman with a two-year-old. She's not going to have a two-year-old forever. Because our department's so small, we've taken it case by case, but it did establish precedent. Right now we have a female officer who went on maternity leave, tried to come back, struggled mightily with guilt feelings, and finally came in and said, I think I need to resign. I said, I'm not going to accept your resignation. We need to look first for alternatives. So we worked out a half-time position. She's going to do a job-share with a second half-time position. We had another woman who lost her babysitter suddenly and she needed to have her schedule moved by one hour to cope with this emergency. She wasn't impacting anyone else's schedule and we did that for four months until she could get something worked out.

We allowed officers to take sick leave time to care for sick children way before the Family and Medical Leave Act became effective, which was a technical violation of city policy. I told the woman who's now half-time that I also was willing to entertain a career break for her. But you can only do that for two years in this State before you lose your certification.

When women officers new to the area asked around, If you were going to have a family, where would you work, they'd hear, Go to Monroe. However, we've also been labeled The Love Police because I expected negotiation and communication skills from the officers first.

Creating a Universe

When I became chief I figured it was my chance to create a universe. I tried to take everything that I thought was important and see if it would work. Our department was rapidly growing so a new culture was being created. If you go into a department that is stable, you're stuck with the culture and only so many innovations will fly. I knew from my organizational development classes that here was a unique opportunity to cultivate values and to control the organization much more by values than by rules. One job of supervisors was to cultivate the attitude that it's important to have a family. Another example is physical fitness. We placed a lot of emphasis and reward on being fit. You get extra points and extra money for exceptional fitness and we also used peer pressure. We test every year. There is no stick. Only carrots and peer pressure. When we began hiring new officers, we said, Here's the standard and you have to maintain it. We use the Cooper's standards.

I brought a rocking chair in for me, because I tend to become hyperactive. I would sit in the rocking chair and rock while I was talking to someone on the phone who was irritating. I originally took down the rocking chair that I had rocked my babies in, but cops started sitting in it so much that it was getting all beat up from their gunbelts. I bought another one in a secondhand store. They'd be upset about something and come and rock in the rocking chair. I had lots of plants in my office, Tootsie Roll pops, a gumball machine, to draw the cops in and keep my office from being a place that nobody went into.

Cindy, one of my sergeants, had kids who were older but she wanted to be able to be a mom and to balance that role with work, so that's why she came here. Then Sheri wanted to have kids and other women told her, Go to Monroe. We worked out a policy so that she could come back to work and still breastfeed. She simply arranged to have someone hold her calls for the time that it took, and they'd bring the baby by and she'd go in and use the rocker in my office and turn on the stereo. She joked about that a lot with the new chief coming in. Shall we tell him there's probably breast milk on that rocker? Tomorrow I'm bequeathing the gumball machine to the sergeant in charge of detectives, because she has kids in and out of her office. I'll give the rocking chair to the other sergeant, and my hope is that it will be a symbol in the sergeants' space that families are important.

I also teach agency administration, how to run a police organization, domestic violence, child physical abuse, child sexual abuse, elder abuse, personal safety. I created a pilot curriculum with my partner, the DT guy, that was recognized with an award from the State School Superintendent. It's still taught in our junior high, to seventh and eighth graders. It tells kids that if an adult lays hands on them, they are not powerless.

Handling a Growing Minority Population

In my nine years as chief the town went from 6% to 15% Hispanic. Dealing with the growing Hispanic population here has been a priority for me. I'm well-known in the Hispanic community and trusted. The first time we put out a call for Hispanics, and made Spanish-speaking officers a priority, was 12 years ago. At that time there was no one who spoke Spanish in the school district or in the city hall. We gave extra points for speaking Spanish and, when I left, out of 30 officers we had four Spanish-speakers in commissioned, and two Spanish-speakers in our noncommissioned staff, including three Hispanics. Plus we had repeated classes for officers in survival Spanish. Half a dozen other officers can communicate well enough to handle most situations and are not totally dependent on translators.

I also worked closely with Hispanic moms through a woman who had a day-care center because it's very hard to keep your children in check and to parent the way we normally would if you can't speak to the parents of your children's friends. We worked with the Catholic church and local hospital to offer survival English classes without asking for green cards. We did a big health fair and got children immunized. My message always was, I don't care whether you're here legally or illegally, if you're just trying to make it here, we provide services. But if you commit a felony, we'll send you away. Their stories paralleled my grandfather's, coming over here from Ireland. They're just looking for a better life.

A group of concerned high school kids came to me several years ago and said there's a lot of racism on our campus and we think it's going to erupt into violence. We have been to our principal, to the superintendent's office, but they're into denial and say there are no problems. This came on the heel of an incident that made the front page of the local paper which said there was a tavern in town that wouldn't serve you if you couldn't speak English, true story.

We did a survey to see what other people thought about racism in town. The questionnaires we got back, said No, there was no racism, which confirmed the denial. Yet, we had seen it, I'd seen it sometimes in officers. I decided we needed some kind of community event to celebrate the differences. The kids also needed a community group at school. They had a multicultural club, but it didn't include any Hispanics. The Spanish teacher agreed to help us. She got together with the multicultural advisor to develop interest in the club and now it just bubbles with energy.

I got five community leaders together and said we need an event and our first was a Cinco de Mayo celebration. We were all Anglos, there were no Hispanics at the table at that time, but I did get advice from those moms who I worked with. They were afraid to come to the meetings. The first celebration was pretty white. I wanted it to be grassroots so once I got some money and community leadership for it, I stepped back, and I didn't come to the table anymore. Three years ago the Mexican Consulate came and we had 4,000 people. That was really cool. The women wanted to cook, so we had the health department come out and do a class in Spanish and the women got their thermometers and health cards so after that it wasn't just restaurants doing the cooking.

Now it's a really big event and is called El Carnaval. They've moved it away from Cinco de Mayo to one week later so that the restaurants could participate better. We chose Cinco de Mayo because we knew that Anglos could understand it and we wanted common ground. El Carnaval still has a Latin flair, but now they have a Trip Around the World Passport and the booths represent many different ethnic backgrounds. If I've left a legacy, it's that these different groups are now embracing each other.

Officer Tana Gwordske

The woman for whom Colleen created a job-sharing position is Tana, born in 1968 and the mother of a 3-year-old adopted son, Jake. Tana practices her Spanish with Jake's relatives in Guatamala por teléfono. Tana's husband is a deputy sheriff. Tana has a BA in sociology and chose police work in 1996 after working as a court clerk. She currently works three 6-hour shifts and then has three days off.

What I Get Out of It

It sounds so canned, but we're looked to for help and I wanted to be a part of helping. It also looked exciting to me, but I wasn't sure I wanted to learn to drive 90 miles an hour. My Mom was a county court administrator so I had been around male police officers since I was young. A lot of her personal friends were officers and my Dad was a firefighter. I also had an interest in firefighting but I preferred service and helping over battling fires.

An example of what I like best is a recent fraud case I put together with another patrol officer I enjoy working with. We walked and talked through it. It was so easy to divide up the work, I'll do this part, and you do this because you're better at it. Another rewarding aspect to the job is that I feel like I have a room full of brothers and sisters. And, thirdly, I like checking up on cases we've handled to continue to be of help. We had a family whose little one was the victim of a crime. I helped get the mother counseling and I check in with her once a week because she's having a baby and she didn't have anything. I put together my version of a baby shower and brought over some of my boy's things. She was very appreciative and I know she will ask me if she needs something. A gal who did a ride-along with me went with me and donated some items as well.

Overcoming the Firearms Hurdle

After I got out of college I knew I'd work in the criminal justice system, I just didn't know how. As a clerk working in the courtroom I had the advantage of looking at all the different players. I started picking people's brains, and I did volunteer work in the probation department. What intrigued me most was the officers' testimony about what they did. I chatted with them and did some ride-alongs.

Initially, I was hired by the county, but at the academy I didn't pass the firearms qualification. I was let go. I started testing again, because the one thing the academy did do was assure me that I wanted to be a police officer. I mistakenly thought they would teach me how to shoot at the academy so I only went out once beforehand with a friend. Most other people had experience shooting. In the end it was, Tana, get back up on that horse. I tested here and it took a year from the date that I didn't pass the firearms qualification to the date that I did pass it. I passed by hiring an instructor to help me learn firearms and gain confidence. She was helping other women as well. I got to know the other women and shot at different ranges.

I've been a field training officer for two years. I pay particular attention to people who have problems with shooting. I explained what happened to me so that they know that it's definitely doable. I'm sort of glad that this initial failure happened because I realized that not everything's going to come to you easily. I went through a hard time over it mentally because would everybody think I shouldn't become a police officer because I couldn't pass this qualification?

Full-Time Mom, Part-Time Officer

After Jake came to us, he was 16 months old, I was off on family leave for three months. Then I came back full-time. As a patrol officer, I get taken from here to there, here to there, from teaching personal safety to eighth graders to working on a case with detectives. Being away from my son was immediately very difficult for me, especially when I had a 12-hour shift. I couldn't say, Can you watch Jake on Sunday mornings for the next two months because of my rotation. My basic objection was over the hours, but I also wanted us to have neighborhood play group friends.

I wanted to handle it all. I wanted to be a great cop, wanted to be able to work long hours, wanted to be the best Mom. And there wasn't enough time in the day for what I was asking of myself. I kept asking myself, Why can't I do this?

I didn't know what to do. My daycare schedule was like putting together a million-piece puzzle. With my husband's schedule, his working nights, me working 12s, he working 12s sometimes and trying to work overtime. It was chaos. My heartstrings were getting pulled. I went into the chief and told her I thought I needed to quit. I didn't hand her a letter of resignation, but I had prepared one. She saw how overwhelmed I was and the others did too, because I didn't enjoy the department anymore.

At the end of our discussion, she said, I think there's something we can do. Part-time. I was not prepared for that. She said, Go, think about this, give it some time. I took two months off to think it through. It would be hard for me to give up law enforcement, but the most important thing was my family. After two months off I came back part-time. It's made a huge difference. It's still chaos on Sunday mornings but I'm continuing my career. Financially we've had to cut back but I'm at home more so we're not paying so much for daycare. As far as being happy at work, I'm sure everyone here could tell you that I am.

My full-time role is being a Mom, but if I get involved in a case, I get involved in a case and that's just part of being a police officer. I have about a 35-minute commute and I try to let the job go before I get home. If something is still on my mind, I talk to my husband about it. And there's everybody here I can talk to and I'm not known for not sharing my feelings. I just had my evaluation and the sergeant said, You should take a leadership role. But right now all I aspire to be is a part-time police officer.

Spanish is important for my personal life but I also spend a lot of time on the streets using it. When we go to a 911 hang-up call where we don't know if it was a child playing with the phone or there was a domestic disturbance, using choppy English and choppy Spanish we can generally figure out what happened. And if someone understands why you pulled their car over, it works out better even if the end result is a ticket. If people understand what's going on, it's better, and I'm all for better situations.

The Emerald City Soccer Club Network

The only women's group I belong to is a soccer team. A couple of years ago, before Jake, a friend called me and said, Do you want to be on this team? We're from Seattle, Redmond, King County, Yakima, Everett, a variety of women from all over on this one team. Every year there's a police soccer tournament. This year it's in Los Angeles. The year I went it was in Vancouver, B.C., and we took the silver medal. Next year it's in New York and I really want to play that tournament. I enjoy this outlet, the soccer practices. Somehow we manage, 13, 14, women all with weird schedules, working nights, working days.

We pay our own expenses. We make T-shirts and sell them. It takes you back to college days. It's also fun to interact with the women on the other teams. Because I'm known as a soccer player, I'll get e-mail: We need an extra player. Could you play on our team? It's a great network. I can call any of the women on my team and get good advice. Our captain has Christmas parties every year and I just got an e-mail invite for a different kind of party she's having. She keeps us all connected, whether everyone goes or not.

On-the-Job Mentors

All cops, male and female, need on-the-job mentors, people within the police family who support them. Retired Officer Trisha King-Stargel recalled a 21-year-old single mom at the tail end of a divorce: "Her parents were Russians who emigrated to Poland, then Canada, and finally to the United States. Not only does this woman speak several languages, she had had incredible life experiences. But she had difficulties with some male officers because she was very quiet, not your flip-the-hair, friendly female officer. They didn't know how to relate to her and she almost quit before she got through probation. Her captain called me and said, I'm afraid we're going to lose her. Can you do something? And I helped her to see that it was worth hanging in there.

Another gal called me in tears. She was in her FTO program on graveyard and she wasn't sleeping and was literally coming unglued on the shift. She was an overachiever and the fact that she wasn't performing at peak was horrible for her. I asked, What are you eating when you get home from work at 6 a.m.? She goes, Nothing. It's not good to eat before you go to bed. And I said, Do you know why you're waking up? Because your stomach is hungry. Your body needs something to do while you're sleeping. It was totally against her health regime, but I said, You've got to do it. You've got to eat. Protein. Eggs, bacon. Things that aren't just complex carbs. So she started eating when she got off work and she started sleeping. It's little things like that to let a person know, This is a minor blip on the screen. This is not the end of the world. The mentor's got to maintain objectivity when the person can't. And if they need some very specific remedial training, identify those areas for them. But, overall, be encouraging and tell them, Hang in, hang in, hang in."

UW Campus Assistant Chief Annette Spicuzza told me that her first male FTO thought it would be beneficial for her if she worked with another woman in the department: "So we worked a couple of nights together and really connected. As a rookie and a woman, the men weren't looking to partner up with me. So hooking up with her was wonderful. And then to have a woman who policed the same way. We knew how not to get hurt. We knew how not to get into a fight. We complemented each other. I would chase because I was faster, but she did better reports. It was a wonderful six-year relationship until I left that department.

We laughed all the time. There were days we couldn't believe they were paying us to do the job. We also cried on occasion together. Outside of work we were very dear friends. We would do dinner, go to shows, concerts. We even took our summer vacations together. So my mentoring started informally. Even though my partner had only been there three years, she showed me the ropes, she taught me, she mentored without knowing she was doing it."

Women need support from many directions to succeed in police work. Mentors' support is as important as family support. And if the support doesn't come to you, you have to find it. The next chapter tackles a third possibility.

15

Support from Women's Organizations

Deputy Detective Debbie Kronk, whom you met in Chapter 4, told me about a tea party Seattle PD women once held. She said the men were so threatened, suspicious, and unhappy about the affair that she'd never do that again. I heard similar stories from other women and came away with the impression that women meeting together at the agency level is counterproductive because of the negative reactions of male colleagues. Women meeting at the State level works and on the national level women's organizations are hugely successful.

But the times, they are a'changing. I attended a day-long conference devoted to women in the Seattle Police Department in the spring of 2004 and observed firsthand that it was roundly supported by the men. Here, now, is what happens at the State and national levels.

Sergeant Renee Winston, Internal Affairs, Tulsa, OK, County Sheriff's Office was born in 1963. She is single and studying for a bachelor's degree in business management. She joined the police in June 1985. When she came to get me in the reception area, she was accompanied by a civilian who shook her hand and thanked her for seeing him. He had come to praise the performance of a deputy, the transcript of which will go into his file. Internal affairs swings both ways. Renee is a good example of a supportive mom and unsupportive dad.

Joining Up

My two best friends got on the year before I did. We all hung around together so I went everywhere they went and law enforcement officers were always there talking about different incidents. My friends ate it, slept it, breathed it. It rubbed off on me. They were telling me, they're having an academy, they're recruiting, they're hiring. Do you want to do this? I thought, Yeah, I'm serious. I've always been the type of person who wants to help people. I like the statement that represents law enforcement, to protect and serve. I'm somebody who wants to make sure that the right things get done. I have never liked to see people or animals wronged or abused. I was always getting people help even before I got into law enforcement, so this is an official way to do that.

Maternal Support

I was a PBX operator at Tulsa Junior College. My mother told me when I said I'm going to do this, I thought you might, one of these days. Because, she said, when I was a kid—I don't know if you remember, there was a detective series called "Get Christy Love" about a Black female detective—I loved that show and I told her I wanted to be just like Christy Love. Renee, you used to say that all the time. So you coming forth and telling me now that this is what you want to do does not surprise me, although it isn't something I would have chosen for you. But you're grown now and have to make your own decisions, live your own life, and whatever you decide to do, I'm behind you 100 percent. If this is the road that you want to go down, I'm with you, although I'm going to worry about you a whole bunch and do some extra praying for you. But my father couldn't understand it. Why would you want to put yourself in that situation? People shooting at you. I told him when it's my time to go, I'll go, but I might as well be doing something I want to do.

If an officer is a bully or rude to people, kids pick up on that immediately—if you want to establish rapport, forget it. You won't even get your feet in. I've had people say, I'll talk to you. Because I'd treated them as my mother taught me, Do unto others as you would have them do unto you. I've had problems in my career with people who didn't like me for the color of my skin, and she would say, You just have to work with that person eight hours a day. You don't have to take them home. They're not paying your bills. You're not feeding them and they aren't putting food on your table. You treat them with a long-handled spoon, be professional, do your job, and don't be rude; if you can't say anything nice, don't say anything at all.

If I go to my mother with a problem, she'll say, You know who you need to go talk to about this. When you found the job you were looking for, I told you what you needed to do if you were stressed, so don't come crying to me. My mother is a no-nonsense, go-take-care-of-it woman. Don't be worrying about it—if you're not going to do the right thing to take care of it, I don't want you coming around here complaining. She is my rock. She's helped me out a lot, and those lessons come back to me, I don't always have to call her. She taught me how to deal with stress, and to deal with people as I would want to be treated. And don't burn bridges. You might need to ask that rude person a question someday.

Just Like Boot Camp

Before I went to the academy, I was taking law enforcement classes at TJC. I had an instructor who used to be a captain at Tulsa PD. I don't know how he did it, but he had a teaching method that at the end of the semester, the material was engraved in your brain. So when I went through the academy, many portions of the course—law, procedures, evidence—I already knew. I had to hold my hand down every time they asked a question because I didn't want to be considered a know-it-all. I told my mother, Wow, I know this stuff already. This is excellent. I was ahead of everyone else in understanding law enforcement.

I quickly realized that they were into head games, just like in boot camp. They get in your face, talk real loud, tell you you're not going to make it. If you think we're going to give you extra privileges because you're a woman, think again. It's to toughen you up. People on the street will talk real bad to you, call you all kinds of names, and you can't be mentally weak. You have to be very stern in handling certain situations.

More and more academies around the United States are becoming very physically demanding, especially the academies that are four to six months long. To be accepted by the other officers, you need to pull your weight. I'm not saying a woman has to be as strong as a man. But a woman should not be the one who is always last in line, struggling to finish up. One day you may be into a physical confrontation and saving your life and other people's lives may depend upon your physical condition and stamina. When I was out on the street, I did all kinds of stuff to make sure that if something happened, I wouldn't let my guys down. Especially when I was in the gang unit, we did foot chases. If my partner runs around the corner, I don't want to be so out of shape I can't catch up with him. I want to keep close enough to him that if he needs it, I can help him. And when I get there I don't want to be doubled over, trying to catch my breath.

I Want to Talk to Her First

Women are more people-oriented than most guys. Women are more sensitive to a broader range of issues than most men. Women dot their I's and cross their T's, have good memories, and don't leave out details in their reports. In law enforcement, dealing with little kids, domestic violence, sexual assault, all put the police in a lot of contact with people where females have an edge. It's very rare to find a woman officer who doesn't know how to talk to people. So while it is still a male-dominated occupation, women play an important role, more so than ever before. Even guys would look at me and my partner and say, I want to talk to her first.

I was in human resources for awhile and I would go to job fairs, which we don't do anymore because our turnover's not that high. We used to have a county jail here, but when the jail was privatized in 1999, we had to downsize and let many sworn officers and civilians go. It's coming up for contract negotiation next year and people say the sheriff's going to get it back. Which means I want to tell a lot of people about this opportunity. But to recruit Latina or Hispanic females—we don't have any—our strategy needs to stress that they would be able to help the people in their neighborhoods. Their role in law enforcement would be to respond in their language to the people's needs. We have a large Hispanic section of town, and our biggest obstacle is the language barrier. They don't come to us for help because we don't speak their language. So first we need to get Spanish-speaking recruiters. Because in the schools in those neighborhoods, English is a second language.

We need to recruit women at neighborhood functions, watch parties. Community policing is recruiting and it's important the way you carry yourself in the neighborhood. The sheriff's Explorer program, which has females, is recruiting. And we recruit on an individual basis. I had a little buddy who I used to pick up so he could work the Kid Print booth. I talked with his mother and had him home at a certain time. He's a senior now, taller than me, he's got to be 6'2". He works here in the summer. He's going to get a college degree, but the day he turns 21, he'll be here putting in an application for deputy sheriff. I see him every now and then. We correspond through e-mail. He knows he's got to keep his grades up because I call and check on them. He'd eaten a bunch over the summer and I said, It looks like you're getting a little soft. You need to be lifting some weights. Get to the gym and get in shape. Last time I saw him he'd been working out and he said, I couldn't let you down.

If a woman is facing a fight—I've seen deputies do it, police, all male law enforcement officers—they try to get in front of you. When I first got into the gang unit, my partner was a male. If the Crips were having a party there might have been 50 kids there, not all gang members, from 15 to 18 years old. Six Bloods would try to get in. We knew them all by name, and we didn't want to let them in. I'd say, Why do you want to go in there? They'd say we have the right, just like they do. I'd say, You know what's going to happen, right? And we're ready for it. But you can't discriminate against them because they're Bloods, so we'd let them in and start getting ready. I'd tighten the band around my glasses. Put my watch and earrings in my pocket. We'd follow them in because we knew what was going to happen. They would get swallowed up and the fight was on. Then we'd break it up.

One time we were arresting multiple suspects in the middle of the street. I had grabbed somebody, but this guy, 6'3", intervened and he cuffed him. I asked him, Didn't you want me to cuff him? I told him, I can handle this. He said, I didn't want you to get hurt. I said, I got a badge and gun just like you do, I've been through the same training, and if I think I'm going to get hurt and need extra help, I'll holler. But in this department, they say, Renee can handle this. She's fine. I want to be treated like one of the guys and get tossed in right with them.

I've never thought about running a department but I have thought about being number two. If you're running things, you have to be involved in politics and I'm a cut-and-dry, straight-to-the-point person, sometimes too blunt, anal I've been told. Dot your I's and cross your T's. It's got to be a certain way. In politics it's you scratch my back, I'll scratch yours. I don't know how doing favors fits with me, hiring or promoting or moving somebody over here because they contributed money. Now I can see putting out signs because you believe in somebody, they're for right, they're fair and consistent. To run for sheriff, I'd need political grooming and political connections. I don't have any. What people know me by is my word. Most people would say, I'm not going to worry about her because she's going to do what needs to be done. Or if something needs to be taken care of, and you give it to her, she'll take care of it.

Everybody Had a Blast

When I became president of Oklahoma Women in Law Enforcement, I wanted the organization to grow. I had a male supervisor who asked, Why should I join? Well, sir, I said, we do training and bring everybody up to what's going on. He said, I can go to this other conference for that. He put me through the third degree, made me do some serious thinking. We were thinking of changing the name because our membership had dropped, but he said, The uniqueness of your organization is because the name is Oklahoma Women in Law Enforcement. If you change it to Oklahoma Law Enforcement or Oklahoma Men and Women in Law Enforcement, you become just like the rest of them. Your specialness is that you cater to females. I like that and you shouldn't be offended. I'm not interested in joining any organizations.

This next year I'd like to get some good instructors for training in scams, computer crimes, identity theft. Good training made everybody go away with smiles on their faces from our state conference in May. We had the conference the last two years in state lodges on lakes and everybody had a blast. There might even be a golf course. It's like a little three-day getaway.

The best thing of all is getting to know different women around the state. But the best conference I've ever been to was the IAWP in Milwaukee. There were women there from all over the world, Brazil, Canada, New Guinea, places I had only heard about. It was mind-blowing. At the opening ceremonies everybody wears their uniforms. We walked down the street in all these different uniforms. That conference did a lot for my overall mental well-being. That's why some women go every year, even though their departments don't give them any time off. They take it as vacation. Most departments don't have the funding, that would be a big chunk out of a training budget, so many women pay their own way.

My Proudest Moment

They did a newspaper article on me when I was the first female in this region to be in a gang unit. They had a picture of me on the front page and an article inside. I had a company put it on a big plaque and I sent it to my Mom. I'd never been in the paper before and after people saw that, they'd recognize me wherever I'd go. Especially when I went into the community policing unit after four years in the gang unit. People never forget stuff like that.

I went to a meat market the other day and the girl behind the counter said, You don't remember me, do you? You remember that time at Central? I said, You were in a gang fight, weren't you? Yeah, and I'm glad you were there because you kept me out of trouble and you turned me around. I appreciate your doing that for me. I want to thank you. There were no tears in my eyes but it's moments like that when somebody tells you, you made a difference in their life, especially a kid, it makes all the headaches worthwhile.

I was going to court in plainclothes and this lady came up and said, Aren't you a deputy? I said, Yes. She said, Did you take me to Lexington? I had been transporting prisoners back and forth. I said, Yes. She said, I remember you. You were the only one that treated me halfway decent. I just wanted to say hi. I said, Hi to you too. Are you doing all right? Yeah, I am. Are you staying out of trouble? Yeah. I just wanted to say I appreciated your being nice.

Intelligence Analyst Kim Kraushar

Kim Kraushar works for the federal government, and has been in Anchorage since 1996. She was born in 1959 in South Dakota, is married to a retired Air Force officer, and has a BS and a MS in business management with an emphasis on quantitative analysis. Prior to her civil service job, which began in 1991, she served nine years in the Air Force. Kim, who is obviously very fond of where she lives, observed that in Alaska, wildlife and fishing events always take precedence over world conditions.

Women's Organizations and the Younger Generation

I've belonged to Women Police of Alaska for two and a half years. Its main purpose is networking with other women because it's a small community up here and sooner or later you end up working with practically every other law enforcement agency in the state. We have meetings once a quarter and we do fun things, barbecues, campouts, picnics. We try to give support to women starting out in law enforcement mainly through telling them of training opportunities, mentoring individuals, giving them advice. A lot of young women won't join the organization, which is a problem we're trying to figure out. Everybody's busy with their own life, all this other stuff they're doing, so they don't want to get roped into doing something else. A second explanation is that they don't want to be perceived as joining an organization that is only for women. They believe it's going to be looked upon as a feminist thing, women off doing things that exclude men.

There are two principal ways we can help young women, scholarships to fund training they want to go to, which is vital for people starting out who don't have money for training that would help them on the job. We also need to let them know when training is happening. If we could get them to come to the meetings, then they would see how much fun we have and that we're not an exclusive organization and not there to put down men.

I've belonged to the International Association of Women Police for one and a half years. In my job I deal with foreigners all the time and I've made connections through IAWP and will continue to get more international contacts to network with. The only big event that I've been to was the conference in Australia. One thing IAWP does that WPA needs to do is more e-mailing, basically of any event that is going on. When you are far-flung as we are, e-mail is the only way we can keep in constant contact.

I also belong to the International Association of Law Enforcement Intelligence Analysts, IALEIA. They have a huge membership. Again, the main purposes are networking, having contacts in other countries, and training. They send out big booklets of the training they are offering over a given year. Currently, if I want to go to any IALEIA training, I have to pay for it myself.

I also belong to the Anchorage Business and Professional Women, a national organization. There are several chapters up here all doing mentoring, networking, offering scholarships for nontraditional women, women who after taking care of the kids go back to work and need various courses to progress, to get promoted. I'm both corresponding secretary and legislative chairperson: bpwusa.org is their web site.

IAWP President Terrie Swann

I know from experience how well-regarded Supervisory Deputy U.S. Marshal Terrie Swann is by the people she supervises, which include private court security officers. One stopped us outside Tulsa's federal courthouse in November 2001 and when I told him I was there to interview Terrie, he beamed, She knows how to do it! Then he made a list of the best barbecue places in town and told us to put some meat on our bones.

Terrie was born in 1952 in Phoenix, Arizona. She is Caucasian, single, and plays mom to Molly, a 4-year-old German shepherd, "who just happens to be a person herself." Terrie is president of the International Association of Women Police.

How My Career Began

In 1974 I was in my third year at Arizona State University in the nursing program, I decided nursing was not my calling. I quit school and was floundering and my uncle said, Why don't you join the Army reserve? See if you like the service. I went to a MP school, fell in love with it, and in 1974 went to work for the county sheriff's office in Phoenix. It was suggested that the best way to get on as a deputy was to become a detention officer and work in the jail. I got promoted to a supervisor's position after only two years and I stayed because I liked it. I got to work in research and development, and ended up as the assistant to the director, doing all the hiring, oral boards, testing.

The sheriff's office utilized me where they recognized my strengths. The federal marshal connected with the Maricopa County Sheriff's Office came into the jail all the time. He said the Marshals Service was really pushing for females. This was the end of the '70s. I took the test, a testing procedure that took a year. I left the sheriff's office and have been with the Marshals Service ever since. I was drawn by the money, travel, and type of law enforcement. My end goal was to become an investigator and the Marshals Service offered me that opportunity, which the sheriff's office didn't.

I have a bachelor's degree in business administration from the University of Phoenix. I chose business because I thought it would do me more good if I decided I didn't want to remain in law enforcement in retirement.

It Was All about Variety

My idea about working in law enforcement was the same most people have, the old cliché of, to help people, to do my part for the community. I felt I could contribute because I am an intelligent, capable person. I wanted to make a difference, take crooks off the street and give back to the community. The things that we do looked exciting, exhilarating. With the Marshals Service there is so much variety in duties and responsibilities, and any number of career paths—witness protection program, fugitive program, task forces, prisoner transportation. We get to travel a lot, all over the country. I've been on special assignments in Guam, I went on an extradition to Italy, I've been to the Virgin Islands. I was also drawn by the opportunity of career advancement in any of the specialized areas.

What Mom and Dad Had to Say

I wasn't in very good favor with my father when I quit school against his wishes and joined the Army. But when I graduated in the top 10% of my military police class, he was very proud of me. Then when I told him I was going to work for the sheriff's office, he railed against it—no daughter of mine is going to be a police officer. Over my dead body am I going to have a cop in the family. But when I graduated and came home and showed him this bright shiny badge and credentials and the fact that I had made it through this 15-week grueling school, he was so proud he couldn't wait to tell the people at work that his daughter was a U.S. marshal. Even though my dad balked at each stage that I tried to control my life, he was always very proud of me when I succeeded. That made a whole lot of difference. On the other hand, my mother is still scared to death that I'm going to get killed. She worries about me every time I travel, she worries about me living away from home. But she knows that I have a job to do, and she may even be a little envious that I've had such an interesting career, make a decent salary, take care of myself, am able to live a very comfortable life.

I'm especially looking forward to the IAWP conference in Australia because my Dad's going with me and we're going to spend a month. We're going to fly in early, spend a couple of days in Sydney, go down to Canberra for the conference, then fly to the Great Barrier reef where he wants to go deep sea fishing. My Dad has wanted to go to Australia his entire life and now he's retired and has the money to do things, but he didn't want to go by himself so I told him he could come with me.

My Role

I am the first female deputy to work this district. For the last ten years I've been the only female criminal investigator in the office. I was promoted to supervisor in 1996. I'm a 23-year veteran and the plan is to retire in December 2003 and get a master's in management or public administration. Also I'm going to get a teaching certificate so I can teach law enforcement at the college level. But for now I want to remain an active, serving law enforcement officer during my tenure as president of IAWP, a position of leadership that I'm very fortunate to have.

I play multiple roles. In a small office such as mine, there are only 15 employees in the entire office. I am supervisory investigator over operations, which entails all prisoner movement, court scheduling, special assignment scheduling. I am also supervisor of the warrants and fugitive section, and I supervise the deputy who works in the seizure and forfeiture unit. I'm also the contracting officer, technical representative, for the court security office where I keep track of the court security officers who work for a private company that the Marshals Service contracts with.

Recruiting Is One of the Biggest Issues

I try to convey to people the variety of different career paths and specialties, pay, flexibility especially in a federal agency, traveling and working in different districts, opportunity it provides for advancement. You just can't beat the adrenaline rush. Breaking down a door, taking down a criminal, and putting handcuffs on him is the funnest thing in the world. It makes your whole day worthwhile after you've spent two weeks tracking someone down and finally catching him. Since

I've been promoted I don't get to go out on the street so much anymore, and I miss it. But I have a particular forte for administrative work so that presents a challenge for me every day.

Recruiting is one of the biggest issues being dealt with by women's organizations. Most agencies now are trying to figure out how to better recruit and retain women. The testing process in some agencies is geared toward failure for those who don't have a college education, those who may not be book smart but are street smart, and women. The testing process needs to be more people-oriented. We've gone from head-bashing police officers who took care of things with force to community policing. It's the wave of the future. It's been determined through dozens of surveys and studies that women can deal with people in community situations better with their communication skills, empathy, and compassion. Men are getting there but women have been there all the time.

Colleges are a good place to recruit. We have a recruiter in our office who goes to job fairs at colleges, one reason being to have a larger pool of women and minorities. The military has one of the biggest pools because it has people who have done their three- or four-year stint, they're disciplined, trained, respectful, and most have a good work ethic. The Marshals Service has recruited at military bases quite a bit in the last two years. We contact a base, let them know we're coming, set a date for the test, and anybody who wants to can take the test that day. Then we interview after basic testing, 25 interviews a day. Then there's physical fitness, background, and the medical. We had one 48-person academy made up entirely of military recruits and it was one of the best recruit classes we've ever had. The group was motivated, hard-working, in good physical shape.

IAWP Goals

We need to nurture working relationships with other women's organizations such as the National Center for Women & Policing, National Association of Women Law Enforcement Executives, and NOBLE, National Organization of Black Law Enforcement Executives, because our goals are basically the same—to get women into law enforcement, get them promoted, and provide them with support to get the job done. We need to make testing equitable for both sexes and all races. We need to make the physical fitness requirement acceptable for both sexes, somewhere in the middle. And have it as a minimal standard. Because when a person's in the academy for three months, they can work on running, push-ups, sit-ups and meet the standard that's required to graduate.

A 5'4" female is going to have a difficult time going over a six-foot fence unless she learns a certain technique. A 5'2" male will have the same problem. Frankly, I see no particular reason for being able to jump a six-foot fence, because if I see someone I'm chasing go over a six-foot fence, before I go over that fence after him, I'm going to want to know, is there a gate I can go through? Or can I at least see what's on the other side and that he's not waiting to ambush me. Common sense would tell you not to go over that fence if you can't see what's on the other side.

Women inherently have weaker upper body strength but they have better lower body strength. Obviously if I'm told, Drag that 200-pound man a hundred yards, I'm going to have difficulty if I've never done it before or had time to practice. If women go into a testing situation and don't know what the criteria are going to be, how can we expect them to pass something like that? It's very important to be aerobically in shape. Running is a good test, women can run just as fast and as well as men. There's no reason to have any disparity in that standard. Just make it reasonable and enforce incentives to keep everyone in shape after they come on the job. With the Marshals Service anyone hired after 1986 has to take a fitness test every six months. So we have to maintain a level of fitness.

For IAWP and most organizations, the Internet is now the best way to reach women. Since we opened our web site in 1998, I get e-mails eight times a week from women saying, I'm getting ready to graduate, how can I get into a law enforcement agency? Or, I've just graduated and applied to an agency and am supposed to take my oral exam soon, how can I prepare? Or, I would like to know who is hiring. I'm willing to move anywhere. If a department has an opening or is recruiting, we will put their job information, requirements, and who to contact on our web site free of charge, as a public service. We also put these advertisements at a reduced cost in our magazine.

At each of our conferences we've had the postal service, postal inspectors, FBI, Secret Service, Border Patrol, INS, U.S. Marshals Service set up booths so you have women from all over the world picking up brochures. Women are apt to switch agencies in order to advance. Our conferences offer a good pool of female and minority females to recruit from as well. You don't have to be a member to come to the conference, anyone can come whether you're a student, professor, writer. The conferences are advertised on the Web, in our magazine, and the regional coordinators talk to schools. Anyone who wants to come can come to the conference for the social affairs, mentoring, networking, training opportunities, and to see what's out there if you want to leave your department and go somewhere else.

Ignore Those 25 Men

When I first was hired by the Marshals Service, my marshal sat me down and said, I only have one piece of advice for you. You are going to be one of 25 women in a class of hundreds of men. It's going to be 25 to 1, men to women, at that academy. My advice to you is ignore those 25 men. Concentrate on what you're there to accomplish and don't try to come home with a boyfriend or husband. You're there to work and study, get through it, and come back to my office and go to work for me.

It was good advice because there was lots of time to play, and rather than run after class, students would go to bars, movies, the mall. And I was in my room studying. I wanted to make sure that I passed every single written test. Push-ups, I could do push-ups all day long. In fact, one other woman could do 50 in a minute; I did 48.

My proudest moment in training was running a mile under eight and a half minutes. Two weeks before the end of the academy I still couldn't get my mile run under eight and a half minutes. I was so afraid of failing it. There were two men and two other women, there were five of us, who were always coming in the last of the pack. The instructor started screaming and yelling and calling us losers and telling us we weren't going to pass. We were going on a long run one day, and he said he was going to run right beside the five of us and every time we even looked like we were going to stop, he was going to boot us. The next day was our longest run, five miles, and not one of us dared stop. When we got done and were totally exhausted, he came over and said, You just ran five miles without stopping. That means you can run a mile in eight and a half minutes. Three days later, we ran preliminary tests to see who was going to need extra help that last week of the academy, and when he said, 8:14, I sat down and cried like a baby. He had taken the effort and time to pull us out of trouble by finding a way to inspire us. Every single one of us passed the final test.

In the academy situation, people tend to bond with each other, form friendships, form groups, and it's vital that you bond with a group that is supportive of getting through and doing what needs to be done to get through.

Mentoring Is So Important

To retain qualified, good, hardworking police officers, deputies, agents, you have to have an equitable system of promotion and merit promotion. You need leaders willing to take on women and who don't have antiquated ideas about women supervisors. Finding mentors for women can be difficult, even among women, who may be afraid that the women they're helping may learn something that surpasses their performance. Women in leadership positions have the duty to mentor, provide networking, work with women who are coming up in the ranks, find their strengths and move them forward. The only way we are going to break that glass ceiling is to develop management skills and push our subordinates to strive for more.

The attitude of subordinates is directly related to the leadership style and management skill of their superiors, all the way to the top. If you have a director, sheriff, or chief who is not supportive of women, it trickles all the way down. It's difficult for women to get ahead under a manager who is bigoted, anti-training, anti-movement forward, who shows a lack of respect for women's capabilities and a lack of plain courtesy. A pat on the back once in awhile goes a long way toward gaining loyalty towards a manager. When you don't get that pat, you figure, what am I working so hard for if I'm not going to be recognized? One of the largest goals of the IAWP is to give awards to women who are out there working hard and who may not be recognized by their departments.

Retention is a responsibility of management to make sure that women are getting respect, incentives to stay on the job, the training they need, and are not subjected to gender bias in promotions or assignments, or subjected to harassment and abuse. Women shouldn't have to take abuse that ends with, Hey, I was just joking.

I was fortunate early in my career to have a leader who wanted women in his department, who wanted to push women forward. He saw my strengths and allowed me to take training and improve myself. And that was very early in the Marshals Service when women were still a novel item. I can't thank him enough.

Families Are Important

There are several ways an organization can help a woman with a family. If she has children in school, say, you might want to put her on an evening shift when her husband's home with the kids. A lot of officers do that, especially when you have two officers in the family. In addition to flexi-time, finding positions within the department that are conducive with giving people the hours they need, not just for family, but to go to school.

The Marshals Service is very flexible in placing married couples in the same district. If a woman's husband gets transferred to another district, even if he's with another law enforcement agency or is non-law enforcement, there are Marshal Services all over the place and we try to get women in offices close to where the husband gets transferred. We've taken a woman here even though we didn't have a position open. If we don't do this, women may quit. Think of all the money and time that go to waste if you can't accommodate them.

My Overprotection Experience

It was close to the end of my probationary period and my turn to do my 90-day rotation in the warrant section, the fugitive section. The women deputies in that office were basically gofers. They ran for lunch, did errands, the men's computer work. When I got there I said, I've been in law enforcement six years and I've located this guy. I know where he is, I want to go arrest him and I'd like to do it tomorrow morning at 6 a.m. Can we meet? No, they said, We've got more important things to do. We can't give you anybody, you'll have to wait. I said, But I've got this all set up. We know he's wanted for probation violation. He gets off at 5:30 in the morning so at 6 we can arrest him and be gone. No. We don't have enough time. So I went downstairs to the operations supervisor and said, Hey, the guys upstairs don't have enough time or deputies to help me arrest this guy in the morning. Can you give me a couple of court deputies at 6 and we'll be back well in time for court? The supervisor said, No problem. Tell me where you want to meet. When the deputies upstairs found out I had gone downstairs to get deputies from court, they were furious. They said, Well, if you're going to be this way about it, fine, we'll go get your guy. They called the supervisor and said, She doesn't need your deputies. We fugitive deputies will get this guy.

So the next morning at 5:30 we got to the house, I laid all the photographs out and said, This is the guy we're looking for. He's in an upstairs bedroom, the roommate's going to open the door for us when we knock, his girlfriend's probably going to be there. So the deputies started saying, Joe Blow, you go to the back door, Terrie you go to the back door. And I said, Wait a minute. What do you mean back door? This is my warrant. I found the guy. It took me two weeks. I made the arrangements. I'm going to the front door. I'm putting handcuffs on the guy. No, you're not. We've had experiences where women were afraid to go through the front door. I said, That was other women. That's not me. I've been in the military police, I've been in the sheriff's office for six years, I have put some handcuffs on some people. Don't judge me by other women's insecurities. This is my case. I don't care where you all go. But I'm knocking on the front door. So we had this five-minute argument, me, the supervisor, and the other deputies. Finally I crossed the street to knock on the front door. They followed behind me and two of them went to the back. I banged on the door. The guy let me in. I went upstairs. The guy was in bed with his girlfriend. I told him to get his rear end out of bed, he was buck naked, made him put his clothes on, put the handcuffs on him, and escorted him out the door. The men were astounded because first I wasn't embarrassed that the guy was in a state of undress, that I stood there and watched him get dressed, took control of him, and walked him out. After that they never told me Terrie, go to the back door, unless it wasn't my warrant. It took a lot of argument and they were really angry. I took a lot of abuse, but I had to show them that I was not going to back down on that issue. If I had gone to the back door, I would have lost the battle for the 90 days I was there. And it made a lot of difference in the way I was treated later on.

Why I Got Promoted

Managers have to find ways to entice women to promote. With the Marshals Service I was fortunate because I got promoted and got to stay in the same office. That hardly ever happens. The only reason that happened is because there was no supervisory position here. It was added. I put in for it. The criteria at the time were that you had to be in the top three to get promoted and normally the number one person was promoted unless there was a mitigating reason not to. I was number one, eight points above number two and number three. Even though they didn't like to promote somebody within the same office, they had to promote the number one person, so I got to stay here. Normally, I would have had to transfer out. If I wanted to become an assistant chief or a chief now, I'd have to move. A lot of women won't move their families and their husbands who have careers to another federal district.

My dilemma right now is, do I put in for a chief's job to promote out of here, and go anywhere, knowing I have only three years to go minimum and nine years to go maximum? Because I have to retire at 57. And do I want to stay with the Marshals Service or do I retire and take on some new career opportunity? If a chief's position became open in Phoenix or Tucson, Nevada, New Mexico, yes. But I would not put in for a job anywhere east of the Mississippi. I've sacrificed in my career. I've moved four times. From Phoenix to San Diego for my first position, from San Diego to Michigan, which was totally alien to me to get a witness security inspector's position, then from Michigan back to Phoenix, giving up a promotion to go home and take care of my mother, and then I came here for a promotion to senior deputy, and got promoted while I was here.

My motivation to be a chief deputy depends on whether the money increase balances out the fact that I would have to start all over again someplace else. This is a consideration for everyone when they think of promotion. I've got guys in my office who will never promote to supervisor, because they don't want to move from their hometown. They'll stay deputies their whole career. Women have to learn that you have to sacrifice to get ahead.

The IAWP and Amy Ramsay

My confidence has grown leaps and bounds every year. I attribute the increase in self-worth to the IAWP. When I joined in 1991 and attended my first conference in 1992 in Miami, I found that I was not alone. Other women were experiencing the same difficulties I was. The support, networking, training, mentoring, social activities they provided, and the friendships I developed boosted my opinion of myself. And in the last two years I can honestly say I have had the best mentor of my entire career in Amy Ramsay, who is my executive director. I didn't know Amy very well until I asked her to be my executive director when I decided to run in Philadelphia in 1999. But through that friendship and working to get elected, I have learned so much from her. I can't tell you how much learning from her has transferred into how I handle things at my job. I knew that she was very intelligent, educated, and well-respected by everyone and that with her support, I had a very good chance of winning.

She's written five books, she has two or three master's degrees, she's just finished her first doctorate and is working on her second. She works for the Ontario Police Service. Where I'm a very emotionally motivated person, and tend to say what's on my mind, rather than being politically correct, she is able to do things in an unemotional, very matter of fact, get it done, factual manner. I thought I was pretty good until I met her. She has taught me how to write better, deal with people better, and lead better. I have learned more from her than any other mentor I have had. She has given me a lot of what I needed to succeed.

At the IAWP Meeting in San Francisco, 2003

Participants could choose among an endless variety of classes: "Achieving your personal best: work within your power zone"; "Domestic violence and crisis negotiations"; "For better or for worse: married to the job"; "Nutrition for the law enforcement officer"; "Physical control techniques"; "Living in balance"; "Have guns, will travel: firearms trafficking and investigations." This supports one of my unexpected themes, that is, women police are constantly into continuing education and training and loving it.

The kind of support women's organizations have to offer apparently is not something women who start early recognize. This is unfortunate and my hope is that this book will help young women give these organizations that can make life so much easier a try.

16

Where Are They Now?

In the spring of 2004 I wrote everyone and asked for updates. This is what came in. Most are brief, but a few are long, including the three who start this chapter off, alphabetically.

Little Rock, AR, Sergeant Jennifer Bartsch: "I am currently working in the Special Operations Division as the Mobile Unit Sergeant. I absolutely love my assignment. I have a squad of five officers (we normally have eight positions) and we work a variety of problems and special assignments—large-scale events and vice and drug related crimes, assisting in undercover capacities. We also help the Detective Division, sometimes in an undercover capacity, looking for wanted subjects, working on robbery or burglary details when we have an influx of those crimes.

I have a great working relationship with the gentlemen who work for me. We have all learned from one another. As their supervisor, on a very regular basis, I point out each of their good qualities. They range from a 16-year veteran to others barely in for three years. After being here for 18 years, I have a better understanding of the closeness of members within the department. Whether good or bad, every lesson I've learned has taught me something about living. I have more patience than ever before and have a closer bond with family and friends. I am thankful and proud to admit that I have kept compassion for people. My skin is definitely thicker but my heart has not changed!"

"Things are great here," said Shoreline, WA Sergeant Michelle Bennett. "I am still on day shift patrol, and, up until maternity leave, I was in charge of first shift patrol duties, storefronts, school resource officers, and the Explorer program at our precinct. There is a captain's test coming up in September and I am mulling over the idea of taking it. I am not sure if I want to move up the ranks, though a day job would be nice.

I am still very involved in the anti-bullying program another officer and I created in 2001 and the conferences associated with that. We have two, possibly four conventions or conferences scheduled this year. One is in Reno, one in Oregon, and two in Seattle. In the last 2 years we presented our anti-bullying curriculum and program at 4 conventions (National COPS, National Youth Crime Watch, National School Resource Officer Convention, and National Sheriff's Association Convention) and won 2 national awards for it.

I am four classes away from finishing my doctoral coursework. I just have to take three comprehensive exams and write a dissertation, no sweat! I hope to graduate Summer of 2005 with my Ed.D.

I am in my sixth year of teaching part-time at Central Washington University satellite campus in Lynnwood. This quarter I am teaching Community Policing and Current Issues in Policing.

On a personal note, a lot of changes. I had a little baby boy in January 2004, Thomas James, little TJ. He is just wonderful and I love him to death. I return to work in a month, so I have been enjoying my time off."

Since we met, Port Townsend, WA, Sergeant Robin Biffle has retired: "Yesterday I sweated as I mountain-biked at a lake east of the Rocky Mountain Front, on the North American Flyway route—hundreds of thousands of migrating birds and water-fowl, with the magnificent 'Bob' (Bob Marshall Wilderness Area) in my westerly sights. Today I've shoveled about three inches (and still falling) of heavy, wet snow. Montana in the spring—what a great place!

I have been caretaking (cleaning, cooking, etc.) at a retreat center in exchange for room and board. I completed an accredited unit of Clinical Pastoral Education (CPE), which was very helpful in my process of figuring out What's Happening Next. The CPE Unit was in hospital chaplaincy, and I learned that that's not the next step for me. It was worthwhile in all sorts of ways, but not my calling.

Next, I'll be starting 'community discernment' of the call to ordained ministry. In the Episcopal Church, an individual responds to a call to ordained ministry, but it must be affirmed in community (one's parish family) and by the Bishop. The parish discernment process will take a few months, maybe beginning after people's summer vacations, and what I'll do after that depends on whether or not others affirm this call. Whatever happens, I'm sure I'll continue my education at least to a master's degree.

I'm enrolled in a theological study program now that is the equivalent, in rigor, (not as we used the term in police work) of a master's program. I'm studying Church History, Theology, Homiletics (sermon preparation and preaching) and Liturgy. It's really great, so much fun to be using a part of my brain that's not about 'fight or flight.' Writing papers is so much easier with a laptop than with the old Olivetti electric typewriter I got from my parents as a graduation present in 1970 before college. Editing is not only possible, but easy, footnotes are automatic, and mistakes can be repaired without having to type the whole page over again. I love it!

I'm finding that having been a police officer has been particularly enriching in terms of learning to be with people in crisis; learning to hear people with all kinds of needs, coming from all kinds of perspectives, learning to live with others in mutual respect and dignity; honing writing and public speaking skills; learning that everyone has a story and there are countless sides to that story; learning to listen; learning patience; and learning the satisfaction of community service—and that's just a bit of it. I could write the book, 'Everything I Need to Know, I Learned as a Police Officer!'

I live in a town that's more than three times the size of Port Townsend. I have friends here who knew me long before I was a police officer and so have 'the long view' of who I am. Mostly, though, I live among people who don't know me at all, or if they do know me, don't know or care that I was once a police officer, except when they find out, they think it's sort of interesting. People love the war stories and I don't mind telling a few, now and then. But it's a wonderful, freeing, new life to go to the grocery store and not see anyone I've arrested.

I don't miss being a police officer. I think it helps being in a new town, and a town where I lived before I ever had an inkling to be a police officer. I still have some 'reflexive,' trained responses. I see an old beater pick-up and I look quickly at the driver and then at the license plate. I saw an officer on a traffic stop that had just turned physical, and before I realized what I was doing I'd pulled in behind him and was about to bail out of the car when another officer drove up. Another time, I came upon an officer in a field interview with a belligerent drunk, and I stood by ready to help if things turned bad. Again, another officer arrived before long. But mostly, I am in a new place, literally and figuratively."

"My rank is still Chief of Criminal Investigations. I'm thinking about retiring in June," thus wrote King County, WA, Chief Fabienne Brooks.

"Still here," Frances Carlson, a King County, WA, Sergeant, wrote. "I'm still a sergeant. Captain Louie will be leaving the unit for greener pastures, so to speak, at least different duties, as a Captain at SeaTac. I went back to school, taking management classes with the University of Phoenix-Online. I actually started taking classes in mid-1998-2001, but had to take a two-year break because of the transfer to this job. I'm enjoying the online classes, a bit time consuming. All of us are being rotated out of IIU because the command staff wants other sergeants and captains to have the pleasure of this fine experience."

Seattle Assistant Chief Cynthia Caldwell has been in charge of the Investigations Bureau since May 2002. She wrote, "I am now planning to retire in 2 to 3 years and work in private security if I can find a good job. There will be a Police Women's History event put on by SPD on March 24, 0800 to 1600 hours. There will be many current and retired SPD women there, huge photo displays of past and present women at SPD, three videos on history, and two panel discussions. Several local female chiefs and I are on these and the keynote address is by state attorney general Christine Gregoire. This is the first time for such an event and after my 27 years I am honored and excited. If you would like to come, let me know and I will put your name down." I did attend and the atmosphere was super positively charged. The big room was packed with women and men and everyone was having a very good time.

"I am still the Detective Sergeant and I wish I had better news to report on my Spanish," e-mailed Monroe, WA Sergeant Cindy Chessie.

Retired Deputy Constable, Harris County, TX and poet Sarah Cortez: "I'm still a reserve officer with Precinct Four and continue to think about going back full-time."

"I am still a patrol Sergeant, although with a new boss and lots of projects on the burner," Sergeant Sheri Crain of Sequim, WA, one of my earliest interviewees, informed me.

King County, WA Commander Carol Cummings: (I had commended her on an excellent taped TV appearance before the county council.) "I really don't like making those appearances. Going to a hot domestic is so much easier. I don't have cable so I never have seen how I come across. Probably wouldn't watch it if I could. Nothing like crossing the middle aged line to make me wish that at least once in my younger life I had bothered with facial products."

"I am still doing the Crisis Intervention Team work, still a Sgt, and still enjoying it," was how Seattle Sergeant Lisbeth Eddy put it.

The Oregon Academy Lieutenant: "I recently retired, due to problems with our retirement system. I had 30 years in law enforcement in October of 2003. I am working my same job as a temp through the end of August, hoping they will hire someone that I can train. As for my future plans, I hope to continue working for the academy part-time, then pick up some private contract work on the side."

"My rank is still patrol officer," responded Port Townsend, WA, Officer Sherry Erickson. "I am currently the department's Field Training Coordinator as well as being an FTO. I am a certified Child Interviewer, Forensic Photographer, and have started, along with the Chief, in giving self-defense classes to women and teens in our area."

"I'm still in Kenmore and doing the same job I was doing at the time of our interview. I've been asked to take promotions, but really enjoy what I'm doing and have decided to stay put," wrote King County, WA Major Robin Fenton.

"I just accepted a new detective position," e-mailed King County, WA Sergeant Belinda Ferguson. "I will be transferring to the KCSO Special Assault Unit (yippee!)."

Retired Boca Raton, FL Captain Linda Forst had been extremely busy. "Just got tenure (yeah), presented at a conference, and am in the final editing stages for my new book. Classes this quarter are very enjoyable but I can't wait for summer so I can slow down a bit."

I asked Evergreen State College, WA Officer Pamela Garland to write about her interest in writing after she had said that she was in the process of moving and once that was accomplished, she would attempt to write her memoirs. "One of my duties as coordinator of Region 9 of IAWP is to write a column for *Women Police*. I enjoy writing the column, but the information is often material submitted by other members. For instance, I ask command staff or members of police departments to relay the recent promotions in their departments, or any news that elevates women in law enforcement. Like a reporter, many times I have to dig for more news. The satisfaction I get in writing is the idea that I can be a tool for conveying the strides women make in law enforcement. If women don't toot their own horn or another woman's horn, than the world will not recognize how instrumental we are in a field that has not fully appreciated the gifts we bring to law enforcement."

Soldotna, AK Chief Shirley Gifford retired not too long after we met. "I am serving as the Interim Chief of Police in Nome, Alaska until May 2004. The previous chief did not have his contract renewed and he left suddenly. They had a homicide of a young woman in August and one of the officers arrested for the crime in November. It is a whirlwind up here, both literally and mentally. Sound like good book material? Nome is a very cool old mining town. Come on up!"

"I'm still a Sgt. in the same Unit, though the Unit's focus and duties have changed to more of a support role with asset forfeitures, drug task forces, and meth labs being the major areas of responsibility," wrote King County, WA Dawn Grout.

And how about the only officer who worked part-time, Monroe, WA Officer Tana Gwordske? "As far as where am I now—same old Tana. I have been working more hours to help with staffing, however, I look forward to going back to part-time when the need for extras is not so great. I am in the middle of adopting our second child and can't wait. My Spanish is coming along. I am involved in some volunteer work where I am using it a lot. All is well with me."

"I am still in a daze, retirement party last night, boxes of 'stuff' to sort through. I know I am going to be doing some consulting and maybe some teaching, but a lot is up in the air. Need a few weeks to come up for air!" Port of Seattle Lieutenant Myra Harmon.

A very big promotion had come to Monroe, WA Sergeant Cherie Harris. "I'm now the Operations Commander at Monroe PD. The job is much different than that of a Sergeant, but I am enjoying it."

Sometimes the answer to my question had more to do with a woman's personal life than work. Port of Seattle Sergeant Jackie Hill said she was not up to much. "Still pounding away at Boston University. Will be completing commencement exercises in May. It's very exciting, though this current course, statistics, is really a bear, but perseverance shall win. I'm still at the Port, but divorced my husband of 20 years and have found my true love. I work with him and he is such a joy!"

"I am where you last saw me, enjoying my assignment in Criminal Investigations Division," wrote King County, WA Captain Mitzi Johanknecht. "Always more work than time of day."

My e-mail found Retired Kent, WA Officer Trisha King-Stargel continuing work on her doctoral degree in Educational Leadership at Seattle University. "I will finish my course work in June 2004, and am currently in the early, early stages of my dissertation proposal. I will focus on police academies' choices of teaching methodology and the resulting preparedness for police patrol work of newly minted officers. I suspect academies are still locked into an instructor focused, lecture-based methodology to impart knowledge. With all we know about adult learning, I believe the results of such methods do not adequately prepare officers for the responsibilities we expect them to fulfill.

I will be co-teaching a class on Race, Gender and Crime next spring. I am also teaching Criminal Justice classes at SU. Need to pay for this Ed.D. somehow. Since retiring in September 2001 I have done some consulting work for Kent PD and remain close with my police gal friends. Just last night I attended a dinner at one of Kent's sergeant's home for one of the gals who had been medically retired. It's a drag when you get hurt on duty and can't come back to full duty. We sat around a table and yakked for several hours. It also gave us an opportunity to reminisce about one of our gals who died of cancer at age 41, and only two years into her career. As you can tell, I miss being an active officer, but have moved to new challenges."

"I'm working graveyard and will probably finish out my career here," said Port of Seattle Sergeant Dianna Klineburger. "Not sure how long that will be. I will have 25 years completed in July. I have been very active away from work and enjoying that. Just need to determine what my next career will be. Walking along the ocean beach?"

Remember the woman who was going to become a PI? Reservist Tania Kohlman: "I'm now licensed as a PI and have started my business (Peninsula Private Investigations). I'm just now getting it up and running and am having a great time. I remain connected with Sequim PD as a Specially Commissioned Officer, but I may go back to being a Reserve as they are requesting I do so and spend more time doing patrol. We'll see. I find it hard to leave law enforcement so will probably always be involved at some level."

"I have accepted a wonderful analyst position on Saint Thomas, U.S. Virgin Islands. It's the same kind of job I have now but with different types of cases. I'll be learning a lot of new things, which will be good for my career. It starts mid-June," so that's when Intelligence Analyst Kim Kraushar will leave Anchorage, Alaska.

NYPD Detective Julia Koniosis said that the conference we talked about went very well. "We're now getting ready for 2004 on March 31 to April 2. It's amazing how much it's grown. We got over 1200 applications this year, which makes me happy since this is my final one with the department. I am retiring in 37 days (but who's counting). Don't know what I'll do yet, maybe just take some time to smell the roses and read your book."

"I have been fairly busy these days mostly going to training and learning new/old things. I am still in Quilcene and loving it. It's an adventure I wouldn't give up for anything," wrote Deputy Detective Debbie Kronk. "Some days I seem to go in all different directions, but that is the nature of the beast. Currently I'm working on some issues at the Teen Center, some juvenile problems, the drug Meth in the area, and emergency preparedness."

Kathleen Larson was no longer King County media person for the Green River homicides investigation and no longer a detective. "I was promoted to the rank of Sergeant in December, 2003. I am currently working at one of our Precincts in the north end of King County."

"I was just transferred to Precinct 4 as their Operations Captain on April 1, 2004," Annette Louie, whom we met as head of King County Sheriff's Office Internal Investigations Unit.

"I am doing the same thing. Unfortunately, due to budget cuts, the Family Violence Unit will not be hiring an advocate to fill the vacancy that occurred when our advocate went on maternity leave and then resigned," wrote Redmond Detective Anne Malins. "So, my partner and I are barely keeping our heads above water. You know the song and dance. 'You are doing such a great job. We appreciate your hard work. So, we'll punish you and not hire an advocate because you'll work hard to take up the slack.'

I am in court reporting school. I have been using my skills here at work and am considering going into closed-captioning where I can make the same money I do here with half of the hours. We'll see."

On March 27, 2004, Seattle PD Sergeant Joy Mundy wrote, "We have sold our home and will soon to retire in Arizona, but I am trying to get a teaching job in the Middle East. I would love to help another government experience democracy." I heard from her again on April 11, 2004. "Hi, headed for Iraq soon. Will work for Dyncorp with their protection service to make sure all American-occupied hotels are secure. They are mostly filled with International Police Officers from the U.S. who are training the Iraq Police Department. I will be there at least one year. I hear there are some women in Iraq joining their police departments, so my goal is to seek them out and determine if they need mentors."

Little Rock, AR Officer Tammy Nelsen: "First of all, I got a divorce. After being divorced for awhile, I met Darrell and we dated for over a year. We got married on March 20, 2004 and just got back from our honeymoon cruise. We went to Cancun, Grand Cayman and Costa Maya. I have truly met the love of my life and he is not in law enforcement. But he supports me in my work and all that I do.

I am still at the Mann Road Alert Center as a COPP Officer, but I am temporarily assigned to the Crime Analysis Unit. It is truly a change from the streets to the desk. It's nice and quiet in here. Since my interview we had an Officer killed in the line of duty. I went to rookie school with him and he was a great officer. He is dearly missed.

My sister was recently hired by the Hot Springs PD (she was with Little Rock PD for 10 years). She quit to have a baby and has been doing nothing for three years, and now that she is back at it, she loves it there." Signed Tammy (Nelsen) Wessel

University of Washington PD Chief Vicky Peltzer: "We now have a Computer Aided Dispatch System (CADS) and Records Management System (RMS). Before, everything was done by pencil and paper. We broke away from Seattle PD and now house our own police reports. We remodeled and updated our Communications Center to include all new equipment, consoles, phones, radios, base stations, wiring, computer, etc. We are in the process of getting nationally accredited and hope to have our on-site assessment in August. This is a grueling process but needed. As a result, our policies and procedures manual has been totally rewritten. We have changed our Evidence section to meet the standards. We are just now doing a pilot project of officers writing reports in the cars.

For the future, we are looking at a possible joint facility with Seattle fire and police departments, and Seattle Emergency Management with our UWPD and UW Emergency Management. We have been given the approval from the Mayor's Office and the UW President's Office to discuss these possibilities. I am working on establishing our own police foundation, have our own police chaplain, and working with a Crime Stoppers program for campus, to name a few other projects."

Chief Denise Pentony reported that all was well in the Shoreline, WA PD. "I am in year 4 of being the chief and loving it. We continue to build on the good police work and community relations. Not much has changed other than our focus is clearly on terrorism detection and prevention. We are working region-wide to improve information sharing and intelligence development. The turf lines are blurred more now than ever and we are all cooperating for the good of our communities." Signed Denise J. Turner (her maiden name)

NYPD Retired Auxiliary Sergeant Judith Rock had moved out of NYC. "I'm now dividing my time between Sarasota, FL and Louisville, KY. We'll probably be partly based in Louisville for the next five years because of my husband's new job. I'm writing and doing guest teaching gigs, with the occasional performance of the show I told you about.

In regard to your recent spine surgery, someone gave me an amazing book called *Learning to Fall* by Philip Simmons about dealing with physical difficulty and loss. I was skeptical when given it—inspiring book by dying person, uh-uh—but it's fantastic. The woman who gave it to me, a sculptor and member of the women artists' group I go to every fall in New Hampshire, categorizes things like surgery as AFGOs. Which stands for 'another fucking growth opportunity.'"

"My husband and I are settling into Cle Elum with our three boys," reported now retired King County, WA Sergeant Susan Sill. "We truly love it here. It is a wonderfully welcoming small community and it is a great place to raise our kids. The deep snow in the winter and hot sun in the summer are perfect for us.

It has taken me awhile to learn to slow down but I am really enjoying the peace I have in my life now. I do miss the job. But it is my law enforcement friends that I miss the most. I will always be a cop in my heart. My nighttime dreams continue to be filled with police work and that will probably never change. We moved here to start a Christ-centered retreat and I know that life will get very busy again once that gets under way, but we are not sure when that will be. We are waiting for God's direction. He never lets us down."

University of Washington Assistant Chief Annette Spicuzza: "Wow! Since 2001, we've been through a lot of changes. Reorganization, decision to pursue National Accreditation, a new CAD/RMS system (Computer Assisted Dispatching/Records Management Systems). Remodel of our Evidence/Property Room, personnel changes. A ton of stuff. Personally, some good things and some bad things. What can I say? Life is life and we live each day to the fullest."

"Terrie is HAPPY in Phoenix and exactly where I want to be, a much happier and healthier environment than the one in Tulsa," said Terrie Swann whose title had been Supervisory Deputy U.S. Marshal. She is now a Supervisory Criminal Investigator for the U.S Marshals Service.

Tulsa, OK Master Patrol Officer L. Jean VanLandingham has retired and reported, "I am staying real busy with IAWP and FOP business. I have an office at my local FOP lodge, where I am during the workweek. I am the treasurer of both my local and state FOP, which keeps me even busier. I just came back from six days in Philly. I will be going to New Mexico for a four-day FOP meeting April 1, then the National Memorial in May in Washington, D.C. I think I have retired, but haven't found time yet to realize it."

"I was Chief in Monroe for nearly nine years under three Mayors and three City Administrators," wrote Colleen Wilson. "In the spring of 2002 the Mayor fired me. There are still times when I wonder if I should have fought to get my job back, but I don't think I could ever have really done the job well there anymore. For a couple of weeks my attorney and I prepared for a lawsuit, one he told me that 'as a lawyer I would love to try.' But he also emphasized the long, drawn-out process involved and asked me what I had come to him to get or preserve and my unplanned response was 'I would like to preserve one, my integrity, two, my home and three, my employability.' In mediation, I received a year's salary and 'retired' from MPD, which preserved some benefits for me.

Due to a long story about LEOFFI and me, I could not yet draw a pension. I need to continue to work. But I did preserve my integrity, my home and my employability, and I did receive my weapon as a retirement gift, but was not allowed to purchase my badge like other retirees.

I then went to work for the State of Washington Criminal Justice Training Commission. I took over implementation of the state's new police officer licensing (certification) law. It was great fun and very different than hands-on law enforcement. I worked with an incredible bunch of people and learned a ton over the next six months. At a Business and Professional Women's conference where I was honored as their 'Woman of the Year,' I said something like, 'Here's how I figure it. The average tenure of a police chief is three to five years. I did nine years and if you're a woman we all know you have to work twice as hard to be considered half as good, so no matter how you do the math, I had a good run!'

I enjoyed my time working for the Training Commission, but I missed being part of a community and I hated the commute. Originally I thought I would wait for something to come open in Snohomish County, but eventually a friend asked, 'Do you really want to run into those people every day at the grocery store?' Then several people told me that Sumner was looking for a police chief and that I would be a good fit for them. I didn't even know where Sumner was and at first I wasn't interested. But when the Chief who was leaving called me, I decided to take a look.

It is a great little community and I really enjoyed my visit and conversation with the City Administrator. They have a well-preserved downtown business district and a community renowned for its involvement and philanthropy, just the place for my kind of policing. The internal organization was in turmoil and the team badly fractured, but the Mayor finally decided I was the best 'man' for the job and I accepted the position. I had great references including my old boss, a local psychologist who had worked with the department on team building, and it was vindicating to have the background investigator find nothing evil in my past.

It was very difficult to sell the Monroe home we had built ourselves and raised our babies in, but once that was done the whole thing turned out to be quite liberating. Once you've faced down the 'I could get fired' demon, it is easier to do the right thing and keep going. To this day I believe I left MPD a better place than I found it, which is all we can hope for. Sumner is a little smaller department as far as commissioned officers go, but I have more employees than I did in Monroe because we run a communication center that dispatches for other agencies and we contract to do animal control for Puyallup.

We have services that respond to a population base of 60,000, but the City's population is only 8,500 which make my callouts less frequent and the stress level lower. So once again, I am learning every day, but mostly I use the same techniques I used in Monroe and Sumner seems very happy with my leadership. We are on target for accreditation next year.

I did a leadership class for Tacoma Community College and discussed 'Women in Blue' in the context of leadership. As Anne Kirkpatrick always says, 'Being a Chief is a three to five year gig, Colleen. That Monroe thing was a fairy tale. Get over it!' I would say that I am getting over it. We have a lovely home in Sumner overlooking the Puyallup valley, Tacoma and the Olympic mountains. I have a great team of people here who have really risen to every challenge I've thrown out.

When I taught in the past I always said that people rise (or stoop) to your expectations, but coming in from the outside and actually trying those techniques has been great fun and very rewarding. After Dave Brame (Tacoma Police Chief) killed his wife, I found myself right in the middle of the statewide response to officer-involved domestic violence. I've often worked to bridge between social services and law enforcement. Being in Pierce County with a DV background made me feel useful again beyond my own department.

I was invited to join a group of responding experts with the Attorney General's office as well as the Pierce County effort and am once again chairing a WASPC Domestic Violence Committee. We worked to shepherd a law through the legislature that cleared both houses with no amendments and the draft model policy now goes out for comment. Fae Brooks from King County was part of this effort, too. She was also there for the the leadership panel I did at the Seattle Police Department's celebration of Women's History month and it was cool to connect with others who have been around since the '70s. It's nearly time to renegotiate my two-year contract for Sumner and rather than the stepping stone I thought it might be, Sumner feels like the perfect place for me to stay for awhile.

I intend to leave Sumner a better place than I found it and am working to implement many of the family-friendly policies I did in Monroe. Some are easier to do when you're an outsider and some harder. I don't know how long I will stay. I am much more open to whatever comes my way now and, I believe, less vulnerable to attack. This time I have a contract that requires cause and a ninety-day out clause in case my political reality changes suddenly.

Some evenings I still lie awake wondering what I did wrong, but most days I am happy with my world and wouldn't change a thing even if I could go back. I know beyond all doubt that the 'Monroe thing,' as we have come to call it, went down the way it did in part because of my gender. But I have remained professional and true to what I believe in so I can hold my head up and believe I still contribute. Besides, as the bumper sticker says, 'Well-behaved women rarely make history!'"

Tulsa County, OK, Sheriff's Office Sergeant Renee Winston reported, "I am still currently assigned to the Internal Affairs Unit, coordinator of the Honor Guard and Crisis Negotiation Team. I was also voted in for the seventh year in a row as president of the Oklahoma Women in Law Enforcement. I am also an officer with the Oklahoma chapter of the National Organization of Black Law

Enforcement Executives. As far as future ambitions, I would like to create and/or supervise a multi-jurisdictional Cyber-crime Unit."

What you have learned is that women police are on the move, sometimes motivated from within, sometimes motivated by other people, administrators, mentors, family. If you like a job where change is always possible, law enforcement could be for you.

17

Summary: Expected and Unexpected Themes

My interviewees confirmed various predictions made over the years in the law enforcement research literature (see, for example, Gitchoff & Henderson, 1985). For example, community policing has, indeed, become the wave of the present. Neighborhood watch programs have expanded and police reserves and civilian volunteers are used everywhere. As predicted, departments have become more racially balanced and integrated, more officers have advanced degrees, and the paramilitary model has been replaced by the bureaucratic management model. Both minorities and women are more accepted in the police family. These expected themes came up repeatedly in the interviews. They, together with some unexpected themes, provide a good way to summarize what this book is all about.

Women Police Have the Same Motives as the Men

Women police join for the pay, benefits, security, and variety in the day-to-day things they do. They also join to contribute something worthwhile to society, "to make a difference," to use their abilities to add to the well-being of others. Sergeant Jennifer Bartsch signed on at a very young age because it was exciting, never a dull moment. She said, "You probably hear this over and over, but I wanted to make a difference in people's lives." Retired Officer Trisha King-Stargel put it this way: "My motives had to do with personal power. Basically I like the challenge of dealing with people in crisis, making sense out of chaos, and giving their life direction."

Sergeant Dianna Klineburger left milking cows and selling real estate: "Because I was looking for enough stability, pay, and benefits to get my kids raised. Sergeant Karen DeWitt was in the same boat, divorced with two small boys to raise: "Two male troopers kept telling me how I'd be really good at being a trooper. I was very athletic, very serious and focused, and had the maturity. It was a career that had great medical benefits."

The Upside of Promotion

Many women ambitious to be promoted crave the satisfaction of changing police procedures and policies and even state laws. King County Chief Fabienne Brooks: "There were three women chiefs at one time. We all made a joke that, Ah, hah, decisions used to be made on the golf course but now they're going to be made at Nordstrom's. One of my units recently developed a regional group of six different agencies. Their mission is gathering and disseminating intelligence information about criminals. Criminals don't understand boundaries so we shouldn't either. You notice today I have on my uniform. I don't generally have to wear it but today I have an interview on a cable TV program where I want to be visible. Today I need to wear it because we've had a lot of tragedy lately and I'm proud to put this on."

Cops' Black Humor

"I heard the girl who answers the phone say, Oh, shut up," said NYPD Detective Julia Koniosis. "I said, Tina, is everything all right? She said, Yeah, fine. Why? I said, Who was this guy? She said, That's just Sherman. I said, Who's Sherman? She said, He works here but he's out on medical. But there's a new class from the academy coming today so they called him down. When new cops come in, they go to the conference room and they're greeted. Sherman puts on the inspector's uniform and he welcomes the troops. The rookies are sitting there and they've been totally indoctrinated in how you have to respect others' ranks. It's great fun to watch, when Sherman gets this uniform on, he's not the neatest guy in the world, and he's supposed to be an inspector. His shirt's hanging out, he doesn't have the right pants on, and he starts saying what he expects from them."

"Part of the camaraderie is our sense of humor," laughed Sergeant Belinda Ferguson. "I got stuck in a window because my rear end was too big and the only people behind me were male officers and I'm saying, Push me. Just push me. Push my rear end through this window. Another time I was standing over this horrific crime scene and my stomach growled and despite the situation, I was very hungry and someone said, That's my girl. She's hungry."

Working with Other Women Really Works

Years ago the men didn't want to put two women together, because how could a woman possibly back another woman up? A lot of effort went into keeping women apart in the precinct and elsewhere. But eventually, when Linda Forst became a Captain of Uniform Operations, 15% of her officers were women and women were backing up other women all the time.

"Probably the best time of my career was when a friend and I were partners in the Special Assault Unit," Detective Sergeant Susan Sill told me. "We worked together as detectives. We kicked butt. We arrested bad guys. We were constantly out, working cases together. We got tons of work done. Our personalities are very similar. She knew she could trust me and I could trust her for anything. We both worked like this (she snaps her fingers repeatedly). We were very good at multitasking and it drove other people in the office nuts."

Challenges by the Men Begin in the Academy

Redmond, WA, Commander Gail Marsh recounted that, "The first day we went to shoot guns they decided I needed a whole eight-hour block because I would probably take that long. We had to shoot handguns and shotguns long enough to reach qualification level and typically it took three to four hours. But it didn't take eight hours until I qualified. We went back to the station and the men told the lieutenant, She's done. He said, Are you sure? Maybe she should go back and do some more.

Even though I did well at the academy, right after I got out they sent me to this class where we had to learn to roll out of a car with a shotgun. They set me up. They loaded my shotgun with rifle slugs, which are very powerful. I was rolling out and shooting and everybody was watching. I didn't say anything. I just finished the class and went home. I'd learned another lesson."

Growing Acceptance by the Men

At the same time that the challenges are still there, the women said that after they had proved themselves, they felt accepted by the men. Redmond, WA, Detective Anne Malins told me, "The guys might tell you that there is a group of us who are okay. They would say, You guys are not like the 'other' women. But that okay group is enlarging and a woman is not assumed to be on the outside anymore." Deputy Detective Debbie Kronk said, "Nowadays men and women are more equal in terms of respecting each other's opinions and abilities and being more honest about accepting what everyone's limits are. When you are working as a team compared to working individually, the team is able to function much better than 25 years ago."

Dealing with Others' Channeling

"There was one attempt to channel me," Chief Shirley Gifford said. "I had been a lieutenant in training, and when a position came open in training there was an attempt by the deputy chief to put me back there. I felt like I was being channeled and I resisted. I just told him outright, No, I don't want to do it. My preference would be to go back to patrol, because traditionally women get channeled into non-confrontational, non-front line, non-operational positions. I was thankful for some recent reading I had done on channeling because otherwise it may not have clicked for me. You need someone in training? Yeah, in my accommodating way I would have acquiesced and not have known what was happening to me. He said, Well, okay and he allowed me to go back to patrol."

Childcare Is a Big Issue for Women Police

The stay-at-home dad is one solution. Detective Katie Larson waited until she was 31 before she got married. "We had our son a year after we got married and my husband was a stay-at-home dad. He did a great job. We had our daughter two years later, so he was taking care of both of them. Then he went back to work part-time on weekends. I had weekends off." In Major Robin Fenton's case her husband retired from the Washington State Patrol when their little boy was born and has been "Mr. Mom" ever since. Other officers used their immediate families. Said one detective, "Fortunately, my parents are very helpful with my little boy. They're constantly taking him in at night when I get called out. He has bedrooms at my sister's house and my parents' house. He doesn't do daycare at all." But what seemed to work best was being married to another police officer so that they could work opposite shifts.

Relationships with Men Suffer

As far as marriage went, if a woman was married before she came to the job, she had a 99% chance of losing that marriage in Chief Denise Pentony's opinion. The woman couldn't help but change as she accepted new responsibilities, and became much more competent and capable. Her excellent wage might also play a role. Denise's perception was that very few men are attracted to women who are successful and competitive and have positions such as hers.

Sergeant Dianna Klineburger said that most women she knew who are cops are single or become single. She said it's an unusual man who can deal with a woman who plays a dominant role. Most men are intimidated. Relationships also suffer when women earn more money. She said she had met men in social gatherings who, when they found out what she did, would turn and walk to the other side of the room.

Chief Shirley Gifford said that she and her husband divorced when their daughter was two, so she was a single mom for 16 years. He was also an officer in the same department and she absolutely believes her job was the cause of their divorce. She had a young child and a career in a department where she was moving up. The job took its toll.

Mentors Are Very, Very Important

There were seven fewer females in Sergeant Michelle Bennett's department when she joined, but other women followed because they had heard it was a great place to work with a female chief who was awesome and mentored them all the time. Michelle felt free to talk to her about issues and to bounce ideas off her for projects she'd like to undertake.

An important mentor in Detective Jessica Belter's life had been her partner for a couple of years. "He is a great cop, the kind of man who has the ability to show compassion. All the guys respect him even though he's the kind of guy who can talk about things from his heart. He taught me that it's okay to be nice to citizens. It doesn't mean you're letting your walls down, or that you're a weak person. He taught me to be more well-rounded and I didn't have to be this black-and-white trained cop."

Preparation for the Academy Includes Physical Fitness

First of all, Sergeant Sheri Crain got a degree in Society and Justice. Then, "I wanted to make sure I had all my ducks in a row, that I knew what I was talking about. I did research. I read books about women in law enforcement and what they were up against. I had myself mentally prepared for the questions I might be asked. I also prepared myself physically. I ski, play softball and soccer, I hike, I bike, I swim, I kayak. You name it, I do it. I've always been athletic anyway, but I spent a lot of time doing judo. Then when I was interviewed I said, These are the things I have done to prepare myself for this job. I had a nice little list. That's what got me the job."

Running and exercising had always been a part of Officer Sherry Erickson's life, but because a couple of weeks before the academy she had to take the Cooper's test—sit-ups and push-ups, run, and a flex test—she did these five times a week to get ready. She had to make sure she was ready mentally and physically because she knew she was taking a gamble at age 41 with four kids to support. So she gave herself every shot for completing training.

Women Have To Go That Extra Mile

Women shouldn't have to go that extra mile, said Sergeant Karen De Witt, but they always feel they have to. She certainly does with her detachment, gets out there and works with them, giving them pats on the back when they deserve them. Retired Captain Linda Forst said, "I always felt the need to prove myself. My husband and others would say, We know you can do the job, you don't need to prove yourself. But it's always there." Sergeant Dianna Klineburger got called into academy chief's office and was accused of cheating, her grades were that good. She said it wasn't the first time this had happened because she goes for excellence. She also said women's high standards for themselves and other women meant a woman had better be a notch up if she was appearing before a promotion or hiring board that had women on it.

Women's Management Style Differs from Men's

In the chapter devoted to "Command Thoughts about Family Life" you read some thoughts about women's management style. Before Chief Vicky Peltzer arrived on the scene, decisions had been made at the top level only. She was pushing decision making further and further down as was Chief Kristen Anderson, who talked about the importance of ownership in the minds of staff. She said if you go to them and ask them what they'd prefer rather than telling them, This is what you're going to do, it works. Likewise in the chapter "A Suburban Commander and a Small Town Chief," both women talked about involving the entire community in getting programs up and running. They both had community policing advisory boards to regularly give department managers input.

Now for some unexpected themes, starting with, "Who would have thought that so many officers want nothing to do with promotion?"

The Downside of Promotion

It was a surprise to me to find people who just wanted to do the job and go home. They didn't want to supervise others. Patrol was what they were after and, as time passed, all they ever wanted. We'll illustrate with a sergeant immersed in neighborhood policing and what she'd miss if she moved up further.

This sergeant said, "If I got promoted I might not get to do things like take a run of animal calls. We had calls that a mother mallard and her ducklings were crossing this major highway. Well, you don't want people slamming on their brakes and hitting something else because they were avoiding these ducks. We went out and shooed them along, making sure we were 'Peking' both ways. Then right after the ducks we got a call about a vicious dog, or 'it could be a pig.' Then after the dog-pig, we had a catnapping call. A cat was urinating in a neighbor's beauty bark so the neighbor stole the cat and was holding it hostage in his house. We responded with a search warrant to get into the house to recover this crotchety old lady's cat from her crotchety old man neighbor who was tired of that cat pissing in his bark. We recovered the cat and gave it back to her."

Handling Situations with Feminine Creativity

A common theme was that women cops talk their way out of situations rather than use physical force. Sergeant Sheri Crain said, "Women need to know that they can get down and wrestle if their backup doesn't show up for half an hour. But I use my mouth to make sure I don't end up wrestling. I say, I'm very sincere about this—you do what I tell you, or bad things are going to happen."

Women extrapolate from using their mouths to handle situations to some unique applications. Sergeant Belinda Ferguson talked about the animal calls they get from rural parts of the county. "We got a call that there was a cow in the road. I'm from Los Angeles, I don't even know what a lasso is. I thought, How do I do this? I reached in my lunch bag and I pulled out a piece of jerky to coax the cow off the road and it worked. The other officer was rolling over laughing.

We have crises deer, they get hit and block the roadway. You have to somehow remove the deer from the road. I got a call about a deer in a very, very rural area. My FTO said, I'll get there to help you. I'm thinking, No, you won't. I'm going to take care of this myself. I got there and this deer is huge and there is absolutely no way I can lift it. How am I going to do this? I moved my car and rolled over the deer, then backed up, and I could see this was making the deer fall apart a little bit. I thought, Hmm, there's nobody here, nobody's watching me, and my FTO is 20 minutes out. I rolled my car back and forth and the deer became sectioned and I dragged the pieces off the road. My FTO got there. You got that thing off the road. How did you do that? It was me. I was stubborn. I was going to do this on my own. I was going to figure this out without help."

Confronting Discrimination Head On

Overprotection in one's early years can still be a given and must be actively resisted and overcome by the woman herself. Likewise, discrimination and harassment must be countered directly, and, if possible, immediately. Like below.

Master Patrol Officer Jean VanLandingham told me her academy classmates had not signed up to work with a woman. "Women were still real new. They challenged me out on the range where we did a night-fire. After you shot your round you dumped your empty cartridges into a dump bucket, a coffee can. When you got through for the night, you'd go through your cartridges and sort out split cartridges because we did reloading and they would jam the machine. One night-fire some of the guys decided they'd be real cute and they urinated in my dump bucket. It was just a ha-ha for them, but to me it was, Okay, I'll show you. I took my dump bucket and poured cartridges, pee and all, in every one of theirs. And turned to the sergeant and said, I qualified. I'm home. I'm out of here. He said, You can't leave. I said, Oh, yes, I can and this is why. To me it was a test of my strength. Okay, is she going to be a whiny butt and cry about this? Or is she going to get back and go on? I overheard them giggling, We got her on this. No, you didn't."

Women Cops Like to Write

Many interviewees said women cops write better reports than the men. For example, Retired Deputy Constable Sarah Cortez: "Women tend to have better verbal communication skills. Women tend to be better writers. I've never lost a case. It might have been plea-bargained out, that's the DA's prerogative in decisions, but I've never lost a case. I'm a good investigator. I'm good at details. The guys, they just want to turn the lights on, and drive fast and break glass. They don't want to write the report that's going to put the person in jail."

Interest in writing apart from the job was high in this group of women. Retired Captain Linda Forst belongs to the Police Writers Association as does Chief Vicky Peltzer who wants to write a book about her career in Albuquerque. Sergeant Michelle Bennett had an article published in a Russian journal. Retired

Auxiliary Sergeant Judith Rock has written a one-woman play, *Response Time*, and Officer Pam Garland and Sergeant Joy Mundy write columns for *Women Police*, for which Master Patrol Officer Jean VanLandingham is editor.

Chief Kristen Anderson's BA is in English with a writing emphasis, so what better vehicle for getting cops and kids together in Port Townsend than a poetry workshop? She is quoted as saying, "This allows the kids to see cops with a motivation other than 'I'm going to nail you.' It allows cops to see kids on a more personal level and where they came from" (Morris, 2001). Like the other participants, Chief Anderson had laid herself bare in the workshop, remembering a tense moment from her childhood—flying pizza and angry words—captured in a somber 10-line poem.

Women Officers Like to Learn and to Teach

Women police have a very strong interest in continuing education. It starts with the academy where the popular perception of both sexes is that women do better than men academically. In this group the most popular subject for a future master's degree was public administration. Other women were interested in advanced degrees in business management, law, organizational development, leadership, theology, psychology, and women's studies. However, if a woman had recently completed a master's, she might respond to "What do you plan to study in the future?" with golf, horticulture, cooking, or a foreign language. The desire for a master's degree was linked with retirement plans which included a career change. Often, that new career was teaching.

Sergeant Dianna Klineburger said that she was a teacher in a different kind of classroom. "I like free-wheeling teaching. Like the other day we had a new officer assigned to the ramp, inside where the airplanes are. He is supposed to stay there for an emergency response to incidents having to do with aircraft. But he wound up way over at the north end of the airport backing up another officer. To teach him that he needs to stay closer to his area I said over the air that I'd appreciate other backup to that area so he could get back to his own. What he heard was, I'm out of my area.

Childrearing—Training Ground for Supervising

Sergeant Joy Mundy described her supervisory role as Mom Mundy. Typically, when she counsels an officer, she will touch him or her on the arm, adding the kind of warmth that mothers give their children. She said she felt like she had a ton of sons and daughters in the department that she'd talked to over the years and helped raise from student officers to adult officers.

"There isn't much difference being a sergeant and being a mom," said Detective Sergeant Susan Sill. "Who's got the better toys? Who is being treated better than the other person? Who got wronged by somebody? These are personnel issues moms deal with and sergeants deal with. To be a good supervisor you have to understand people and be good with people and being a mom really helps in that respect. The same theories that go with raising children go with supervising detectives. We could all use cookies and a nap."

Women Police Reward in Myriad Small Ways

This theme is "unexpected" because I hadn't thought about it at all. I felt that these women were very cognizant that praise went a long way toward making officers feel good about themselves. Sergeant Lis Eddy felt that rewarding outstanding performance aided retention. The Officer of the Year for each precinct is based largely on supervisors' nominations but anybody could make a nomination. She said her agency also had employee recognition awards, which come with a day off, which is a real incentive that doesn't cost the city very much. But the basic, day-to-day commendations she uses are "atta boys and atta gals."

Sergeant Jennifer Bartsch felt she had a special relationship with 98% of the people who worked for her. She writes them up frequently to receive police commendation bars and civic achievement awards. When we met, she had just recommended an officer who had a degree in education and tutored kids afternoons. He had developed a program that combined helping the elderly with helping youth. He'd recruited retired teachers who lived in his area to help with his after-school program.

Recruitment by Word of Mouth Is the Best Way

Chief Vicky Peltzer is a big proponent of getting officers out talking with kids. Explorer posts give high school students the chance to see what the job is and if they're comfortable with the environment. Her department has seven students who meet on a regular basis. They have practice crime scenes and go to a week-long exercise in the summer where they do accident investigations. They are sent out in uniform and attend crime prevention groups when they're set up on campus, so they're another recruitment tool.

"We go to the recruiting fairs and colleges, but to get more women, there has to be a lot of word-of-mouth recruiting," said Detective Anne Malins. "When I was looking for a legal advocate, I went out myself and recruited the legal advocate I wanted. I truly make it a point to talk to women when I know we're hiring. You get them yourself. Solely sending out a male training officer doesn't usually bring in women."

There Is Tremendous Variety to Police Jobs

While Detective Kathleen Larson is content with the rank of detective, she has worked a variety of jobs, crucial to getting promoted. She was impressed that during her county internship they put her with a number of units so she was exposed to many different activities. She saw immediately how easy it was to move on if you got bored with your present job.

"I work in this personnel capacity but I also support a number of other units," said Sergeant Belinda Ferguson. "I'm a member of the hostage negotiation team and I support undercover. I work in vice and narcotics, money laundering. I keep my hand in as many things as I can because you disconnect yourself from patrol when you go into a specialty position. For me it's very important to feel like a cop."

Women Channel Themselves into Child-Centered Community Policing

If she'd been channeled, she had no one to blame but herself, Commander Gail Marsh told me. She said it was no coincidence that when women began to enter policing that laws around child abuse, domestic violence, and family issues started to change. On a more personal level, she recalled rescuing an eight-year-old from a violent stepfather and getting her settled with her dad. Twelve years later the young woman stopped in to thank her.

Women who were involved at the ground level included Dispatcher Mel Larson, who coached and umpired kids in basketball, baseball, and softball. Reservist Tania Kohlman is a behavior interventionist for her school district and counsels children who have home and social problems, while Patrol Officer Deborah Allen says she spends the majority of her time dealing with high school kids, encouraging dropouts to get their diplomas and talking about pros and cons of the job of police officer.

Women who have played major roles in getting laws changed include Major Carol Cummings who worked to get the Revised Code of Washington revised to lower the bar for investigating cases of child neglect. Another is Sergeant Susan Sill who developed a Drug Endangered Children Program to be able to charge meth lab parents with criminal neglect. Susan said that almost everyone who becomes a cop thinks they are going to save the world and she is saving the children's world.

Research Departments Thoroughly Before Choosing

How many women had this advice for prospective police? Sergeant Cherie Harris did ride-alongs all over the Seattle area and contacted officers she knew had moved here to ask about various departments' reputations as far as women were concerned. She wanted a family and went for family-friendly policies. Detective Anne Malins also did ride-alongs everywhere to help her decide where to go: "One of my big questions was, How many women do you have? Because if the department has no women or can't keep women, don't go there."

Chief Denise Pentony said every woman should make sure a department is the kind she wants to work for. What's their leadership like? Their vision? Would she fit in? If so, great, she will be successful. But a woman should never, ever go to a department where she is bound to be unhappy.

Young Women's Aversion to Joining Women's Organizations

"Most young women don't join a women's organization in their first few years, partly because they're saving face, partly because they don't understand they're going to need this, nor what they can get from it," said Retired Auxiliary Sergeant Judith Rock. "Women need to be approached when they're in the academy about the IAWP. Then we have to keep getting to them, offering the opportunity until they finally realize they need this. We can reach them through female supervisors and female academy instructors. There were days when I would have quit for ten cents and then a female instructor would show up for a day or two, and I would think, Okay, I'll stick around."

Intelligence Analyst Kim Kraushar said Women Police of Alaska was having a hard time giving support to women starting out in law enforcement because they wouldn't come to meetings and enjoy the parties and barbecues and learn of training opportunities and scholarships for training. She thought their perception of the WPA was that it had a feminist agenda and would be seen by the men as exclusive.

Now to Summarize Yourself

How about your motives? Do you also want good pay, benefits, and job security together with contributing in a very worthwhile way to the community?

Can you imagine yourself as a top ranking officer whose agenda is to revamp outdated policies and programs and to mentor other officers?

Do you have a good sense of humor? How about black humor?

Could you work in an environment where women are in the minority? Would you be able to seek out and find other women to share assignments with?

Are you willing to prepare mentally and physically for the academy and know where you'd get the emotional support you need if challenged by the men?

Suppose you run into one of those guys who is not all that accepting? Which woman in this book was most inspiring in terms of how to handle him?

And if others try to channel you into areas you are not interested in, which woman here was the most inspiring "resisting marginalization"?

As the introductory chapter asked, are children in your plans and how would you handle the childcare issue as a police officer?

What about these stories of how relationships with men can suffer as a woman progresses through her induction into the police? Could you live with that?

Do you currently have mentors? Are you willing to seek out mentors if mentors don't come to you?

How athletic are you? What sports do you play? What physical shape are you in? Are you willing to add to your exercise routine to succeed at the academy?

Were you surprised that women police feel they have to go that extra mile to be accepted? Could you do it?

Whose management style did you admire the most? Are you good at management and organization?

Which officers did you most identify with, those who stayed in patrol throughout their careers or those who sought supervision and administration?

Which side of promotion could you relate to better, up or down? Who did you most admire who resisted promotion and who did you most admire who sought it?

Do you think of yourself as a person who can come up with unique solutions to unexpected problems and situations? Think of a recent example.

Discrimination and sexual harassment are not completely dead. Could you handle them with confrontation?

How good a report writer are you? What's behind women officers' greater writing ability?

Clearly women police enjoy continuing their education. Is lifelong learning one of your values?

Do you see the connection between childrearing and supervising a group of alpha males? What have you learned here about how to handle challenges to your authority?

Why do you think women police are so good at rewarding day-to-day behavior?

Okay, word of mouth is the best recruitment tool. What ideas do you have about finding women police to find out more about the job and if it fits you?

You've read about a host of assignments and duties. Are you more likely to seek out what attracts you the most and stay with it, or to change your work roles frequently?

Does child-centered community policing appeal to you or not? Why?

What sort of police department would be right for you? What questions would you ask when you do your research to compare agencies?

You've learned the advantages and benefits of being a member of women's police organization. So where do you stand on whether to join and when to join?

If this self-reflection does what I intend it to do, you now know a lot more about yourself and whether that self is a good fit for law enforcement. Good luck.

Afterword

Patricia Lunneborg's book paints pictures of strong, resilient, caring, and intelligent women in their own words. With perceptive self-reflection, often sprinkled with humor and humility, these police officers describe being pioneers in a profession that has gradually evolved from resistance to acceptance of their presence, thanks to the perseverance of people like themselves. The unexpected themes described in the last chapter are the most interesting part of the book, as women clearly have not simply attempted to fit into their departments by doing things the way men did them: they talk about using verbal skills to diffuse situations and write effective reports, choosing the involvement with the public that led them to the profession over career ambitions that would remove them from direct service, learning to respond directly to discrimination and harassment that lingers in male-dominated fields, and the ways in which maternal roles inform their work. While many of Lunneborg's respondents might not describe themselves as feminists, they affirm tenants of feminist psychology that emphasize how women cope, persist, and ultimately change professions to which their entry has been resisted.

Margaret E. Madden, Ph.D.
Provost and Vice President for Academic Affairs, The State University of New York, Potsdam
President, The Society for the Psychology of Women

Bibliography

Bartol, Curt R., Bergen, George T., Volckens, Julie Seager, and Knoras, Kathleen M. (1992). Women in small-town policing: Job performance and stress. *Criminal Justice and Behavior, 19*, 240-259.

Bennetto, Jason. (4 February 2003). Met chief says police stations need crèches. *The Independent*, page 3.

Campbell, Deborah J., and Christman, Bryon D. (November, 2000). Improving the recruitment of women in policing. *The Police Chief, 62*, pages 18, 20, 23-25, 27-28.

Daum, James M., and Johns, Cindy M. (1994). Police work from a woman's perspective. *The Police Chief, 61*, #9, 46-49.

Duke, Brynn C. (2001). *Heart to Heart: For teens who have lost a parent, From one who has been through it*. Shoreline, WA: Shoreline Community College.

Equality denied: The status of women in policing: 2001. (2002). Los Angeles, CA: National Center for Women & Policing.

Gitchoff, G. Thomas, and Henderson, Joel. (1985). What goes around, comes around: Policing America, 1999. Taken from Blumberg, Abraham S., and Niederhoffer, Elaine (Eds.) *The ambivalent force: Perspectives on the police* (3rd edition). New York: Holt, Rinehart and Winston, Inc., 419-424.

Green, Sara Jean. (18 September 2003). Promotion a milestone for trooper and Patrol. *Seattle Times*, pages 1 and 16.

Haarr, Robin N. (1997). Patterns of interaction in a police patrol bureau: Race and gender barriers to integration. *Justice Quarterly, 14*, 53-85.

Haarr, Robin N., and Morash, Merry. (1999). Gender, race, and strategies of coping with occupational stress in policing. *Justice Quarterly, 16*, 303-336.

Leinwand, Donna. (26 April 2004). Lawsuits of '70s shape police leadership now. *USA Today*, pages 13A and 14A.

Morris, Keiko. (19 October 2001). Port Townsend workshop has rhyme and reason. *Seattle Times*, pages B1, 5.

Heidensohn, Frances. (1992). *Women in control? The role of women in law enforcement.* Oxford: Clarendon Press.

Lunneborg, Patricia W. (1989). *Women police officers: Current career profile.* Springfield, Illinois: Charles C Thomas.

Lunneborg, Patricia W. (1990). *Women changing work.* Westport, CT: Greenwood Press.

Ratchford, L. Faith. (Summer 2003). Hiring the "total package." *Women Police*, page 4.

Recruiting & retaining women: A self-assessment guide for law enforcement. (2001). Los Angeles, CA: National Center for Women & Policing.

The Sisters Wells. (2001). *Food, drink, and the female sleuth.* Lincoln, NE: Authors Choice Press, an imprint of iUniverse.com.

The Sisters Wells. (Winter 2001). Fictional women police: How close to the facts? *Women Police*, page 16.

About the Author

Patricia Lunneborg is a former Professor of Psychology and Adjunct Professor of Women's Studies at the University of Washington. *Women Police: Portraits of Success* is her fourth book since retirement concerning women in law enforcement, the others being *Women Police Officers: Current Career Profile*, *Women Changing Work*, and *Food, Drink, and the Female Sleuth*. The author lives in a rustic cottage on Lake Washington, Seattle, with her forbearing husband of 45 years.

Index

Sergeants, in the office 2, 72-90
Service orientation x, 105, 187
Sexual assault cases 26, 63, 64, 122
Shift work 21, 22, 42, 128, 180
Shoreline, WA, PD 114, 212, 264, 272
Sir John Stevens 227
Soldotna, AK, PD 197, 268
Specially commissioned officer 34, 36, 270
Sports, involvement in 27, 96, 218, 229, 244
Starting early 2, 24, 53, 105-128, 128, 217
Starting late 2, 129-149
Stereotypes 13, 92
Strengths 34, 129, 254, 259
Style of policing viii
Supervision, by women 61, 69, 105, 118, 138, 285
Supervision, of women 32
Support from women's organizations 246-263
SWAT vii, 12, 60, 68, 98, 117, 147, 184, 213, 224

T

Talking to deal with situations. See Women's ways of policing
Teamwork, women's ideas about 59
The Sisters Wells 294
Top command positions ix
Traffic problems 51
Training: 24; academy 106, 170
Trainings, conference 49, 63, 87, 173, 215, 251, 252, 262
Transforming policing. See Changing police culture
Transition from officer to mother. See Job-home switch
Travel on the job 43, 117, 254
Tulsa County, OK, Sheriff's Office 246, 275
Tulsa, OK, PD 5, 8, 273
Turnover 249

Two-officer marriage 48, 50, 72, 91, 94, 95, 118, 125, 143, 151, 155, 160, 164, 176, 197, 200, 218, 241

U

Unexpected themes ix, 3, 263, 277, 282, 291
Uniforms 42, 87, 88, 89, 142, 174, 251
University of Houston, TX, PD 129, 131
University of Washington, WA, PD 172, 271, 273

V

Variety of roles 220, 254, 287
Verbal command training 10
Village Public Safety Officer, VPSO 18, 19
Visibility of women 54
Volckens, Julie 293

W

Washington Association of Women Police 87
Washington State Patrol 51, 118, 150, 184, 280
Washington State University PD 91
Why women leave ix, 86
Women Changing Work ix, x, 55, 105
Women in Control? 169, 294
Women partners 245
Women Police of Alaska 22, 252, 288
Women Police Officers: Current Career Profile ix, x
Women supervisors 259
Women's management style 173, 282
Women's ways of policing 53, 62, 66, 89, 93, 97, 115, 121, 138, 148, 154, 163, 248, 283
Work experience, previous 1, 23
Working with other women 125, 132, 252, 279
Writing 10, 20, 53, 84, 94, 97, 112, 118, 129, 131, 133, 135, 136, 137, 154, 160, 169, 176, 177, 186, 265, 266, 268, 272, 284, 285, 290

0-595-32075-9

Printed in the United States
22063LVS00004B/49-285